KW-406-987

# The Machinery of Change in
## Local Government 1888-1974

*To*
*E.H.*

# The Machinery of Change in Local Government 1888-1974

## A study of central involvement

CLIFFORD PEARCE

*Formerly Under Secretary, Department of the Environment*
*Honorary Research Fellow, University of Birmingham*

For the
Institute of Local Government Studies
University of Birmingham

GEORGE ALLEN & UNWIN

London      Boston      Sydney

First published in 1980

GEORGE ALLEN & UNWIN LTD
40 Museum Street, London WC1A 1LU

**British Library Cataloguing in Publication Data**

Pearce, Clifford
    Machinery of change in local government, 1888–1974.
    1. Local government – England
    I. Title    II. University of Birmingham.
    *Institute of Local Government Studies*
    352.042    JS3091    80–40609


ISBN 0-04-352091-X

Set in Press Roman 10 on 11pt by Katerprint Co. Ltd., Oxford
and printed in Great Britain
by Biddles Ltd., Guildford, Surrey

# Contents

# Preface

This study derives from my service in the Local Government Division of the Ministry of Housing and Local Government and then of the Department of the Environment, during which I was personally involved in the implementation of the proposals of the Hancock Commission and the promotion and implementation of the London Government Act 1963 and the Local Government Act 1972. I should make it clear, however, that any views expressed or implied are entirely mine and are not necessarily those of the Department.

I would also like to record my gratitude to the many people and bodies by whom I have been helped – and especially to the University of Birmingham and the Nuffield Foundation under whose aegis the study was written, to the Department of the Environment who allowed me the use of official accommodation and papers, to the Controller of Her Majesty's Stationery Office for permission to quote from a wide variety of government publications and to my friends and former colleagues V. J. Lewis, Douglas Milefanti and Hal Summers who read the work in draft.

C.J.P.

*Chapter 1*

# The Background to Change in Local Government

## PURPOSE AND SCOPE OF THE STUDY

No system of government can remain static and survive. It must always be responsive to social, economic and political developments in the community, and the machinery for adaptation is itself an essential part of the wider machinery of government.

The purpose of this study is to examine the machinery through which changes have been made in one part of that field – to local authority areas and to the structure of local government in England since 1888. The period extends from the last quarter of the nineteenth century, when a series of statutes gathered up the threads of earlier developments and defined the system which was then to operate for the best part of a hundred years, until the comprehensive reorganisations effected by the London Government Act 1963 and, in the rest of England and Wales, by the Local Government Act 1972.

The machinery of change in local government has itself changed over the years, and the study therefore attempts to answer the question: what procedures have been adopted at different periods and what factors have helped or hindered their effective operation? In so doing it looks primarily at the mechanics of change rather than at the changes themselves. Some account is needed, of course, of the local government structure and of the modifications actually made but the study does not aim to describe these in comprehensive detail nor to assess the merits or success of the policies pursued.

During this period the scope of government, as a whole, has steadily expanded and the role of the central government has become more important. The study necessarily looks, therefore, at the part played by the central government in formulating the machinery of change in local government and in the working of that machinery. In particular it examines the practical problems facing the governments of the day when they undertook direct responsibility for the recent reorganisations, first in London and then in the rest of the country. The 'central government' in this context refers to the executive, not to Parliament, and especially to the minister generally responsible for the working of the local government system and his department, that is, the Local Government Board (LGB) until 1919, the Ministry of Health until 1951, the Ministry of Housing and Local Government (MHLG) until 1970 and the Department of the Environment (DOE) thereafter.

Local authority services and the way in which they are financed (which lie outside the scope of this study) have been subject to incessant change over the years. No session of Parliament passes without the enactment of further statutes affecting the activities of local authorities which then need to be supplemented by orders, departmental circulars and other forms of literature. But the administrative areas within which local authorities operate have changed very much more slowly. There are several reasons for this. A practical problem of mechanics is that even a minor boundary alteration involves a lot of detailed work. If a new boundary has to be defined it will need to be inspected on the ground and then recorded on large-scale and properly authenticated maps. The cumbersome difficulty of defining a new boundary in words is illustrated by the London Boroughs (Boundaries) Order 1963[1] which described, *inter alia*, a new stretch of boundary about a mile long between the London boroughs of Barking and Redbridge. The process required twelve lines of print and referred to geographical features in five different Ordnance Survey plans. The order also provided (as is now usual) that the boundary should be mered by Ordnance Survey. Mereing (from the Anglo-Saxon word meaning a boundary) is the process whereby boundaries are related, with definitive exactitude, to existing physical features, for example, roads, fences, streams, railway tracks. Local government boundaries, as thus mered, are agreed between Ordnance Survey and the local authorities concerned.

More important than these practical considerations is the fact that boundary changes affect authorities on both sides of the line, possibly at more than one level. A boundary between two counties, for instance, is also the boundary between two districts and possibly between two parishes. A modification of such a boundary will affect all three levels of authorities as well as the pattern of electoral divisions at each level; it will require the jurisdiction of one group of authorities to be extended and of the other group to be correspondingly restricted; staff, assets and liabilities may have to be transferred along with territory; there will be implications for other activities whose organisation is related to local government areas, such as the national health service and the administration of justice.

If an area change is substantial, involving (say) the amalgamation of two authorities or the division of a local authority area, then the administrative upset will be correspondingly greater; local authorities are going concerns, some on a very big scale, and major changes will disrupt arrangements both before the appointed day and for a long time afterwards. Boundary alterations will have consequential effects on the incidence of local taxation as well as on the political complexion of local authorities; and, because parliamentary constituencies are defined by reference to local authority boundaries, changes may ultimately have repercussions for parliamentary representation too.

Last, but by no means least, boundary changes are almost always opposed by local public opinion. Most people are initially against change of this kind, and proposals to shift boundaries often arouse fierce opposition based on loyalty to history and the *status quo*, supported by fears of an increase in the rates. 'I am well aware' (said Mr Balfour introducing the London Government Bill) 'that there is probably no more ticklish question to be dealt with in this Bill than this question of areas. It invariably arouses jealousies, feelings, local passions and local rivalries in a way which has proved very embarrassing to every government which has endeavoured to deal with the complexity of our existing local areas and which has, I am afraid, stood in the way of many important and useful reforms' (Commons Hansard, 23 February 1899, col. 356).

Supporters of the *status quo* have often used a more general argument against change. They ask to be shown in what respect an existing authority is inefficient or is falling down on the job, and demand proof that the proposed new arrangement will work better. Neither demand can be met to the satisfaction of the authorities concerned because changes in the machinery of government must be based more on political judgement than upon statistical data. The answer was given however by the Permanent Secretary of the Ministry of Housing and Local Government (Dame Evelyn Sharp), when giving evidence to the Royal Commission on Local Government in Greater London, and her remarks on that occasion define the ultimate basis for all action taken with the aim of improving the local government system, whether in particular areas or the country as a whole:

Reorganisation is not being proposed because authorities are thought to be inefficient; it is being proposed because in some areas the conditions for the greatest efficiency do not exist. A local authority cannot be fully efficient if it is constantly engaged in friction with other authorities; if it has no room to carry out its functions; if its area, population or resources are inadequate to enable it to provide a complete service or to warrant a full range of well qualified officers to advise it. Within the limits of the conditions in which they are working many local authorities of all classes and sizes are very efficient. Efficiency depends largely on the quality of councillors and the quality of officers; and you will find good quality in authorities of all shapes and sizes. You cannot prove a need for reorganisation by pointing to efficiency or inefficiency. What you can do, I think, is to point to the conditions in which efficiency has the best chance; to the conditions most likely to attract the good councillors and good officers on whom efficiency so largely depends; and to the conditions in which those councillors and officers will be able to work most effectively.[2]

The formal procedures of change during the period covered by this study have involved general legislation, local Acts, royal charters, orders made by ministers, by the Boundary Commission and by county councils; some of these orders have been subject to confirmation by, or to challenge in, Parliament. To dwell on the minutiae of procedures in comprehensive detail would assuredly induce confusion and boredom. But they cannot be ignored altogether for, to borrow the phrase from Sir Henry Maine which Maitland adopted, the substantive law has the appearance of being secreted in the interstices of procedure.[3]

Machinery and policy go together, and the relationship between the two is a recurring theme of the present study. The existence of an effective policy with regard to local government change implies, *inter alia,* that the proposed developments affecting areas, status or structure have been clearly defined and presented; that they have been the subject of full public discussion; that they command sufficient support for their implementation to be politically feasible; and that the central government are possessed of the necessary determination to carry through the policy, notwithstanding that they may encounter general or local unpopularity in the process. The machinery of change has to be considered against the background of the policy it is intended to implement. It must include processes of consultation which are thorough and which ensure that the bodies affected can give their views and hear the views of others. But it must not be so long drawn out or so hedged around by opportunities for re-hearings and appeals that the policy is frustrated – which may happen if individual proposals of types which are already agreed to be necessary are rejected when examined in isolation; or if the procedure creates so much delay and friction that support for the whole general policy evaporates.

The period covered by this study was a period of rapid and profound social upheaval during which the local government system had to change in order to adapt itself to the expanding needs of the community. The machinery for such change, being itself part of the system, had to be adapted too, and the main part of this study is an examination of the mechanics of change which have operated at different times since 1888. The study is not, therefore, merely an account of the processes through which the recent reorganisations were carried out – first in Greater London in 1963-5 and then in the rest of the country in 1972-4 – but aims to trace the evolution of the machinery of change throughout the whole period. Such machinery was, at each stage, related to contemporary thinking with regard to local authorities and the role of local government and, as each stage led on to the next, useful lessons were to be learned from the way in which different procedures for change operated in practice - lessons which may be relevant in the future, too.

Before proceeding to the main purpose of the study a preliminary look is needed, first at the background influences and pressures which have required changes to be made in the structure of local government and, secondly, at the elements of the local government system, as inherited from the nineteenth century, which have affected the processes of change. These had a powerful influence on subsequent events; some features became clear candidates for reform while other characteristics operated so as to resist change.

## BACKGROUND PRESSURES AFFECTING
## LOCAL GOVERNMENT CHANGE

Social, economic and political changes during the twentieth century have influenced all aspects of government, both central and local, and have interacted on each other. Amongst these, changes in the *size and distribution of the population* have been fundamental. Between 1750 - at the commencement of the industrial revolution - and 1901 the population of England and Wales increased from about 7 million to 32 million and there was a massive move into the towns. The rapid and uncontrolled growth of towns produced appalling conditions of urban squalor with overcrowded housing, inadequate sanitation and acute problems of crime and disorder. Inevitably the history of local government in the nineteenth century is largely the history of municipal authorities attempting to tackle the urgent environmental problems of towns.

During the twentieth century the population continued to rise, though not at such a rapid rate. But, for England and Wales, the increase from 1901 to 1971 was nevertheless 50 per cent (from 32 million to 48 million) which meant another 16 million people to cope with. And within this total important changes were taking place in the age distribution of the population. The nineteenth century was a period of high birth-rate and high, though declining, death-rate. In the twentieth century the death-rate continued to decline but the birth-rate came down too. Wider knowledge of birth control was reinforced by other factors - the changing role of women, especially in employment, the desire (strongest in the middle classes) to give children a better education (which meant restricting numbers on economic grounds) and the competition of other ingredients in rising living standards such as holidays, housing and cars.

The lower birth-rate, coupled with the fact that people lived longer, meant that the proportion of children gradually declined while the proportion of elderly increased. The decline in the proportion of those under the age of 14 was offset by the fact that the population continued to increase; in terms of absolute numbers this group remained at about 10 million. But, at the other end of the life span, the proportion aged 65 and over has risen from 5 to 12 per cent of the population – from 1·5 million to nearly 6 million.

A higher proportion of the population get married, people marry earlier but families are smaller. From the local government point of view all these changes mean a constant demand for school places, an increasing demand for housing and a very substantial increase in the demand for health and welfare services for the elderly. Whereas elderly relatives used to be looked after within the larger families of earlier decades the smaller families of today (with the wife going out to work too) do not permit this, and an increasing number of old people have to be cared for by public authorities. The population has been growing older; and politicians are not likely to ignore the fact that 1 in 5 of all voters are now entitled to the old age pension.

Developments in *science and technology*, many of them accelerated by two world wars, have enormously changed the economic and social life of the community. Motor cars and aeroplanes in mass production are twentieth-century phenomena. So are the oil, chemical and plastics industries; so are antibiotics and man-made fibres, electronics, telephones, radio and television; and so are all the new subsidiary industries that support these developments.

There are three immediate ways in which these changes have affected local government. In the first place, and quite apart from the growth in population, there has been a greater demand for local authority services. The need for more and better roads to meet the needs of motor traffic is an obvious example. Another has been the rising consumption of water by industry and by domestic users, with complementary demands on the sewerage system. To an increasing extent industrial effluents are discharged into public sewers instead of into rivers or the sea, and such effluents, with new chemical and perhaps radioactive ingredients, are more difficult to purify. As in the case of gas and electricity, both water supply and sewage treatment have now been taken out of local authority hands to be organised on a national basis.

Secondly, technological advances have been reflected in the quality of services which local authorities can and are expected to provide. This applies in virtually all fields of local government from the police and fire services to medical care and the welfare services.

Thirdly, changes in the distribution of industry with the rise of modern light industries and the decline of the old staple industries of coal, ship-building, cotton and wool have created social problems in which local authorities are closely involved. The newer industries are not tied to the coalfields and have expanded in the south-east and the midlands, both of which regions have grown rapidly in population. In these areas local authorities have had to provide services for incoming families and new firms; in the north, and in Wales, authorities have had the uphill task of maintaining services and tackling obsolescence against the background of far more difficult economic conditions.

Technological advances have been accompanied by equally important developments in *social thinking and public attitudes*. One such development has been a new approach to unemployment and poverty. Social attitudes in the nineteenth century were very much bound up with the administration of the poor laws, founded on the belief that it was chiefly up to the individual to meet his own needs and find employment; public relief was discouraged by the principle of 'less eligibility' and the stigma of pauperism. Widespread unemployment caused by the depression of the 1880s and followed by the reports of the Royal Commission on the Poor Laws, which sat between 1905 and 1909, led to acceptance of the view that unemployment is more often the result of wider impersonal forces over which the individual has little control and should be tackled by prevention, not deterrence.

The second aspect was the growing realisation that social ills are interconnected. The investigations of Booth and Rowntree at the turn of the century emphasised the close relationship between poverty, high death-rates, ill health, bad housing, unemployment and the plight of the destitute elderly.[4] The social services of the twentieth century were developed to meet those needs and the movement was logically followed up by the Seebohm Committee who recommended the unified administration of the local authority personal social services, to reflect the fact that families and individuals have needs which need to be looked at together and not dealt with in watertight compartments (Cmnd 3703, 1968).

Thirdly, there has been a great expansion of all governmental activities, especially in the social services, accompanied by a change in the role of the central government. A wider distribution of the benefits of greater national wealth required the government to play a more positive role in order to eliminate poverty, to maximise welfare and achieve a greater degree of both economic and political equality. The assumption of this role has led to the great twentieth-century change in the whole concept of social policy embracing social security, health and welfare services, education and the improvement of the environment. In the local government field this has resulted in a significant change of emphasis; the main services are no longer those needed to meet the environmental problems in urban areas - they are the personal services aimed at individuals, whether they live in towns or in the country; county councils have eclipsed the town authorities as the providers of the most important local services. Similarly there has been a change of emphasis in the balance between central and local government. The part played by central government in prescribing what services should be provided, and to what standard, has enormously increased and these decisions in turn depend upon the national economy and the ability to pay.

The fourth change has been in the general attitude to services provided by public authorities, whether central or local. State intervention on behalf of general welfare is now regarded as permanent and desirable and not (as before) something to be deplored. Participation in benefits thus provided, whether through social security, the NHS, local authority housing or education, is now more generally demanded as of right than regarded as an indication of moral failure.

*Financial implications* have inevitably to be taken into account. The growing complexity of government, the wider range of services (including those provided by local authorities) and higher standards, have meant a steady growth of governmental expenditure both absolutely and as a percentage of the gross national product. At the turn of the century total governmental expenditure amounted to just over 10 per cent of the GNP; by 1970 the figure was 50 per cent. And, within this total, expenditure on social services grew even faster from 2 to 24 per cent of the GNP. In short, while all governmental expenditure increased fivefold between 1900 and 1970, expenditure on the social services increased twelvefold. 'Social services' in this context is necessarily a wide term as the nature of these services has changed over the years, but the figures quoted include national insurance (unemployment, sickness, retirement pensions, and so on), national assistance (relief of poverty, family allowances), housing subsidies, education, child care and the health services.

Two important services – the relief of the poor and the hospital element of the NHS – were transferred after the Second World War from local to central government but, even so, local government expenditure has risen rapidly in the recent postwar period, largely through the big expansion of education, housing and the personal social services. 'Local authority expenditure is one of the faster growing elements in public expenditure' (said the 1971 Green Paper, Cmnd 4741). 'Throughout the first half of the 1960s it grew about 6 per cent a year in constant prices – about twice as fast as the growth of the economy as a whole.'

An important aspect here is the fact that many local services are labour intensive. About two-thirds of local authority current expenditure goes on pay – a higher proportion than in the economy generally – and these services are not easily geared to concepts of productivity; indeed higher standards may imply lower 'productivity' in the form of (for instance) smaller school classes and fewer pupils per teacher. Figures quoted by the Layfield Report on Local Government Finance (Cmnd 6453, 1976, table 22) illustrate the fact that local government manpower in Great Britain rose in the decades before reorganisation both absolutely (from 1·45 million in 1952 to 2·70 million in 1973, though about one-third are part-time workers – many in the school meals service) and as a proportion of the total working population (from 6 to 10 per cent). This was part of a more general shift of manpower out of manufacturing into service employment.

These trends have had repercussions for the financial relations between central and local government. Because of the relative inflexibility of rates as a source of income the proportion of local authority expenditure provided by the central government has had to increase as costs have expanded. In 1913 the central government contributed 15 per cent of all local government expenditure; in 1973 the figure was 45 per cent. If housing rents and other receipts are left out of the calculations, the proportion of expenditure financed out of central as against local taxation is even higher, with government grants exceeding 60 per cent and rates now less than 40 per cent (Cmnd 6453, table 26).

Central government thus provides the major part of the cost of local government services and is necessarily involved in decisions affecting the share of the national cake allocated to local authorities as against (say) defence, social security or the NHS. In the first place local government expenditure is an important component of public sector spending, and the general management of the economy must include some control over it – especially as the substantial numbers employed by local authorities are an important element in public sector wage negotiations. Secondly, the taxable capacity of the community has to be considered as a whole; if local authorities raise more money by rates (or any other source of revenue) then the central government's ability to levy taxes is reduced. And thirdly, the central government is directly interested in the amounts paid to local authorities by way of grants – not only in the total payments, but also in their distribution and their effect in remedying inequalities between one authority and another.

*Political developments* are relevant to local government change too. Local authorities share one essential characteristic with the House of Commons and with no other body – they all derive their authority from direct election. Appropriately, there have always been close links between democracy in Parliament and in local government because if democracy is to work effectively, it must operate at all levels. Parliamentary reform in 1832 was logically followed by municipal reform in 1835. The extension of the franchise in 1884 was followed by the establishment of representative government in the counties through the LGA 1888. The twentieth century has seen the further extension of votes to all resident adults, the abolition of the business vote (except for local government elections in the City of London) and the complete assimilation of the parliamentary and local government franchise. It has also seen the growth of mass political parties, and various developments have gradually drawn local authorities into the realm of national politics.

One of these has been the increasing tendency for local councils to be run on party lines and this has been accompanied by the merging of central and local political activity, both in machinery and policies. Candidates for parliamentary and local elections are seeking the support of the same voters, and the local machinery of the national parties is geared to both sets of elections. The fact that local government elections are so arranged as to take place in local authorities of one type or another each year, instead of all being concentrated on one day every three or four years, is not accidental; regular elections help keep the local party machines in working order. Similarly in policies: the national programmes of the main parties cover not only the functions of central government but also services which are in the hands of local authorities; party organisations are dedicated to pressing policies which can be implemented only by joint central and local action. And as the limelight of press, radio and television concentrates attention on the national political leaders, local government elections are increasingly fought on national issues and are seen as indications of the popularity (or otherwise) of the central government.

Summarising the preceding pages: it would be wrong to think of 1900 as a special turning-point, because the general trends referred to had their roots in earlier decades. But some generalisations can be offered on twentieth-century developments in the local government field. There has been a steady expansion of local government services. Some admittedly have been transferred to other bodies – to nationalised undertakings in the case of gas, water and electricity and to the central government in the case of poor relief and the NHS. But new services have been provided and others have been expanded, especially since the Second World War. Services have not only had to meet the needs of a bigger population but also to match the growing expectations of the public as regards standards. Modern services are more technical and more sophisticated; they require more manpower and especially more highly qualified manpower; they require a greater expenditure of effort on management and planning; they are inter-related in their organisation and effectiveness. Finally, and of special importance in the context of this study, they require bigger areas for their efficient organisation and, being much more expensive, need larger financial resources.

The trends which lead to pressures for larger areas of local administration lead also to the greater involvement of the central government in all aspects of local government. Indeed, increasing centralisation is itself a contributory cause of such trends because the expansion of local government services and their higher standards have been substantially due to initiatives, encouragement and even control from the centre. Finance has played an essential role; as the share of local government expenditure attributable to grants has increased so too has the influence of the central government over the rate and direction of expansion of local services. The services provided by local authorities are increasingly governed by national policies, and these pressures towards increasing centralisation have been further strengthened by the concentration of political attention on national leaders in London and the blurring of the distribution between central and local government in party politics. And it must be added that the growing influence of the central government is a trend which is temperamentally congenial to ministers (and civil servants); they may deplore it in public but in practice they find it difficult to reverse. For motives which in most cases are entirely laudable, those in a position to exert some leverage through the central apparatus feel they ought to do so when there appears to be a need to be met or a shortcoming to be remedied; it is not easy for ministers to disclaim responsibility, even for matters within the competence of local authorities, and thus to appear to have less influence than wishful thinking would prescribe.

## THE STRUCTURE ESTABLISHED AT THE END OF THE NINETEENTH CENTURY

The impact of social developments and the processes of change in local government cannot be considered without a brief look at the system as it stood at the turn of the century and the various roots from which it had grown.

The main outlines of the system can be shortly stated. The principal units were the counties and county boroughs. In the county boroughs single-tier government operated; the county borough council were the sole authority in their area and all local government services were concentrated in their hands. In the administrative counties (and leaving London on one side for the moment) the county district councils constituted a second tier of three types: non-county boroughs, urban districts and rural districts. In the rural districts the parishes constituted a third tier of local authorities. But two important services still remained outside the system of compendious authorities: education (which was transferred to local authorities from the school boards under the Education Act 1902) and the poor law (which remained with the Guardians until the service was taken over by county and county borough councils under the LGA 1929).

*The county* (the old English 'shire') was the oldest and clearest division of the country. The unit was still associated with two ancient functionaries - the sheriff, dating back to Saxon times, and the lord lieutenant of Tudor origin. But, since then, county business had increasingly passed into the hands of the appointed justices on whom had been heaped a mass of duties both judicial and administrative. Some of the work was done by justices sitting alone, some at the petty sessions for divisions of the county and some required the authority of the full bench of county magistrates at quarter sessions. Gradually at quarter sessions judicial and administrative affairs were separated and the clerk of the peace was joined by a growing band of county officials.

The administrative functions of the county were few compared with later years though efforts were made – not entirely successfully – to build these up. The Local Government Bill 1888 proposed, for instance, to transfer the licensing of public houses to county councils and to place them in a position of hierarchical superiority over county districts (both of which proposals were dropped because of opposition). And to pave the way for the devolution of substantial powers from central departments to the new county councils powers were enacted in section 10 of the Act – though never used. When the LGA 1888 was passed, therefore, county functions were chiefly connected with certain bridges and main roads, reformatories and industrial schools, pauper lunatic asylums, various licensing functions and the police. But this was by then the only level at which local government was not on a representative basis and one of the main purposes of the Act was to establish elected councils for the newly constituted administrative counties.

One basic question which had to be settled was: which areas should be adopted for this purpose? There were already two kinds of counties in existence: the counties 'at large' and the counties of cities (or of towns) – the counties corporate. The expression 'county at large', as contrasted with 'county corporate', appeared in earlier statutes, including the Act of 1888, but after that date was replaced by references to administrative counties. The counties corporate were a small group of towns in England and Wales which claimed the status of county, by charter or prescription, and which had their own sheriffs.[5] But, in addition, the holding of assizes and quarter sessions had also come to be associated with county administration and some of the counties at large were subdivided for this purpose. In the end, possession of a separate court of quarter sessions – in effect the existence of a county administration as a going concern – carried most weight in deciding whether an area should be constituted as an administrative county. Curiously enough the 1888 Act (unlike its later consolidating successor, the Local Government Act 1933) contained no list of the counties but, in section 46, referred only to the special cases. It constituted the three Ridings of Yorkshire as administrative counties, the three Divisions of Lincolnshire, the two Divisions of Sussex and Suffolk and made separate provision for the Isle of Ely and the Soke of Peterborough. One further administrative county, the Isle of Wight, was created by order in 1890 but otherwise the pattern of counties remained unchanged until 1965, when Cambridgeshire and the Isle of Ely were amalgamated, as were Huntingdon and the Soke of Peterborough, by order under the LGA 1958, and changes made to the Home Counties by the London Government Act 1963.

*The county boroughs* constituted in 1888 were a new statutory type of borough. Before the reform of the municipalities in 1835 there was no single kind of borough but an infinite variety of origins, powers and constitutions. Nevertheless there were certain broad characteristics which all shared. The first related to the exclusion of the town from the organisation of the county. To a greater or lesser extent the incorporated towns obtained their own rights and privileges – to hold their own courts, collect (and sometimes compound) their own taxes, and enjoy other rights of self government. The maximum degree of freedom was achieved by the counties corporate – those boroughs and towns which could claim to be counties in themselves. The two other characteristics of boroughs which gradually became accepted as criteria were the existence of a corporation – a juristic personality with rights and duties separate from those of its members – and the foundation of borough privileges in a royal charter – or presumed charter, where none could be found.

The Municipal Corporations Act of 1835 was the product of the same pressures for administrative improvement that had reformed Parliament in 1832 and the poor law in 1834. It did not create any further boroughs (Birmingham and Manchester were still unincorporated at that time) or extend borough functions (which were generally very restricted). Its main purpose was to establish a new and uniform constitution for boroughs and to restore a concept which had been widely ignored by the self-perpetuating oligarchies into whose hands many boroughs had fallen – the view of the corporation as the legal personification of the local community, represented by a council which was selected by, acted for and was responsible to the inhabitants of the borough. The constitution laid down for boroughs, with an elected council, open proceedings and publicly audited accounts, became the prototype for all later classes of local authorities.

The idea behind county boroughs – of big towns standing on their own – was very natural in the 1880s when local government reform was under discussion. There was the historical fact that about a hundred boroughs with separate quarter sessions already stood substantially outside the county system, with a further degree of constitutional separation recognised in the case of the counties corporate. In addition the emphasis of local government development during the nineteenth century was on the urban problems of the growing towns – health, sanitation, housing, highways, law and order – most of which were tackled on a purely local basis. On the other hand the new status of county borough ought not to be granted too freely; if the new county councils were to be a success they needed to be able to call on the rateable resources of urban areas and to recruit able members from the towns as county councillors.

The government finally adopted a population of 150,000 as the guiding principle in naming ten proposed county boroughs in the Bill, not on the basis of any scientific calculations but because, as the President of the Local Government Board explained when introducing the Local Government Bill

1888, there were some boroughs 'so large and so important that they point themselves out for removal' from county jurisdiction (Commons Hansard, 19 March 1888, col. 1657). Mr Walter Long, the Parliamentary Secretary to the LGB (later Lord Long of Wraxall), underlined the pragmatic approach when he was subsequently asked by the Onslow Commission why the population limit of 150,000 had been adopted: 'There was no special reason for selecting that number' (he said); 'we thought on the whole that it probably represented as good a local government area as any other.'[6]

But even here consistency was difficult. The original candidates – Liverpool, Birmingham, Manchester, Leeds, Sheffield, Bristol, Bradford, Nottingham, Kingston-upon-Hull and Newcastle-upon-Tyne – were not the ten biggest, nor did they all reach 150,000; Newcastle's population had been only 145,000 at the last census (but it was a county of a city) whereas Salford's was already 176,000 (but it did not have its own quarter sessions). Inevitably, parliamentary pressures built up. The government lowered the limit first to 100,000, then to 50,000 and finally agreed to grant county borough status to counties of cities even below this figure which brought in Exeter, Lincoln, Chester, Gloucester, Worcester and Canterbury. In the end the Act listed sixty-one county boroughs instead of the original ten and as Lord Long said later, 'We came to the 50,000 line for a reason which very often obtains in the House of Commons – because we could not help ourselves'.[7]

*The county districts* – the second-tier authorities within each administrative county (outside London) – had a confused ancestry. Strictly speaking, in the terminology of the LGA 1894, there were only two types: urban districts (including non-county boroughs) and rural districts, but this study adopts what became the accepted but narrower application of the term 'urban district', which did not embrace boroughs. The county districts were therefore the boroughs which had not been given county borough status, the urban districts and the rural districts.

Urban and rural districts owed much, in their origins, to the inability of the parish to cope with the drastic changes in social conditions brought about by the industrial revolution. Originally a unit of church government, the parish had gradually superseded all other local institutions as the smallest unit of local government. The 15,000-odd parishes included many variations derived from custom and tradition but the common elements were the obligation resting on all men belonging to the parish to render unpaid services and to fill one of the ancient offices as constable, surveyor of highways or overseer of the poor, coupled with the direct participation of all householders in parish affairs through the vestry meeting. Local government in the expanding industrial age could not be conducted on a basis of part-time unskilled service, however, and a great variety of *ad hoc* bodies were summoned into existence to meet urgent needs.

The first measure of general reform, aimed at the local administration of the poor laws, came with the Poor Law Amendment Act 1834 and was prompted by the big increase in pauperism during and after the Napoleonic wars. It was based on the Report of the Royal Commission on the Administration of the Poor Laws (1834); it strongly reflected the views of Bentham and the Philosophical Radicals and was in total opposition to the historical spirit of local self-government which had inspired the reform of the municipalities. The poor laws were reformed on principles of efficiency and utility; new units of administration – the unions (there were about 650 unions at the end of the nineteenth century) – were defined by grouping parishes around the market towns which were their natural centres; a Board of Guardians, part elected with *ex officio* justices, became the poor law authority in each union, employing full-time officials; and a strong measure of central control and inspection was established coupled with a centralised audit system. Central control was exercised at first by the Poor Law Commissioners (the 'Three Bashaws of Somerset House'), a body which was transformed into a government department (the Poor Law Board) in 1847. It was later absorbed into the Local Government Board in 1871.

Attempts to tackle problems of urban squalor had started earlier but on a piecemeal basis. Between 1750 and 1835 a stream of local Acts set up *ad hoc* bodies of Improvement Commissioners for virtually all towns with populations of 10,000 or more, including many boroughs where, at first, the Commissioners existed side by side with the borough council. The main tasks of the Improvement Commissioners were connected with paving, lighting and cleansing of the main thoroughfares but some expanded into other activities and promoted further private Bills to enable them (for example) to abate nuisances, improve and widen streets, and provide sewers and a piped water supply.

But the work of the Improvement Commissioners touched only incidentally on public health. The need for action in this field was underlined by outbreaks of cholera, reinforced by the reports coming from the Poor Law Commissioners and the newly established Office of the Registrar General (the registration of births and deaths – and also the causes of deaths – started in 1836). Eventually the first steps towards a general system of public health administration were taken by the Public Health Act 1848 which contained a comprehensive code covering, *inter alia*, water supply, drainage, nuisances, the regulation of dwellings, burial grounds, public baths and recreation grounds. But this code did not apply automatically; it needed to be adopted – or it could be forced on a town with a very high death-rate. In boroughs the code could be adopted by the borough council but elsewhere a new *ad hoc* authority – the Local Board of Health – had to be brought into existence and its area of jurisdiction defined. Public health remained on a permissive basis until 1872 when, for the first time, a complete system of health administration was established for the whole country, covering areas and authorities and obliging all sanitary authorities to enforce the public health code. The Public Health Act 1872 (consolidated in the Public Health Act 1875) was described by Mr (later Sir Gwilym) Gibbon to the Onslow Commission as 'on the whole the most significant date in modern local government'.[8]

The urban sanitary authorities designated in 1872 were the borough councils, the Local Boards of Health and the (now comparatively few) Improvement Commissioners, and these urban sanitary districts were adopted as the county districts for urban areas by the LGA 1894 when the Local Boards of Health and the remaining Improvement Commissioners were abolished.

In the rural areas, that is, in the unions less the areas of the urban sanitary authorities, the PHA 1872 named the Poor Law Guardians as the rural sanitary authorities. An earlier Act (the Nuisance Removal Act 1846) had already placed some limited public health obligations on the Guardians and the 1872 Act preferred to rely on the newly established and more effective machinery (even though it had been established for poor law purposes) rather than go back to the rusty apparatus of the parish. These rural sanitary districts were adopted as the new rural districts in 1894 and a uniform constitution for the urban and rural district councils was established, based on direct elections. The rural district councils were separated from the Guardians in law, though they retained a close link in practice in that rural district councillors also sat as Guardians for rural areas.

To sum up: the county districts for urban areas had three separate sources of ancestry – boroughs to which royal charters had been granted at various times over many centuries; towns for which Improvement Commissioners had been established by local Acts during the late eighteenth and early nineteenth century; and towns which had chosen to set up Local Boards of Health since 1848. The rural districts, on the other hand, were based on the poor law unions from which these urban areas had been 'punched out'.

*Parish government* had fallen steadily into decay during the nineteenth century until the LGA 1894 made a determined effort to revive the ancient machinery. The relative importance of many parish functions had declined; others had been transferred to other bodies. The establishment of the Guardians had left the overseers with very few duties; in 1856 police had become an obligatory county function; after the Highways Act 1862 parishes could be forcibly grouped under Highways Boards for the maintenance of roads. Parishes generally had been reduced to the levying of the poor rate, the administration of parish property and charities, and such functions as might have been undertaken under a small group of Adoptive Acts, the most important of which dealt with lighting and with burials.

The reorganisation of county districts in urban areas and the consolidation of urban powers removed the need for another level of authorities in the towns, so the LGA 1894 concentrated on the 13,000-odd parishes in the rural districts in England and Wales. Hitherto the ultimate authority in the parishes had been the vestry - the assembly of all householders. This assembly, the parish meeting, was retained as an annual statutory requirement but where the population exceeded 300 a parish council had to be elected as well, for the regular exercise of day-to-day business on a representative basis. When the population was between 100 and 300 a parish council could be established if the county council agreed. The new governing bodies of the parishes took over all civil functions of the old vestries together with some new, though still very local, powers connected with, for example, allotments, recreation grounds and village greens.

*The metropolis.* London - the built-up town as a whole - has always played a special role in social history, not least because its very size intensified its urban problems of sanitation, housing, highways and public order. In 1700 the population had already reached some half a million - the largest city in Europe - and it continued to grow steadily. The area which became known as 'the metropolis' was in fact that covered by the bills of mortality in 1836 (when the Registrar General's office was established) and which was adopted as a unit for the publication of population statistics. Bills of mortality were the weekly lists kept by parish clerks showing the numbers who had died in each parish and the causes of their deaths. The original purpose of these lists was to give an indication of the prevalence of the plague in the London area so that the Court, and others, could leave if necessary. The area within which the bills were kept was not static: parishes were added as London grew. The area thus adopted as the metropolis in 1836 - which owed little to the consideration of local government needs - eventually became the administrative county of London and still survives, for some purposes, as 'inner London'.

Within the metropolis lay the City of London, a county of itself with its own lieutenancy, sheriffs and arrangements for the administration of justice - and implacably opposed, over the centuries, to any changes which would have diminished its ancient privileges. Outside the City the local government bodies matched those in the rest of the country, though with greater confusion. In the mid-nineteenth century there were over 100 vestries, nearly 100 bodies of Improvement Commissioners and sundry Commissioners of Sewers, Boards of Guardians, Turnpike Trusts and others - some 300 authorities in all. The situation required the rationalisation of this jungle of authorities and the establishment of a body with jurisdiction over the whole of London for at least certain services.

The first effective attempt to reform London government in this way was made in 1855. At the more local level elective vestries were established in twenty-three of the largest parishes, and the others were grouped into fifteen districts each with a District Board. These bodies absorbed the various Improvement Commissioners and were given responsibility for paving, lighting and improving their areas, and generally for public health – responsibilities which they discharged with indifferent success, however. The overall body set up in 1855 was the Metropolitan Board of Works, indirectly elected by the City (whose area was included within the Board's jurisdiction) and the thirty-eight newly organised vestries and District Boards. The immediate task of the Metropolitan Board of Works was to construct the main sewerage system which London so badly needed but, in addition, they were given a range of other functions including highway improvements, building regulations, housing and slum clearance, London trams and the fire brigade (Captain Shaw, apostrophised by the Queen of the Fairies in *Iolanthe*, was Chief Fire Officer of the Metropolitan Board of Works). On the other hand the Board's existence did not deter the creation of other metropolitan bodies with special functions, for example, the Metropolitan Asylums Board in 1867 (which became responsible for a wide range of hospitals) and the London School Board in 1870.

At that time the London area was made up of parts of Middlesex, Surrey and Kent but in 1888 these portions were detached to form the new administrative county of London with its own directly elected county council, though the LCC (which inherited the functions of the Metropolitan Board of Works) had much wider responsibilities than the other counties. The LGA 1894 which established the county district councils in other counties did not apply to London where a Royal Commission were investigating the possibility of amalgamating the City and the County of London. Their recommendations in favour of amalgamation (C. 7493, 1894) were not followed but they also recommended strengthening and improving the status of the second-tier authorities. This part of their report bore fruit in the London Government Act 1899 under which the thirty-eight vestries and District Boards were reduced by amalgamations to twenty-eight and each new unit given the status of metropolitan borough – a borough by Act of Parliament instead of by charter. The additional powers in the hands of the LCC meant, however, that there were fewer to be exercised by the metropolitan boroughs, who never had the range of functions possessed by non-county boroughs elsewhere.

## SUCCESSIVE APPROACHES TO LOCAL GOVERNMENT CHANGE

The social, economic and political pressures during the present century have pointed to the need for fewer and larger authorities to provide a widening range of services – services which have aimed at constantly rising standards for everyone, without differentiation between town and country; services which need more highly qualified staff and which absorb a far higher proportion of the nation's real resources. At the same time these background pressures have enhanced the role of the central government in central/local relations; increasingly local authority services, substantially paid for out of central taxation, are provided within national policies, and increasingly the central government have become involved to ensure that local authorities collectively are efficient and effective organisations capable of implementing those policies. Is it possible, albeit with the wisdom of hindsight, to identify aspects of the structure as it stood at the end of the nineteenth century which were likely to create problems, to require modification or to stand in the way of the changes needed to meet these pressures?

The three Acts of 1888, 1894 and 1899, taken together, constituted a further step in the continuing evolution of local government. They virtually completed the process of extending representative democratic government at local level and, although education and the relief of poverty still remained in the hands of special bodies, most other *ad hoc* authorities had been superseded by a coherent structure of elected councils. But it was a structure strongly shaped by its historical antecedents, with features explicable only by reference to the way in which it had developed.

In the first place the structure included two different types of local administration: single-tier all-purpose authorities in the county boroughs and two-tier arrangements in the administrative counties, with a special variety of two-tier government in London. The strength of the former was derived from the clear advantages to be gained in planning, administration and local accountability when all services in an area are concentrated in the hands of the same authority. The arguments in favour of two tiers are related to the administrative requirements of different services, some of which need wider areas while others can and should be dealt with on a more local basis. At the turn of the century, when local government services were far less fully developed and when attention chiefly concentrated on the environmental problems of the urban areas, these two systems existed side by side without difficulty. But services expanded and county functions became more important; at the same time there was a steady stream of applications to establish new county boroughs or to extend existing ones and, inevitably, there was friction and rivalry between the counties and the county boroughs.

The second feature of the structure derives from the fact that it was constructed of units already in existence. The counties, other than London, were essentially those into which the country had been divided for nearly a thousand years; the boroughs (county and non-county) were towns which had been incorporated at different times over the centuries; the urban and rural districts were units which had originally been brought into being for different and more limited purposes at various periods throughout the preceding hundred years. No attempt had been made to rationalise boundaries or to eliminate weaker authorities, with the result that, at each level, there were wide variations between the biggest and the smallest units and, especially among the county districts, a great number of small and potentially inadequate authorities. Notwithstanding the elimination of many *ad hoc* bodies, the number of authorities was still formidable; at the turn of the century there were over 1,700 county districts in England and Wales.[9]

Thirdly, the separate development of local government in the towns, largely because of public health and other problems there, had resulted in a divergence between the powers possessed by urban authorities as against those in rural areas – a divergence which was in due course to demand modification in times of greater mobility and more unified standards.

And, finally, the system, while substantially the creation of statute law, contained within itself a class of authorities – the boroughs – which claimed a special position by virtue of antiquity and their rights derived from royal charters. This claim, as the study will show, had important repercussions for the machinery of change.

To these particular features of the structure have to be added the general reasons – not least of which is the invariable expectation of local opposition – which made local government change a contentious and unrewarding topic (see pp. 0–0 above). The way in which successive governments have approached it forms the substance of the remainder of this study.

The background developments which required consequential change in local government took place gradually, though with drastic acceleration during and after each of the two world wars. Only by stages did they come into collision with the structural problems inherent in the system bequeathed by earlier centuries. Only by stages, too, were governments forced to grasp the problem of reform. 'Reform' and 'reorganisation' are, by the way, terms which have frequently been used in relation to local government change. Governments wishing to give the impression of boldness and drastic innovation have tended to use the former; those more influenced by the evolutionary approach have favoured the latter. In practice it is difficult to discern any real difference, so this study uses both terms without implying judgements of any kind.

Broadly the years covered by this study fall into three periods, though there is no absolute distinction – they overlap each other. The first period from 1888 to the LGA 1929 was one in which all changes were dealt with piecemeal. Boundary alterations were left to be proposed individually, and each was examined in isolation. There was no question, of course, of changing the main framework of the system – the coexistence of unitary authorities in the county boroughs with two-tier local government in the counties – which at that time had been only recently defined. Proposals for altering the boundaries or status of the individual authorities were initiated within local government, usually by the authority concerned, and each was dealt with on its merits through procedures which in some instances required the decision of Parliament.

The second period was one of limited attempts at reform - a period in which it was agreed that the county/county borough basis of the system should be retained but that, within this framework, systematic reviews should be carried out. Local government areas would be considered in relation to each other with a view to reducing the number of small authorities and rationalising boundaries in a redrawn pattern of units. Three separate efforts of this kind were made. In each case the government provided that the detailed work should be carried out by an agency other than the government itself, but operating within general guidance from the centre. The first moves of this kind stemmed from the second report of the Onslow Royal Commission on Local Government (Cmd 3213, 1928) on the basis of which county councils were given the duty, in the LGA 1929, to review the boundaries of county districts (counties and county boroughs being left meanwhile to the piecemeal procedures). The county reviews under the 1929 Act were carried out in the 1930s. After the Second World War further attempts at rationalisation were undertaken successively by the Local Government Boundary Commission (the Trustram Eve Commission) set up under the Local Government (Boundary Commission) Act 1945 (see pp. 59-70 below), and then by the Local Government Commission for England (the Hancock Commission) set up under the Local Government Act 1958 (see pp. 71-83 below). A separate Local Government Commission for Wales was also established by the 1958 Act under the chairmanship of Sir Guildhaume Myrddin-Evans. The terms of reference of both the Trustram Eve and Hancock Commissions included counties and county boroughs and went beyond county districts but in each case they were appointed to improve, though not to replace, the existing county/county borough structure. The last proposals made by the Hancock Commission were published in 1965; their work was not completed but local government reorganisation had by then moved into the third phase, and the Commission were formally dissolved by the Local Government (Termination of Reviews) Act 1967.

The third period overlapped the second and was the period of direct government action when, driven to the conclusion that the existing structure needed to be replaced and not merely amended, the government of the day accepted responsibility for preparing the necessary proposals, presenting them to Parliament in the form of major legislation and then following them through with all the further administrative action needed for their implementation. These affected local government in Greater London, where the London Government Act 1963 was closely based on the recommendations of the Herbert Royal Commission on Local Government in Greater London (Cmnd 1164, 1960) and then the rest of England

and Wales when reorganisation, under the LGA 1972, had been given powerful impetus by the publication of the report of the Redcliffe-Maud Royal Commission on Local Government in England (Cmnd 4040, 1969). From the point of view of the central government this last period of direct responsibility for the timing and machinery of change was the most demanding; it therefore receives fuller treatment in this study, which also looks at the various types of decisions and actions which the government had to take during the process of reorganisation.

## NOTES: CHAPTER 1

1    SI 1963 No. 231.
2    Herbert Commission Oral Evidence, Day 68 (12 January 1960), Q. 15,542.
3    F. W. Maitland, *The Forms of Action at Common Law* (Cambridge: CUP, 1936), p. 1.
4    Charles Booth *et al.*, *Life and Labour of the People in London* (London: Macmillan, 1892–7); B. Seebohm Rowntree, *Poverty, a Study of Town Life* (London: Macmillan, 1901).
5    The counties of cities were (in addition to London): Bristol, Newcastle-upon-Tyne, Norwich, York, Exeter, Lincoln, Chester, Gloucester, Worcester, Canterbury and Lichfield. The counties of towns were Nottingham, Kingston-upon-Hull, Southampton, Berwick-upon-Tweed, Poole, Carmarthen and Haverfordwest (Boroughs in England and Wales: classified statement by the Local Government Board, August 1888, HOC 316). In addition to those which were counties corporate many other boroughs had their own quarter sessions, too.
6    Onslow Commission Evidence, Pt III, Q. 8,772 (Lord Long).
7    ibid., Q. 8,786.
8    ibid., Pt I, p. 16 (Memorandum by Mr I. G. Gibbon, Ministry of Health, para. 29).
9    David Butler and Anne Sloman give the following figures for 1900: counties 62; county boroughs 67; non-county boroughs 250; urban districts 800; rural districts 663; to which have to be added 28 metropolitan boroughs and the City of London (*British Political Facts, 1900–1975*, London, Macmillan, 1975).

## Chapter 2

# The Period of Piecemeal Change

## BOUNDARY PROBLEMS OF THE NEW SYSTEM

The piecemeal approach to local government change characterised the period down to the Second World War so far as counties and county boroughs were concerned – and it was the problems of these authorities which bulked largest. For county districts, and particularly urban districts and rural districts, a new approach was heralded somewhat earlier by the LGA 1929; the affairs of these authorities are dealt with more fully in the next chapter.

The Acts of 1888, 1894 and 1889 had adopted the various units as they then existed and had done nothing to solve the boundary problems inherited from earlier times. The ancient county boundaries still included lengths which were uncertain or subject to dispute and there were many instances of a detached part of one county forming an island of territory within a neighbouring county. Borough boundaries were often based on the traditional extent of the town and frequently had little relation to the built-up area; sometimes the boundary included wide stretches of open country but more frequently the suburbs had overspilt the limits of the corporate authority so that, by the end of the century, the boundaries of all the big boroughs were out-of-date. The urban districts and rural districts, derived from their predecessor sanitary authorities, were based on areas originally defined for more limited purposes and at varying times. In the metropolis the area of the new county of London went back to an area adopted for statistical purposes in 1836 and the new metropolitan boroughs were based on parishes or groups of parishes.

It was natural that the general statutes applied to the country as a whole should make no attempt to review individual boundaries in detail. This was left to the machinery devised for the purpose but, meanwhile, the new settlement created additional problems which needed to be given priority. They arose from the aim to create a pattern of authorities whose areas should be logically related to each other, a pattern in which each county was to consist of a group of districts wholly contained within that county and in which districts were similarly to comprise a group of parishes none of which overlapped into other districts. No such principle had been followed before and there were many instances of poor law unions, boroughs, urban districts and parishes straddling county or district boundaries. When the Local Government Bill 1888 was introduced 172 unions (relevant here as the forerunners of the rural districts) were situated in more than one county, as were sixty-five boroughs and urban districts and sixty parishes.

There was an immediate need to eliminate these 'straddlers' in order to achieve, if only as a preliminary to further rationalisation, the set of self-contained areas which was an essential element of the new structure. This problem had in fact received a good deal of attention during the preliminary discussions and some advance steps had been taken to tackle it. Under the Local Government (Boundaries) Act 1887 Commissioners had been appointed for England and Wales to consider each county (outside the metropolis) and to report on the best method of adjusting boundaries so as to arrange that no union, borough, sanitary district or parish was situated in more than one county, and also on the best method of dealing with the detached parts of counties. At one stage it had been in mind that Boundary Commissioners should be appointed who would themselves prepare boundary alteration schemes for direct submission to Parliament. But the task of initiating any action (except in the case of the unions) was eventually laid on county councils and county borough councils; section 53 of the Act of 1888 merely provided that these councils should consider the Commissioners' reports and make such representations to the Local Government Board as they thought expedient for adjusting the boundaries of their county, and of other areas of local government, so as to secure that no such area should be situated in more than one county.

The LGA 1894 (section 24) made a more direct, if somewhat arbitrary, attack on the problem of overlapping districts in the rural areas by providing that any rural sanitary district which, on the appointed day under the Act, was still lying partly in one county and partly in another should be divided along the line of the county boundary, and that with certain exceptions each part should become a separate rural district. The exceptions were those instances where such a method of division would leave the major part of a district in one county and only a very small rump in another. The criterion adopted was whether the rump would return fewer than five councillors to the rural district council; in such cases the Local Government Board were empowered to direct that the rump area should continue, as an interim measure, to be administered as part of the district of which it originally formed part, though separate financial accounts had to be kept. In most cases, however, each part of a divided district became a separate unit and this approach in the Act of 1894 disposed of the main problem of overlapping districts; what remained was left to be tackled under the general machinery for boundary adjustments.

## GENERAL MACHINERY FOR BOUNDARY CHANGES

The general statutory provisions in the Acts of 1888 and 1894 contemplated that boundary alterations would be made by order, but the procedure differed according to the type of authorities to be affected; a fundamental distinction was drawn here between counties and boroughs (including both county boroughs and non-county boroughs) on the one hand, and urban districts, rural districts and parishes on the other. The London Government Act 1899, however, made no provision for altering the boundaries of the metropolitan boroughs or the City, so any changes to the areas of these authorities would have required legislation.

In the case of alterations affecting counties and boroughs[1] the initiative had to come from one of the local authorities concerned in the form of representations to the Local Government Board asking that an order be made; unless the Board 'for special reasons' considered that the representations should not be entertained, they were obliged to hold a public inquiry in all cases; then, if an order was made, it was provisional only and required to be confirmed by Parliament. Such provisional orders were brought before Parliament scheduled to Provisional Order Confirmation Bills where they followed a parliamentary procedure which was closely akin to that applicable to private Bills. These requirements reflected the special importance of the two major classes of authorities under the new system – the counties and the county boroughs – and (a consideration which also embraced the non-county boroughs) the special position historically accorded to municipal corporations who were, *inter alia*, entitled as common law corporations to seek boundary alterations direct from Parliament by way of private Bill. In all these instances Parliament retained the ultimate control when alterations were being proposed.

In the case of alterations affecting urban districts (other than boroughs), rural districts and parishes the essential characteristics of the machinery were different at all points. The proposals were formally initiated by the county council (not by the authorities most immediately affected); they reached the Local Government Board in the form of an order made by the county council (not as a request for an order to be made by the Board); the Board were not obliged to hold a public inquiry unless the county council's order was the subject of objections; and, finally, the county council's order became fully effective if confirmed by the Local Government Board (no confirmation by Parliament was needed and there were no parliamentary proceedings on these orders).

It is proposed to look in more detail at the first of these two contrasted pieces of machinery and in particular at the way the processes of change operated in connection with the creation and extension of county boroughs. This must necessarily involve references to the parliamentary procedure through which local legislation is dealt with, so it is best to consider private Bill procedure before examining the statutory machinery laid down by the Act of 1888.

## Private Bill procedure

Statutes are classified under three headings: public general Acts, local Acts and personal Acts (relating to the affairs of particular individuals or estates).

Local Acts were an important feature of the development of local government, especially between the mid-eighteenth and the mid-nineteenth centuries. During this period hundreds of local Acts were passed establishing *ad hoc* bodies, defining their functions, their constitutions and the areas within which they were entitled to operate. Local legislation has declined in volume and importance since then (so far as local government is concerned) largely because of the increase in public general legislation establishing classes of authorities and regulating their functions.

Essentially a private Bill, as promoted by a local authority, seeks special powers for the authority itself or proposes to extend or to modify the general law applying within the locality. Often an application for special powers arose from the need to acquire land or to carry out works, but a private Bill could also seek a change of boundaries or status, or both.

Although a private Bill (not to be confused with a Private Member's Bill, which is a public Bill but one which has been introduced by a private Member, not by the government) goes through the same main stages as a public Bill in each House of Parliament – first reading, second reading, committee, report and third reading – there are certain important differences in procedure. A public Bill originates in a motion by a Member for leave to introduce the Bill; a private Bill originates in a petition to Parliament. Standing Orders impose no procedural requirements on public Bills before introduction; in the case of private Bills a number of preliminary requirements, some statutory, some laid down by Standing Orders of the two Houses, must be observed. Public Bills have their committee stages on the floor of the House or in one of the Standing Committees; private Bills are invariably examined by a Select Committee.

Local authorities may promote private Bills only if they have the power to do so. Municipal corporations, being (until 1974) common law corporations, have always claimed this right, which was in effect converted into a statutory power for boroughs and for other urban authorities by the Borough Funds Act 1872[2] but was made subject to important procedural limitations. County councils were not at first given the power to promote private Bills though they could oppose Bills promoted by other authorities (under section 15 of the LGA 1888); they gained power to promote Bills under the County Councils (Bills in Parliament) Act 1903. The power to promote private Bills was given to rural district councils by the LGA 1929 (section 55). It has never been possessed by parish councils though such councils may oppose private Bills (if necessary), relying on inherent powers to take any action needed to protect their interests or those of their inhabitants.

The *preliminary procedural requirements* which had been applied by the Borough Funds Acts to the promotion of private Bills by boroughs and urban districts afford an interesting example of the relationship between procedure and policy. The numerous procedural obstacles placed in the way of such Bills (and particularly requirements relating to town meetings and town polls) were regarded by opponents of municipal trading as safeguards against the spread of socialism and cherished for that reason. Briefly the requirements were these:

(a) a special meeting of the council had to be held to consider the proposal that a Bill be promoted;

(b) a resolution to promote the Bill had to be passed by an absolute majority of the total council membership (and not merely a majority of those attending the voting, which is the normal rule in local government);

(c) after the meeting the terms of the resolution had to be published twice in local newspapers and submitted to the Local Government Board for approval; (the Board (and their successor departments) had to wait seven days for objections but in practice consent was always given if the procedural requirements had been complied with; this stage of central government approval of the council's resolution was never used to veto a private Bill even though the government might not agree with its contents and might later oppose it in Parliament);

(d) the next stage was to deposit the petition and draft Bill in Parliament, after which another special meeting of the council had to be held at which the council had to confirm their intention to go ahead with the Bill, and again an absolute majority of the total membership was required;

(e) simultaneously with arrangements for this second meeting of the council, the authority was required to seek the approval of the town as a whole through the procedure of the town meeting and (if necessary) town poll.

This last item in the procedure (originally borrowed from the Local Government Act 1858, which defined the steps to be taken before the public health code was adopted in the locality and a Local Board of Health established) required the council to arrange a meeting open to all electors at which the Bill's provisions were orally explained, and a motion put to the meeting to approve the Bill *en bloc* or by each provision individually. The outcome of this procedure at the meeting could be challenged in either direction, in which case a poll was arranged by secret ballot, on the same lines as a local election, at which the local electorate voted on whether the Bill should be promoted. Such polls usually attracted little attention and, with a very small turnout, it was not difficult for opponents to whip up a sufficient number of votes to defeat the Bill as a whole or specific parts of it – hence the attraction of this procedure (which vanished only with the LGA 1972) to opponents of innovation.[3]

Only if the Bill cleared all these hurdles did it proceed; if it failed to retain support at the second council meeting, or at the town meeting or town poll, the Bill had to be withdrawn in whole or in part. The obligation to arrange a town meeting and (if necessary) a town poll applied only in the case of the promotion of a Bill by a borough or an urban district, however; it did not apply to Bills promoted by county councils or rural district councils though they were required to follow all the other procedural stages.

Quite apart from the statutory requirements, promoters of private Bills must strictly observe certain requirements laid down by the two Houses of Parliament in Standing Orders. These are broadly of two kinds: Standing Orders which specify the dates by which documents shall be deposited in Parliament and the way in which those documents (including the draft Bill and any supporting plans) should be prepared, and Standing Orders which require a promoter to advertise the objects of the proposed Bill and serve individual notices on the owners and occupiers of properties which would be specially affected by the Bill's provisions.

When a private Bill becomes subject to *proceedings in Parliament* the preamble assumes much greater significance than in the case of a public Bill. The preamble to a private Bill sets out the facts on which the petitioners rely, it asserts the desirability of their objectives and claims that these objectives cannot be achieved without the special powers or provisions contained in the Bill whose passage they seek. It is essential to the promoter's case, therefore, that they should 'prove the preamble', that is, convince Parliament of the desirability, in principle, of the case for the Bill, quite apart from the need to satisfy the two Houses on the details of each clause. In the great majority of cases the merits or demerits of private Bills are not discussed on the floor of the House in either the Commons or the Lords. The first, second and third readings are normally formalities, the real consideration being concentrated in the committee stage, including the process of 'proving the preamble'.

This is not invariably the case, however, as a private Bill may raise general issues of wider importance and may seem to be objectionable in principle, in which case the second reading may be blocked by one or more dissenting Member (possibly with government approval or encouragement), in which case a debate is arranged. But a second reading debate on a private Bill has a different effect from this stage in a public Bill. When a public Bill is read a second time the House clearly accepts the objectives and need for the Bill in principle. But if a private Bill is read a second time (whether debated or not) the House is deemed to have done no more than accept the Bill in principle on the assumption that the allegations in the preamble are correct; the preamble still has to be proved in committee, and it is the committee stage which is the real equivalent of the second reading of a public Bill. If a private Bill is refused a second reading in either House it is, of course, killed stone dead, but even if it is given a second reading it could still be rejected on merits in committee or (again very exceptionally) on report or third reading.

The *committee stage* is therefore the most important in the parliamentary proceedings on a private Bill, but the present arrangements are very different from those obtaining in the eighteenth and early nineteenth centuries. It was then usual for MPs with constituency interests to sit on private Bill committees considering Bills in which they were closely involved. But modern rules exclude from Select Committees on private Bills any Member or Peer with a personal or constituency interest. This change reflects a completely different attitude to the nature of the committee proceedings. No longer are those proceedings governed by manoeuvres aimed at maximising the supporting (or opposing) votes of numerous committee members who may or may not have heard the arguments. Unopposed private Bills and the unopposed provisions of opposed Bills are examined (in the Commons) by the Unopposed Bill Committee, presided over by the Chairman of Ways and Means and (in the Lords) by the Lord Chairman of Committees sitting alone. Opposed Bills are examined by Select Committees appointed separately for each Bill, with four members in the Commons and five in the Lords and the proceedings are more akin to a legal than to a political process.

> In passing private Bills, Parliament still exercises its legislative functions, but its proceedings partake also of a judicial character. The persons whose private interests are to be promoted appear as suitors for the Bill; while those who apprehend injury are admitted as adverse parties in the suit. Many of the formalities of a court of justice are maintained; various conditions are required to be observed and their observance to be strictly proved; and if the parties do not sustain the Bill in its progress, by following every regulation and form prescribed, it is not forwarded by the House in which it is pending. If they abandon it . . . the Bill is lost, however sensible the House may be of its value.[4]

Opposed proceedings before a private Bill committee indeed closely resemble those in a court of law. The promoters are invariably represented by counsel, instructed by parliamentary agents, and the onus is on them to prove the substantive case for the Bill and for each of the separate provisions. Those who are opposed to the Bill's general objectives or to particular provisions appear (generally through counsel) as petitioners, provided they have a *locus standi*. But once a local authority has decided, through the prescribed procedures, to promote a private Bill this decision also binds individual electors; no elector may petition against a Bill promoted by his own authority unless he is personally affected (for example, through property that he owns) in some way that is special to himself. When valid petitions are lodged, however, each side may call witnesses, who are examined and cross-examined, and the case for and against the Bill rests on the evidence thus adduced and the arguments placed before the committee.

Government departments are not parties to these quasi-judicial proceedings before private Bill committees but Standing Orders of each House ensure that they are brought into the picture. Promoters are required to lodge a copy of each private Bill with certain specified departments, which include the Treasury and the department with general responsibility for local government – the Local Government Board and their successors. Departments report to Parliament in writing on those parts of private Bills which impinge on matters within the jurisdiction of their responsibe minister and each report is referred to the committee considering the Bill in question. The committee may, if they think fit, hear an officer of the department in explanation of the report. Civil servants attending private Bill committees on such occasions do so, however, only as Spokesmen for their minister and they speak (literally, as well as figuratively) from the sidelines; they are not subject to examination or cross-examination by the promoters or petitioners though counsel may put questions to departmental representatives through the chairman of the committee.

The central government contribution may nevertheless be significant. Departmental reports normally contain detailed and factual information on the extent to which powers proposed in the Bill have been precedented in earlier local Acts, or the way in which clauses differ from provisions already allowed by Parliament in other cases. In some circumstances, however, departmental reports may deal with matters of policy raised by the preamble, and may contain recommendations from the responsible minister as to the proof of the preamble or the acceptability of particular provisions. The committee are not bound to accept such recommendations but they are required by Standing Orders to take notice of them, and to state their reasons for dissenting if they do not follow a ministerial recommendation – a requirement which has not always been followed in recent years.

Broadly, a minister has three courses of action when considering a private Bill presented to Parliament on a subject within his jurisdiction. He can, if he is wholly opposed to the objects of the Bill, make sure that the Bill is refused a formal second reading (by arranging for a Member to cry 'object' when the formal motion is read out) so that a debate is held on whether the Bill should be given a second reading at all. In such a debate he may speak against the Bill and advise its rejection. It is unusual for the whips to be put on to ensure the defeat of a private Bill, even one which is unwelcome to the government (or to ensure that a private Bill approved by the government receives a second reading) but this course is not absolutely unknown. Alternatively, a minister concerned could take no action at second reading but use the machinery of the departmental report, supplemented by any oral explanation which his civil servants may be invited to give, to try to persuade the committee to reject or accept proposals contained in the Bill. Thirdly, he may offer only factual comments on the Bill, without any recommendation for or against on merits, and leave the decision entirely in the hands of the committee to decide on the evidence and arguments used by the parties. And it is interesting to note that this was the course normally followed by the President of the Local Government Board on private Bills promoted before the First World War to create or to extend county boroughs.

In practice, prudent local authorities who contemplate the promotion of a private Bill contact the responsible government department very well in advance, so that they may gain an early idea of the minister's likely attitude. These advance discussions can go a long way towards removing possible sources of disagreement and hence reducing the risk of an adverse ministerial report. It is only when advance discussions have failed to produce agreement that the minister has to resort to formal steps during the parliamentary proceedings.

The proceedings before an opposed committee on a private Bill may, therefore, be prolonged (and correspondingly costly), with all the arguments for and against deployed in full with the assistance of counsel and witnesses - expert and otherwise. It is important to remember, too, that private Bill procedure offers the opportunity for objections to be pursued in exactly the same way in the second House. Objectors who are unsuccessful in the first House may well decide not to incur the additional expense of repeating their objections in the second. But they are entitled to pursue those objections if they wish (and can afford) to do so, and private Bills which deal with matters of deeply felt controversy may well be argued in full in each House.

## Provisional orders

Private Bill procedure is relevant in the context of this study not only because many changes in areas and status have been effected by private Bills but also because provisional orders may follow the same procedure when before Parliament. Provisional orders were introduced by the Public Health Act 1848 and were developed and extended during the latter half of the nineteenth century. Some orders are still made under this procedure which was devised to provide an alternative route to local legislation which would be more convenient, cheaper and quicker than private Bills while re-lieving Parliament of much detailed work – though not the ultimate control.

In a number of statutes Parliament devolved order-making powers to government departments within defined fields, and prescribed procedures which very frequently included the holding of a public local inquiry. Within the limits of the enabling powers, and subject to the observance of the procedural requirements, departments could make orders granting powers to individual local authorities who would otherwise have had to promote their own private Bills. Such orders were 'provisional' however and had no effect unless and until confirmed by Parliament. This confirmation was sought by annexing the order – or, more often, several orders – to a Provisional Order Confirmation Bill which, if passed, gave parliamentary approval to the scheduled orders and brought them into force.

As in the case of private Bills, the initiative would have come from the interested authority but the main investigation would have been under-taken, not by parliamentary committees, but by the responsibile depart-ment which, in the case of the boundaries and areas of local authorities was, of course, the Local Government Board and their successors. The local inquiry was more convenient to the parties, both promoters and objectors and, as most provisional orders were unopposed, the parliamen-tary proceedings were both quicker and less expensive than proceedings by way of private Bill.

But in granting such order-making powers Parliament did not divest itself of all – or indeed any – of its powers to scrutinise the proposals in detail or to decide the ultimate shape of any local legislation which emerged. A Provisional Order Confirmation Bill starts its parliamentary life as a public Bill (that is, no preliminary procedural requirements are imposed by Standing Orders in addition to those laid down in the enabling statute) but after introduction it becomes subject to the procedure governing private Bills. Notices and local advertisements are required, and persons or bodies who would have been entitled to petition against the proposal if they had come forward as a private Bill have exactly the same power to petition against a provisional order. For its committee stage the confirmation Bill is remitted in each House to an Opposed or Unopposed Bill Committee (as a private Bill would be) and the same quasi-judicial proceedings are followed. In the case of an opposed order the onus is on the promoters (that is, the local authority whose initiative led to the making of the order) to prove the case for the order, just as a promoter has to prove the preamble of a private Bill.

The preliminary procedures for which government departments are responsible – and especially the department's opportunity to reach a conclusion and draft the order after having heard all the views expressed at the public inquiry – has meant that, in practice and looking at provisional orders as a whole, they have usually been unopposed in Parliament, so that the proceedings there have been easier and cheaper than private Bill legislation. But this has not invariably been the case, and certainly not in the field of local government authorities and areas. In 1913, for instance, the Local Government Board's Bill to confirm three provisional orders which would have given county borough status to Cambridge, Luton and Wakefield was given a very rough ride in Parliament and rejected by the Commons on third reading;[5] and in 1914 the Croydon extension order was rejected at the second reading stage of the confirmation Bill. Orders involving the areas and status of local authorities were, moreover, frequently opposed at the committee stage of the confirmation Bill in one or both Houses. Between 1888 and 1923 the Local Government Board and the Ministry of Health brought a total of 173 provisional orders to Parliament for the extension of county boroughs or non-county boroughs; seventy-five of these were opposed in Parliament and, for orders affecting only county boroughs, the proportion was even higher (forty-four were opposed out of seventy-two).[6]

These figures are significant for two reasons. First, because they underline the point already made that proposed changes in the local government map are frequently controversial. And, secondly, because the opposed proceedings before the Houses of Parliament, triggered off by petitions from objectors, were additional to the public inquiry held by the department at which the same parties would have been engaged. So while provisional orders as a whole were generally unopposed in Parliament this generalisation by no means applied to orders affecting boroughs and county boroughs; in those cases it was not uncommon for the proposals to be argued three times – at the public inquiry and before each House. The procedure which aimed at being cheaper and quicker than private Bills could in fact turn out to be the reverse.

This last point would have weighed with local authorities among the matters to be taken into account when deciding whether to apply for a provisional order or to promote a private Bill. The Borough Funds Act 1872 prohibited the promotion of a private Bill for an object which could be achieved by provisional order but this was only a partial deterrent. Most initiatives for the extension of county and other boroughs between 1888 and 1923 were applications for provisional orders (262, as against seventy-eight applications in private Bills) but the number of private Bill applications was still substantial. In many cases, no doubt, local authorities applying for extensions by private Bill would have proceeded in this way because they were also seeking powers in connection with other matters for which provisional orders were not available.

## THE CREATION AND EXTENSION OF COUNTY BOROUGHS

The detailed provisions of the LGA 1888 (section 54) applying to the creation of a new county borough and to the alteration of borough boundaries have to be considered against the way in which these two procedures – for private Bills and provisional orders – worked in practice.

The Act required the initiative to be taken by the council of a county or of a borough, who were empowered to make representations to the Local Government Board (and the Board's successors) to the effect that it was desirable to make the boundary order sought, or to constitute a borough (with a population of not less than 50,000) into a county borough. Where any such representations were made the Board might take the view 'for special reasons' that the proposals should not be entertained, but in all other cases a public inquiry was obligatory. The Board might make an order on the lines requested, or with modifications, or they might refuse to make any order at all. If, in the light of the inquiry, an order was made it was provisional and required to be confirmed by Parliament.

In the decades following the passing of the Act many alterations to county boundaries were made. Generally they were small and caused little controversy, consisting in the adjustment of parish boundaries or the transfer of parishes detached from the county by which they were administered to the county with which they were geographically connected.

But proposals to create new county boroughs and to extend existing ones became a major source of conflict with the counties who stood to lose territory, population and rateable value. In the period 1888–1922, twenty-three new county boroughs were created but as two of the original county boroughs were merged into others (Hanley into Stoke-on-Trent and Devonport into Plymouth) the net addition was twenty-one – making a total of eighty-two county boroughs in England and Wales. During the same period no fewer than sixty county boroughs were granted boundary extensions.[7] Taken together these new creations and county borough extensions involved a loss to the counties of some 350,000 acres, 3 million in population and £14·5m in rateable value. Twenty-seven of the sixty-one counties outside London were affected and these counties lost in total about one-fifth of their population and rateable value.[8]

All these new county borough creations and most of the county borough extensions had taken place before the First World War. In most cases they had been opposed by the county councils, whose collective disquiet was quickly reawakened after the war by the extension proposals put forward by Leeds, Bradford, Sheffield and Nottingham. The West Riding County Council was particularly agitated by the proposals of Leeds and Bradford to swallow up all the territory lying between these two cities and naturally had in mind that there were seven other county boroughs in the West Riding as well. If they all entertained aspirations on this scale the county council would be faced with impossible problems of finance and organisation in what remained of their area.

The situation led to a revival of a proposal, made earlier by the counties in 1913, that the whole question of county borough creations and extensions should be re-examined by a Royal Commission and this was the course followed by the government after the then Minister of Health (Sir Alfred Mond) had failed to extract an agreed approach from informal talks with the County Councils Association (CCA) and the Association of Municipal Corporations (AMC) - to which representatives of the other two main associations, the Rural District Councils Association (RDCA) and the Urban District Councils Association (UDCA) had not been invited (as these associations discovered to their subsequent vexation). The Royal Commission on Local Government, under the chairmanship of Lord Onslow, was appointed in 1923 with the task of inquiring into the existing law and procedure relating to the extension of county boroughs and the creation of new ones. The decision to set up the Royal Commission had been announced the previous year (Commons Hansard, 13 June 1922, cols 306-7) but the actual appointment was deferred because the Royal Commission on London Government (the Ullswater Royal Commission) were then sitting (see below, pp. 89-90). The full terms of reference of the Onslow Commission were 'to inquire as to the existing law and procedure relating to the extensions of county boroughs and the creation of new county boroughs in England and Wales, and the effect of such extensions or creations on the administration of the councils of counties and of non-county boroughs, urban districts and rural districts; to investigate the relations between these several local authorities; and generally to make recommendations as to their constitution, areas and functions'.

When the Commission got down to work the CCA were the first local government witnesses to be heard. This was appropriate, as the setting up of the Commission was primarily occasioned by the dissatisfaction of the county councils at the way in which the machinery for change was operating. The views which they elaborated to the Commission were in fact partly on procedure and partly on related aspects of policy.

On machinery, they were not happy about the provisional order procedure. This was suitable for simple and uncontroversial cases but contested boundary proposals were in practice often fought out on three separate occasions - at the ministry's initial statutory inquiry and then in each House of Parliament. Figures produced in evidence showed that the level of costs incurred at the public inquiry was often much the same as during the parliamentary proceedings; in other words the preliminary public inquiry doubled the costs in controversial cases.[9]

This multiplicity of battles might be reduced, at any rate from three to two, in alternative ways, both of which were discussed by witnesses. The first possibility would be to abandon the provisional order procedure altogether in these cases, along with the departmental inquiry, and to require applicants to proceed by way of private Bill. Alternatively, if the provisional order procedure and departmental inquiry were retained, the way to reduce the number of confrontations would be to hold only one parliamentary investigation into the Provisional Order Confirmation Bill – by a Joint Committee of both Houses – instead of separate hearings in each House. This suggestion had already been made in the context of provisional orders generally, not only those dealing with boroughs and county boroughs, and had received an approving nod from the Acquisition of Powers Sub-Committee of the Reconstruction Committee in 1918 (Cd 8982).

The attitude of the two main associations on this point reflected the extent to which their members appeared to gain or lose by the existing procedure. Both favoured reducing the number of separate hearings but the AMC wished to retain the departmental inquiry as one of these, and hence supported the idea that parliamentary proceedings should be before a Joint Committee. The CCA, on the other hand, preferred to eliminate the departmental inquiry and wanted contested proposals to be dealt with through the private Bill procedure. This view was not based solely on grounds of economy in money and effort. It sprang also from a distrust of the role of the Ministry of Health in connection with provisional orders – a distrust which attached itself to the mechanics of handling provisional order applications, to the criteria applied by the ministry and indeed to the whole attitude of the department to applications put forward by borough councils.

The Local Government Board (and the Ministry of Health) had, for instance, regularly issued instructions telling local authorities how and when to submit applications for provisional orders. But these instructions were sent by the department only to borough councils and not to county councils, though the latter were equally entitled to propose area alterations. This almost appeared as if the department were inciting one class of authorities to make proposals altering the *status quo* whereas strict impartiality would demand that such instructions were sent to all types of authorities affected. There was no sinister motive, said the department, but purely a matter of convenience based on experience.[10] In practice virtually all such proposals were initiated by borough councils and hence it was sensible to aim the instructions at them.

When representations were received the department had a domestic conference of the officials concerned for a preliminary consideration of the proposals, and then it was not uncommon for an inspector to visit the locality for an informal discussion of the issues. The object, as explained to the Royal Commission, was reasonable and potentially advantageous – to find out whether all or any part of the proposal should be rejected at once as a non-starter (thus saving further expense), to promote whatever measure of agreement might be possible between the parties, and to identify the main points at issue.[11] But to the county councils, who generally figured as objectors, this informal inquiry almost looked like an irregular examination of the merits of the issues. They feared, moreover, that by the time proposals reached the public inquiry stage the department would, consciously or unconsciously, already be regarding them as prima facie acceptable because they had passed through the preliminary stages of the departmental examination and the inspector's informal visit.

The formal inquiry followed and the inspector reported to the minister; in the great majority of cases his recommendations were accepted. Here again were possible grounds of apprehension, based on the inspector's qualifications and his independence. Such inquiries were held by engineering inspectors, partly because engineering services connected with sewerage, water supply, refuse disposal, highways and housing figured prominently in any consideration of the level of local government services, and partly because, in their everyday work in these fields, engineering inspectors inevitably acquired a wide knowledge of local government and considerable experience in the technique of holding inquiries. To those who were less impressed by these considerations it appeared that too much weight was often given to the public health services and that the inspector, being an officer of the department, could never be regarded as wholly independent.

When the procedural requirements had been complied with the moment arrived consider the merits of the proposals and, in connection with county borough extensions, the department listed eight considerations which the minister took into account.[12] The overall aim was to ensure 'efficient and economical local government with reasonable regard to the wishes of the inhabitants'. Under the general heading of efficiency and economy the minister looked at such matters as whether the enlarged area would make a good local government unit, at the borough's record of administration, at whether the proposed added area was in fact an outgrowth of the borough, at the likely financial repercussions, at the community of interest between the borough and the added area, at any claim by the borough based on the need for further land for development and of course at the effect on other local government areas if territory was transferred to the county borough.

All these matters could raise difficult problems but the sharpest controversy often arose over the wishes of the inhabitants which were (and are) notoriously difficult to ascertain and to assess. Nor had this task been significantly eased by the 'Kintore decision' in the report of the Joint Committee (under Lord Kintore) which considered and rejected the Birkenhead Extension Order 1920. The Committee expressed the view 'that (subject to special considerations of public advantage) no provisional order for borough extensions should be brought before Parliament for confirmation which has not previously received the substantial support of the ratepayers in the areas proposed to be incorporated'. Exactly how the 'substantial support' should be sought and obtained was not clear, nor was guidance vouchsafed on the meaning of the saving clause 'subject to special considerations of public advantage'. The best the department's witness could say on this point to the Onslow Commission was that the wishes of the inhabitants were of course given 'the very closest consideration' but that they were not conclusive.[13]

It was a cause of dissatisfaction to the counties that the matters listed by the ministry as requiring to be considered when reaching a conclusion on a borough application looked like a list of positive tests on which, if the borough could score points under each heading, they would be granted their application. Witnesses for the CCA would have slanted the approach differently. Mr Vibart Dixon strongly urged that principles should be laid down in the interests of local government stability. In its shortest form the essential rule sought by the Association was that the onus should rest firmly on those who proposed change to prove its desirability, and that unless they were able to discharge this onus of proof the *status quo* should be maintained.[14]

This question of the onus of proof has cropped up at frequent intervals in the history of local government change and is obviously important when the accent is on formal procedures akin to those of a court of law. But when section 54 of the 1888 Act spoke of making changes that are 'desirable' it was clearly intended to give this term a wide interpretation so that all considerations could be taken into account. The advantages to one authority would need to be weighed against the disadvantages to another, and the Onslow Royal Commission quoted with approval the interpretation put on the word 'desirable' by Mr Asquith (when Prime Minister) when he said that a proposal must be desirable in the interests of all persons concerned, and that if the interests of various local authorities in the same proposal were divergent, the question whether the proposal was desirable must be settled upon an equitable and judicial balance as between all the divergent interests (Cmd 2506, para. 1235).

The CCA felt, however, that in operating the provisional order procedure the ministry were not completely impartial but brought to each proposal a mind already predisposed to favour the municipal form of local government. The department's whole attitude suggested (according to Sir Ryland Adkins) 'that the Ministry were so much more closely associated by tradition with boroughs taking the initiative than with counties acting on the defence'.[15]

The same thought was prompted in the minds of some of the Commission by the department's memorandum which said, apropos new applications for county borough status, that the department looked to make sure the 50,000 population minimum had been achieved, that the town was well administered and that the severance of the town would not seriously detract from good county government, but that once satisfied on these points the minister 'would favourably consider such an application'. As Mr Gibbon explained on behalf of the department, if these requirements were met there was a presumption that the application would be granted.[16]

Indeed it is difficult not to think that the presumption worked in favour of the municipalities, particularly in the light of the Local Government Board's decision to make orders conferring county borough status on Cambridge and Luton. At the time - in 1913 - Cambridge had a population of 56,000 out of the total county population of 128,000; the borough had nearly half the total population of the county and more than half the rateable value. The population figures in the case of Luton were 53,000 out of 197,000; the borough accounted for about one-quarter of the total population and rateable value of Bedfordshire.[17] Despite these figures the department gave the boroughs the benefit of the doubt, in coming to the conclusion that severance of the towns in question would not seriously harm the county administration. Parliament took the opposite view however - that the damage to the counties would outweigh the benefits to the boroughs - when the Provisional Order Confirmation Bill was rejected on third reading in the Commons (Commons Hansard, 26 March 1914, cols 654-96).

So although the Royal Commission's terms of reference spoke of the machinery of change, the real issue was one of substance rather than machinery and emerged as the balance between the county system of local government with different levels of authorities and the unified system represented by the county boroughs.

Both the main antagonists claimed the authority of history. 'From time immemorial', said the CCA, 'local government in this country had been preserved in unbroken continuity on the same basic system, namely, the county as the main unit, the hundred (or district) and the borough as the intermediate units, and the township (or parish). From time to time new methods of procedure have been established and new powers and duties have been conferred in order to meet changed social and economic conditions, but the system has remained unaltered, subject only to one exception. That exception is the county borough unit, which was established by the Local Government Act of 1888 to provide autonomy for what were apparently then regarded as special areas'.[18] 'Municipal corporations' (asserted the AMC) 'are the oldest existing form of local authority in this country, and they differ from all other forms of local government authorities in that they are common law corporations created by royal charter, whilst all other local authorities are statutory corporations.'[19]

The CCA placed considerable emphasis on the point that county boroughs should be regarded as exceptions to the basic system of local government. This was underlined (in their view) by the fact that the Bill for the Local Government Act 1888 had not, as originally introduced, contained any provision for the creation of additional county boroughs in the future. And now the balance between counties and county boroughs was being upset by the way the machinery for change, imported into the Act as it went through Parliament, was being used, namely, 'to effect such a redistribution of areas as would amount to the virtual destruction of the system adopted by Parliament in passing that Act. It would be against all principles of public policy to effect fundamental changes of this character by a piecemeal process of departmental orders, made ostensibly for alterations of boundaries. If the altered conditions of local government demand a re-arrangement of areas, it is essentially a matter to be determined by general legislation applied to the country as a whole.'[20] As the machinery was being applied, county boroughs (it was alleged) thought of the areas of administrative counties merely as a reservoir from which they could draw additional supplies of territory and rateable value whenever they so desired.[21] 'The interpretation of the section [section 54, LGA 1888] is therefore a direct issue between the counties and the county boroughs'[22] and, in pressing for a review of the whole issue, the CCA also urged that the minimum population figure for any further creations should be substantially raised to take account of the great increase both in the population of the country and in local government functions since 1888; the reduction from 150,000 to 50,000 had been unwise in 1888 and Parliament should now revert to the original figure, or even one of 250,000.[23]

This was not how the AMC saw things. The movement of the population into urban areas had continued and was continuing, and it would be for general benefit if the form of government developed for towns was correspondingly extended. 'In order to secure efficiency and economy in local government it is necessary to simplify the administration whenever possible, to reduce by means of amalgamations the number of local authorities each having its own separate staff and services, and whenever practicable to arrange that only one local authority should have jurisdiction over a given area.'[24] Sir Robert Fox, speaking for the AMC, robustly rejected any proposal to raise the minimum population figure; it had been arrived at after considerable discussion as the point at which a claim for county borough status might be initiated, experience had shown it to be a very fair figure, and general changes in the population since 1889 were irrelevant.[25] The Royal Commission were hearing (as later Royal Commissions were to hear again) the opposed view of the shire tradition of local government with two or even three levels of authorities based on the different needs of different services, as against the administrative advantages of concentrating authority in the hands of a single council. The opposition between these points of view came through starkly; as one member of the Commission put it, 'the extreme borough view is that they are oases in a desert; the extreme county view is that boroughs are mere details of the county; the truth lies between the two'.[26]

Figures produced by the Ministry of Health showed, however, that even during the first quarter of the century the general trends in local government services were already clear. It is true that between 1891 and 1921 the proportion of the population (outside London) living in county boroughs increased from about 33 to 38 per cent and that the total rateable value of the county boroughs had increased far more rapidly than in the counties. But during this period local government functions had expanded and they now included education and maternity and child welfare. Significantly, in the counties, these functions had been substantially given to the county councils, thus increasing their importance in comparison with county districts on the one hand and county boroughs on the other. Higher education was entirely a county function; elementary education was a county responsibility save for those boroughs with populations over 10,000 and urban districts over 20,000; maternity and child welfare functions were exercised concurrently with borough councils, urban district and rural district councils. It was in the field of these services that expenditure was growing most rapidly. The total current expenditure of all local authorities in England and Wales (excluding trading services) had been £50m in 1895/6, out of which education accounted for £8m or 16 per cent; in 1919/20 the total expenditure was £185m but education was now easily the largest single service and accounted for £57m or 30 per cent. In other words, the way in which services had expanded since the beginning of the century had tended to enhance the role of the counties in the local government system.

## THE ONSLOW COMMISSION'S RECOMMENDATIONS

The Commission's first report, published in 1925 (Cmd 2506), was entirely devoted to the creation of further county boroughs and the extension of existing ones. It was a long and weighty document, much of which consisted of summaries of the evidence put before them. The general purport of their recommendations, however, was a vindication of the views advanced on behalf of the counties – that the provisional order procedure was unsatisfactory in contested cases (which could involve three separate hearings) and that its operation by the Local Government Board and the Ministry of Health in practice favoured the municipalities at the expense of the counties.

The Commission's two main proposals were: first, that no further county boroughs should be created by provisional order; all new applications should be by way of private Bill, whose procedure had not attracted the same criticisms. Bills promoted solely for the purpose of seeking county borough status (or the extension of an existing county borough) should be exempt from the provisions of the Borough Funds Acts with regard to town meetings and town polls but the minimum population figure for new county boroughs should be raised from 50,000 to 75,000. And secondly, that the provisional order procedure should remain available for county borough extensions, but only for proposals which were unopposed by any other interested local authority; opposed cases should proceed only by way of private Bill. The provisional order procedure (as provided by the 1888 Act) was retained, however, for the union of one county borough with another, that is, for proposals which did not involve a conflict between a county borough and a county. These proposals, which required legislation, were accepted by the government and they were given effect in the Local Government (County Boroughs and Adjustments) Act 1926. The revised figure of 75,000, which became the minimum qualifying population before a claim for county borough status could be made, was in no case a test of whether such a claim should be granted but only a bar to prevent unreasonable proposals from being put forward. The Commission declared that this population limit was one of the most difficult they had to consider, and it appeared that they reached their conclusion on broad and general considerations without the scientific assessment of the requirements of different services attempted by the Redcliffe-Maud Commission (Cmnd 2506, paras 1259–63).

In 1926 there were twenty-two non-county boroughs and urban districts with populations exceeding 50,000 but only seven of these were over 75,000.[27] An attempt was made during the committee stage in the Commons to exempt those towns which had already reached the 50,000 mark (for example, Cambridge) from being caught by the new and higher figure, but this was defeated; the only exception allowed was Doncaster, who had made an earlier application in 1921 and who had renewed it by lodging a private Bill before the County Boroughs and Adjustments Bill had been introduced.

The Onslow Commission's recommendations, and the legislation based on them, essentially aimed at re-establishing a situation of balance as between the counties and the county boroughs within the framework of the system as laid down by the 1888 Act. The solution did not prohibit further change – though, in the event, no further county boroughs were created by private Bill after Doncaster in 1926 – but it ensured that such changes would be made by procedures in which the main contenders had confidence. Major proposals would henceforth require to be pursued through private Bills. The Minister of Health would, of course, report on such Bills and give his views on their merits and on their possible repercussions elsewhere. But the modified procedure laid greater emphasis on the parliamentary settlement of contested proposals, each of which would be considered as separate issues by a quasi-judicial tribunal.

## THE CREATION OF NEW BOROUGHS

County boroughs were a class of authorities created by statute and were a clear and self-contained element in the structure of local government. Constitutionally, however, all boroughs – county boroughs and non-county boroughs – shared certain characteristics and made up the quite separate class of municipal corporations, which cut across the county/county borough dichotomy.

The early history of boroughs is complex, and mercifully lies outside the scope of this study; but some of their ancient characteristics (already referred to at p. 13 above) survived to influence more recent events – the exclusion of the town, to a greater or lesser degree, from county jurisdiction; the existence of a separate juristic personality; and the foundation of borough status in a royal charter. It was the charter, granted under the Prerogative, which created the legal entity, and in the borough this differed from the corporation created by statute in the case of all other types of authorities. Municipal corporations were common law corporations embracing all the inhabitants of the borough, and they claimed the right to do anything which a natural person could do, subject to any limitations contained in their charter or imposed on them by statute. Where local authorities were created by statute, however, the corporate body was the council and did not include the inhabitants of the county or district; and, being a statutory corporation, it was entitled to do only such things as were expressly or impliedly laid down by statute.

During the course of the development of municipal institutions the applicants for charters of incorporation would have been towns which, in practice, had already achieved a degree of corporate personality – places which were recognisable entities, each with its own sense of community from which sprung the desire to regulate its own affairs. In such circumstances the legal incorporation of the town was, in effect, the acknowledgment that a *de facto* separate municipal personality already existed.

The procedure for granting charters had been standardised by the Municipal Corporations Act 1882, section 210 of which required, in the first place, a petition to the sovereign from the inhabitant householders of the town praying for the grant of a charter of incorporation. If granted, the charter was still an act of the Prerogative but the statute required the petition to be referred to the Privy Council and permitted the charter to apply the provisions of the Municipal Corporations Acts, that is, to give the town all the statutory aspects of borough government. It also provided for the consequential arrangements as between the new borough and other authorities to be settled by a scheme.

Once lodged with the Privy Council Office the petition, if prima facie acceptable, was made the subject of a public inquiry which reviewed the adequacy of local government services in the town and sought to discover 'whether such elements of civic life exist as would entitle it to the form of government prayed for'.[28] It is tempting to see this requirement as an echo of applications in earlier centuries, when the sovereign's advisers must have considered whether the town in question already possessed a corporate existence which warranted acknowledgement by legal incorporation. Sir Almeric FitzRoy explained this to the Onslow Commission somewhat differently however. The purpose, he said, was to establish that the town 'is not a mere accumulation of industrial workers. What we want to aim at is to get a district which is representative of every phase of civic life . . . men of substance, employers of labour, a residential population engaged in business, a certain leisured class . . . representatives of the classes from which in most cases the better administrators and the more responsible persons are drawn.'[29]

The most obvious consequence of the grant of a charter was on the ceremonial side. The chairman of the council became the mayor, the council was expanded by the addition of aldermen, the clerk of the council became the town clerk and local government usually adopted more elaborate forms of ceremonial and regalia. Some persons were indeed so uncharitable as to see these trappings as the mainspring of civic enthusiasm for the whole concept of incorporation. The applicant towns themselves put these considerations on the higher plane, and claimed that the status of chartered borough promoted civic pride, a more efficient local government service and a more willing performance of public duties.

But more tangible matters were at stake too. The grant of borough status could have repercussions with regard to functions as differences still persisted between the functions of non-county boroughs and of urban districts. Boroughs could have their own independent police force if the population exceeded 20,000 at the last census before incorporation (if the town had been a borough before 1881 the limit was 10,000) but under no circumstances could an urban district have an independent force. A borough became an elementary education authority if the population of the district exceeded 10,000 in 1901 (in contrast with 20,000 for urban districts) and this lower figure for boroughs also applied in the case of a number of lesser functions including diseases of animals, food and drugs, and explosives. These functional details were vestiges of the special position historically accorded to boroughs and their claims to exemption from county jurisdiction. The creation of a new borough was therefore, potentially, a derogation from county services but in practice it was common for the prospective borough to buy off opposition from the county by agreeing not to claim the full range of borough functions; in such cases the bargains would be reflected in the charter and the scheme. Similarly borough applicants customarily sought to deflect opposition from the Local Government Board (and its successors) by agreeing in advance not to exercise another privilege which was open to boroughs (but not to any other type of authority), namely, to adopt professional audit instead of district audit.

Between 1888 and the consideration of this topic by the Onslow

Commission over fifty new boroughs were created in England and Wales, though nearly twenty applications had been, for various reasons, refused or withdrawn. It was expected that the number of applications would grow and this possibility led the Ministry of Health, the Privy Council Office, the Home Office and the Board of Education, as the four departments most concerned, to place a jointly agreed set of proposals before the Commission in 1929 when they were engaged on the second part of their inquiry.[30]

The four departments suggested that the whole process of creating boroughs by charter was an anachronism. While necessary in earlier centuries, when no other way of creating corporations existed, it was no longer appropriate in view of the movement during the nineteenth century towards the creation of classes of authorities by statute - including, in the case of the metropolitan boroughs in London, boroughs by statute and not by charter. A systematic statutory machinery had been created through which county councils and urban and rural district councils could be established or their areas modified, and the general trend was away from common law and privilege and towards parliamentary regulation.

Boroughs, it was suggested, should remain as a type of local authority and the charters, privileges and functions of existing boroughs should remain untouched. But future creations should no longer depend on the Prerogative or on separate applications, each of which needed to be individually examined. Instead, each urban district reaching a prescribed minimum figure (for which 20,000 was proposed) should be entitled to constitute itself a borough by resolution. The resolution would be subject to confirmation by the Ministry of Health by an order which would be subject to annulment (that is, negative resolution) by either House of Parliament. In future, it was suggested, boroughs and urban districts should have identical statutory powers though boroughs would be entitled to the constitutional and ceremonial accessories of a mayor and aldermen.

The Onslow Commission were not prepared for such a break with tradition, however, and favoured the more conservative reactions of the AMC who were loth to depart from the ancient characteristics of chartered boroughs and common law corporations. The Commission felt, moreover, that if existing boroughs retained their status and charters it would add to the complexity of local government to create another class of statutory (and, by implication second class) boroughs. Their recommendations on this subject were therefore of a modest kind, and they suggested no change in the existing procedure for creating boroughs by charters of incorporation.

They proposed that the petition from the resident householders should be abandoned in favour of a petition from the district council passed by an absolute majority of the whole number of the council at a special meeting and confirmed by a similar majority at a subsequent special meeting - a procedure which followed the requirements of the Borough

Funds Acts governing the promotion of a private Bill (Final Report, Cmd 3436, paras 249-71). This change was given statutory effect when local government legislation was consolidated in 1933.

The Commission proposed (though this did not require legislation) that the limit of 10,000 unofficially adopted by the Privy Council office as the minimum population for a new borough should be raised to 20,000; in the LGA 1929 (passed shortly before the completion of the Commission's final report) this figure had in fact been given support as the level at which urban district councils could claim the right to maintain classified roads.

On the incorporation of boroughs, therefore, the Onslow Commission suggested only modifications to the existing processes; they did not propose any changes of principle. The same was true of their recommendations on the creation of new county boroughs and on county borough extensions. The machinery they examined had been framed with an eye to local alterations affecting individual authorities. Each proposal was to be examined on its merits through procedures which could ultimately include quasi-judicial proceedings before Select Committees of the two Houses of Parliament. When these arrangements were devised they contemplated local improvements within the county/county borough system. No positive attempt was made by the government to dictate a pattern of change and departmental reports on private Bills usually refrained from making any recommendations on individual applications for county borough status or borough extensions.

But in practice the changes which took place were all in one direction and led to substantial losses of territory and rateable value from the counties to the county boroughs. Nor would it be surprising if these changes (especially before 1914) were encouraged by a predisposition on the part of the Local Government Board to favour the towns as against the counties; the Board would have inherited many attitudes from the nineteenth century when municipalities were the major units.

The voice of the county councils was heard with increasing clarity, however, as services expanded and as the role of the counties became more important. Largely through their influence the machinery was modified; and by accepting and legislating on the Onslow Commission's proposals the government may be said consciously to have adopted a policy towards change as it affected the structure of local government. The need for such a policy had not been apparent in the period immediately after 1888 but had emerged from the way in which the machinery for change was operating in favour of the county boroughs. The minimum population for new county borough claims was therefore raised, and in future such claims and all contested extensions had to proceed by way of private Bill. Further change was not prevented, nor was there any departure from the proposition that changes should be initiated by the individual authorities affected. But it was now implicitly accepted that the balance of counties and county boroughs should be broadly maintained as it was, and that individual proposals should not cumulatively add up to a fundamental alteration in the system as a whole. This was the basic policy which underlay the next period covered by this study.

## NOTES: CHAPTER 2

1 Proposals affecting counties and boroughs were dealt with in LGA 1888, section 54; those affecting other county districts and parishes in LGA 1888, section 57 as extended by LGA 1894, section 36.

2 Strictly speaking the Borough Funds Act only authorised the authority to charge to the rates the expense of promoting the Bill; it did not give statutory authority for the promotion itself.

3 The procedure was described in detail, and the drawbacks as seen from the promoter's angle, in the written and oral evidence given on behalf of the AMC to the Joint Committee on Private Bill Procedure, 1955 (HL 14, 58-I; HC 139-I).

4 Erskine May, *Parliamentary Practice*, 13th edn (London: Butterworth, 1921). These carefully chosen words, quoted from the edition current when the Onslow Commission were sitting, appear unchanged in later editions.

5 The Wakefield order was revived later and given effect in 1914.

6 Onslow Commission Evidence, Pt I, p. 207 (Appendix XLII to Mr Gibbon's memorandum). In addition to extension orders the LGB, during the same period, made twenty-three provisional orders for the creation of new county boroughs; nine of these were opposed in Parliament.

7 ibid., Pt I, p. 181 (Appendix XXIII to Mr Gibbon's memorandum).

8 ibid., Pt III, p. 452 (Memorandum by Mr F. Dent, CCA, para. 23).

9 ibid., Pt I, p. 186 (Appendix XXIV to Mr Gibbon's memorandum).

10 ibid., Pt I, Q. 2,095, 2,112 (Mr I. G. Gibbon, Ministry of Health).

11 ibid., Pt I, p. 85 (Mr Gibbon's memorandum, para. 211).

12 ibid., Pt I, p. 99 (Mr Gibbon's memorandum, para. 222).

13 ibid., Pt I, Q. 2,496-7 (Mr Gibbon).

14 ibid., Pt III, Q. 10,827-8 (Mr W. Vibart Dixon, CCA).

15 ibid., Pt I, Q. 2,129 (Mr I. G. Gibbon).

16 ibid., Pt I, Q. 2,358 (Mr I. G. Gibbon).

17 When Luton was made a county borough in 1964, on the recommendation of the Hancock Commission, its population was 123,000 but the remainder of the county then had a population of 230,000 and was a substantial unit even without Luton. The county council did not then oppose Luton's application for county borough status – though they did not actively support it.

18 Onslow Commission Evidence, Pt III, p. 437 (Preliminary Memorandum by the CCA, para. 1).

19 ibid., Pt III, p. 439 (Preliminary Memorandum by the AMC, para. 2).

20 ibid., Pt III, p. 438 (CCA Preliminary Memorandum, para. 18).

21 ibid., Pt III, p. 465 (Mr Dent's memorandum, para. 24).

22 ibid., Pt III, p. 437 (CCA Preliminary Memorandum, para. 5).

23 ibid., Pt III, Q. 6,561 (Mr Dent, CCA).

24 ibid., Pt III, p. 440 (AMC Preliminary Memorandum, para. 18).

25 ibid., Pt III., Q. 7,380-1 (Sir Robert Fox, AMC).

26 ibid., Pt III., p. 467 (Sir Ryland Adkins).

27 Hornsey B, Willesden, Rhondda, Tottenham, Walthamstow, Leyton and Ilford UDs.

28  Onslow Commission Evidence, Pt II, p. 213 (Memorandum by Sir Almeric FitzRoy, former Clerk of the Privy Council, para. 6).
29  ibid., Pt II, Q. 3,316–7 (Sir Almeric FitzRoy).
30  ibid., Pt XIV, p. 2519 (Further Memorandum submitted on behalf of the Minister of Health by Sir Arthur Robinson).

## Chapter 3

# Moves Towards Improvements within the Existing System

## LIMITED ATTEMPTS AT REFORM

The period now to be considered starts from the second report of the Onslow Commission in 1928. It includes the county reviews of the 1930s and the work of the postwar Commissions – the Local Government Boundary Commission set up in 1945 and the Local Government Commissions for England and Wales established in 1958. It was a period which accepted the framework of the existing structure with two (or, in rural areas, three) tiers of authorities in the counties and all-purpose authorities in the county boroughs. But within that framework deliberate attempts were now made to review local government areas, to consider them in relation to each other, to reduce the number of very small units, and generally to rationalise boundaries. The machinery of change was geared to this end in three successive approaches to the subject: the county reviews tackled the county districts; the postwar Commissions looked at the pattern of counties and county boroughs as well.

## THE COUNTY REVIEWS

The permanent machinery established in 1888 governing changes to counties and county boroughs applied to non-county boroughs too. But, as already noted above (p. 25), different procedures applied to urban districts (other than boroughs), rural districts and parishes.[1] In these latter cases the formal responsibility lay with the county council. Where a county council were satisfied that a prima facie case existed for altering the boundaries or the pattern of these authorities they were empowered (and later, after 1933, obliged) to hold a public inquiry. If, in the light of local consideration, the county council remained of the view that change was 'desirable' they (not the Local Government Board) made the necessary order. The order needed confirmation by the Board, however (or later by the Ministry of Health), but the role of the confirming authority was limited. If no objections to the order were lodged the Board had no option but to confirm it. If objections were lodged by the council of any county district affected or by one-sixth of the local government electors in any such district, an inquiry had to be held, in the light of which the Board could confirm or reject the order; if confirmed the order thereupon became effective and no parliamentary proceedings were involved. When confirming an order - whether or not objections had been lodged - the Board (later the Ministry of Health) could make such modifications as they considered necessary 'for carrying into effect the objects of the order' but - an important limitation - it was held that this power did not allow the Board to alter any proposed boundary defined in the order. This limitation was removed when the minister's power to make modifications was extended by section 48 of the LGA 1929.

The machinery was frequently in use between 1888 and the examination of this aspect by the Onslow Commission, both to alter boundaries and to create new districts. Boundary modifications were chiefly minor adjustments to rectify anomalies, though in some cases the limits of urban authorities were extended to include built-up areas. The powers of county councils allowed them not only to create but also to extinguish districts but, because of an understandable dislike of upsetting the *status quo* and offending local people, the abolition of a district council (as against the creation of a new one) was rarely contemplated.

Between 1888 and 1927 a total of 270 new urban districts were formed - mostly in the early years of the new system, before 1900. Many of the areas given urban status were in what are now known as the conurbations, where population and urbanisation were both increasing and, indeed, eighty-seven of the new creations were in only five counties: Essex, Middlesex, Surrey, Lancashire and the West Riding of Yorkshire. Even so the new urban districts were, for the most part, only small towns on creation; 183 of the 270 new urban districts had had populations below 5,000 at the last census before the change of status. The reasons why towns pressed for urban status were various but one was that, under section 229 of the Public Health Act 1875, the cost of public works, for example, for water supply and sewerage, carried out by a rural district for the benefit of a particular parish was defrayed by a special rate levied only within that parish. In such cases the parish argued that they would be better off as a separate urban district, with control over their own services.

A total of 118 new rural districts were created during this period, too, though different considerations applied here. All but three of these new creations resulted from the subdivision of rural sanitary districts which straddled county boundaries[2] - though, even in 1927, there were still nine rural districts in which the small rump of a former district in one county was administered by the main part of the former district in another (see p. 24 above).

The practical operation of the machinery of change did nothing, therefore, to reduce - indeed it tended to aggravate - those weaknesses of the system which arose from the multiplicity of authorities (especially county districts), the wide variations between the biggest and the smallest of each type, and the excessive number of small and weak authorities. At the 1921 census, for example, 972 county districts (nearly two-thirds of the total) had populations below 10,000, while 494 (nearly one-third of the total) were below 5,000 (Cmd 3213, para. 19).

Population was not everything, of course, but a very restricted population base meant that the district would almost certainly lack financial resources and the ability to pay for public services. Of the 494 districts with populations under 5,000, 430 had a penny rate product of less than £100, 200 of these were under £50 and in thirty-five districts a penny rate brought in under £20.[3] Not much could be done with resources as low as this even when the pound was worth more. The situation as regards the employment of medical officers illustrated this. In 1927 only 120 county districts out of 1,698 had a full-time MOH. In all others the MOH was a part-time appointment. In some cases the MOH was shared between two or more local authorities and worked full-time in the public service, though for more than one authority, but in two-thirds of all county districts the MOH was a part-time appointment of a doctor in private practice.

Parliament, in response to public demand, was steadily increasing the range of duties of local authorities of all types, and county district councils had heavy and growing responsibilities in connection with public health, housing and highways. This trend demanded fewer and stronger authorities, not more smaller ones. But the machinery already in existence was not suitable for anything save a piecemeal approach to individual boundaries and authorities; it was not designed to meet the needs of a widespread and coherent attack upon the structural shortcomings of the system. It is true that considerable responsibility was formally vested in the county council but, in practice, county councils did not act as initiating agents; they responded to requests from the district councils and any county council which adopted a positive and reforming role was likely to meet with considerable opposition. The machinery had, moreover, a number of in-built limitations. It did not apply to boroughs but only (at county district level) to urban and rural districts, so it could not in any case be used for a genuinely comprehensive review of county districts. Even within these limits it had further drawbacks. It provided, for instance, no right of appeal for an urban or rural district council which had been pressing for changes but whose pleas were being ignored by the county council. And it gave a very narrow role to the minister as confirming authority; he had no alternative but to confirm a county council order which was unopposed and no power (even where such an order was opposed) to modify any boundary which it defined.

Finally, although section 57 of the 1888 Act said that the county council should be satisfied that a change was 'desirable' it gave no guidance on the criteria to be adopted. This was not in itself a bad thing, because the desirability or otherwise of any particular proposal necessarily involves a complex balancing of advantages (to some authorities) and disadvantages (to others). The Royal Commission had discussed this very topic in their first report in connection with the 'desirability' of changes affecting county boroughs, and had come down against any attempt to define too closely something which must in the last resort be a matter of judgement (Cmd 2506, paras 1234–5). But in the case of changes involving urban and rural districts it meant that changes were left to the judgement of sixty-one different county councils, and the scope for variation was considerable.

The fact that the Onslow Commission were in existence suggested that their scrutinising eye should be turned on problems connected with county districts, as well as counties and county boroughs, and their terms of reference were duly extended in 1926. As regards areas and boundaries this was a well-timed and successful move because the Commission adopted, in its entirety, a set of proposals for county reviews placed before it by the Ministry of Health[4] – proposals which all the local authority associations broadly supported. The Commission's recommendations were given effect when the LGA 1929 provided a legislative opportunity.

Section 46 of the Local Government Act 1929 required county councils to make a first review of 'the circumstances' of all county districts and parishes wholly or partly within their counties 'as soon as may be' after the commencement of the Act, and in consultation with the councils of the local authorities concerned. Such consultations were to include any county borough council sharing a common boundary with the county. Following this review they were to report to the Minister of Health on their proposals for change by 1 April 1932 or – a wise precaution – by such later date as the minister might allow. These could include the redrawing of boundaries, the amalgamation or division of districts and the creation of new districts. A county council could submit one report on the whole of the county or it could subdivide the county and submit separate reports on each part.

The Act also, and with the acquiescence of the AMC, modified the special position of non-county boroughs. Under the original machinery of 1888 no order could be made affecting a borough unless the initiative came from the borough itself, and then any change was subject to the provisional order procedure. But a comprehensive approach to the pattern of county districts had to include the boroughs along with urban and rural districts. This was, to a large extent, permitted by the 1929 Act but, even so, some reservations were made in favour of boroughs. A county council could propose the transfer of territory from a borough to another authority, or the extension of a borough so that it absorbed the whole or part of an adjacent district. But, because each borough owed its original incorporation to a royal charter, it was deemed inappropriate that any subordinate body should have power to abolish an authority created under the Prerogative, so the county reviews could not propose the amalgamation of two boroughs, or the abolition of a borough by its inclusion in some other type of authority.

When the county council's proposals were submitted to the minister there was the customary period for representations and, if objections were lodged, the minister was required to hold a public inquiry. The minister's powers were then wide enough to permit him to accept the county's proposals, modify them or reject them. The changes in the district pattern to which the minister decided to give effect were embodied in an order which was not subject to any parliamentary procedure. The Onslow Commission had considered whether these orders should be subject to annulment but had reached no conclusion and made no recommendation (Cmd 3213, para. 44(j)). The government seemingly had no difficulty in resisting the idea of negative resolution, fortified by the precedent of the 1888 Act, no doubt; changes to the boundaries of urban and rural districts made under section 57 of that Act involved no parliamentary proceedings.

The Act provided for subsequent reviews after the first, however, and here the special position of boroughs re-emerged. The procedure was otherwise the same but if, in any second or subsequent review, an objection was lodged by a borough council then the minister's order became subject to the provisional order procedure, thus allowing the borough council (and others, too) to have their case judged by Parliament after a quasi-judicial hearing by Select Committees of each House. Such subsequent reviews were to take place when each county council thought fit (or when the minister directed), but were not to take place more frequently than once in ten years. 'We are of the opinion', said the Commission, 'that frequent changes are detrimental to local administration and are therefore undesirable' (Cmd 3213, para. 45).

The Ministry of Health issued a series of memoranda for the guidance of local authorities affected by the Act of 1929 and two of these, on county reviews, contained some thoughts on the 'considerations to be taken into account' by county councils.[5] But they were so general as to be of little help. The Onslow Commission's words were quoted to the effect that the need for a general review of the areas of county districts and parishes had been established, that the local authority associations had not dissented from the view that 'there are at present authorities who cannot efficiently discharge the functions entrusted to them, and that a review of areas should be undertaken in order to see how far ineffective units can be eliminated by reorganisation' (Cmd 3213, para. 39). But at what point can a district be regarded as too small in population or rateable resources to be effective?

The ministry gave no specific guidance, but left each county council to interpret as best they could some exhortations of baffling imprecision.

Financial strength and general good government must of course be taken into account but it did not get one far to be told that 'in order to be in a satisfactory financial position a district should, wherever possible, have sufficient resources to provide all the necessary sanitary and other services without special assistance. The advantage of being able to employ fully qualified whole time officers should be borne in mind.' The weight given to the wishes of the inhabitants is always a problem. 'Due care will no doubt be taken' (said the memorandum) 'to see that the case for the alterations is fully explained to and appreciated by local electors, and their views will be carefully weighed. In the last resort, however, the consideration of the public advantage must prevail.'[6] The equity of local burdens and the need to consider community of interest were similarly mentioned, but what the county councils really wanted was something more concrete. Having launched the exercise the government presumably had some criteria in view? Many asked, therefore, whether the minister could not lay down some general rule, either by reference to population or the product of a penny rate, which could be applied in deciding whether a new urban district should be constituted or an existing one retained.

If the government had been in a position to offer clear guidance this would have been the occasion to do so. But the minister declined to pronounce on such a controversial topic. 'Differences in the standards of administration, in the nature and needs of individual districts and special local circumstances would make it impracticable to apply any general rule of this kind. All that can be said is that it obviously requires exceptional reasons to justify, under modern conditions, constituting or continuing an urban district with a population not sufficient and a produce of a penny rate not adequate to render the district a unit of local government strong enough to deal with modern requirements and to ensure the provision of the necessary services. Each particular case must, however, be treated on its merits.'[7] County councils could hardly have found this piece of prose of much help in formulating their proposals or in trying to get local agreement on them.

The possibility of suggesting a minimum population for urban districts must have been discussed when the 1929 Act was in preparation, which makes it all the more surprising that no account was taken of the possible repercussions of the county reviews on educational administration. Under the Education Act 1921 the authorities responsible for elementary education included the councils of boroughs whose populations exceeded 10,000 in 1901 and urban districts whose populations at that date had exceeded 20,000. If, as a result of boundary extensions during the course of a county review, a borough or urban district took in land which had the necessary population in 1901 then the county district council concerned could take over the administration of elementary education in their area from the county. This situation was particularly alarming to the West

Riding County Council who wished to eliminate many of the smaller authorities in their county but not at the expense of disrupting the county education service. This consequence had to be forestalled by the Education (Local Authorities) Act 1931 which prevented any non-county borough or urban district not already exercising education powers from acquiring them save by special Act of Parliament.

The county reviews placed a considerable burden of new and unprecedented work on county councils at a time when they were also fully engaged absorbing the work of poor law administration. The minister suggested that there would be organisational advantages if each county council appointed a special *ad hoc* committee to supervise the review of county districts, and most county councils followed this course. The normal procedure was for the county council to circularise their local authorities, asking for the necessary statistics and information about services and administration, and then to frame draft proposals. These were discussed with representatives of district councils at the conferences which were required by section 46 of the LGA 1929. The statutory obligation to consult the district councils by way of conferences was new, and it was an important stage in the whole procedure; a full and frank exchange of views in an informal atmosphere greatly increased the chances of avoiding conflict and friction at the later stages.

Having framed their proposals, the review committee would next place them before the county council; when approved by the council the proposals were submitted to the minister who became the recipient of considerable masses of information backed by tables and maps. Objections were lodged against proposals in nearly all counties and public inquiries (held by engineering inspectors) were arranged. These, too, were often lengthy and in some counties more than one inquiry was held. The whole exercise occasioned a vast amount of work and the procedures were cumbersome; many counties found themselves unable to keep to the 1932 deadline. The final scheme was received by the department in January 1935, and the last county review order (for the West Riding of Yorkshire) was made in 1939 only shortly before the outbreak of war.

The results of the first reviews were uneven – which was not surprising. Three counties (Radnor, Rutland and the Soke of Peterborough) decided to make no proposals for change, while the others tackled their tasks with greater or less vigour according to their zeal and the extent of the opposition. The procedure, involving consultations between the county council and its district councils, debate within the county council itself, representations to the minister, a public inquiry and the possibility of ministerial amendment, offered many opportunities for opposition and for whittling down controversial proposals. In those counties where an effective rationalisation was achieved this was usually due to the efforts of one or two individuals, either an outstanding member of the county council or the county clerk.

In Cornwall the total number of urban and rural districts was reduced from thirty to eighteen, in Cumberland from twenty-one to eleven and in East Sussex from twenty to eleven. Elsewhere the results were less impressive in terms of numbers. In the final result 206 urban districts were abolished and forty-nine created, a net reduction of 157; 236 rural districts were abolished and sixty-seven created, a net reduction of 169. The terms of the Act precluded the abolition of any borough so the total net reduction at county district level was 326.[8]

In the course of the reviews a number of long-standing anomalies were eliminated or reduced. At every level - county, district and parish - there had been numerous examples of local government areas with detached parts; most of these disappeared and a final onslaught was made on the problem, inherited from 1888 (see pp. 23-4 above) of districts which straddled county boundaries. Even so, one straddler remained until 1955 - the parish of Pennal in Merionethshire which was administered by the Machynlleth RDC in Montgomeryshire.

But the county reviews were no more than a step in the right direction. Quite apart from the fact that boroughs, however small, were immune from abolition, 149 urban districts and thirty-seven rural districts still remained with populations under 5,000, and there was still a total of some 450 urban and rural districts with populations under 10,000. Some county councils had seemingly regarded the first review as a rehearsal for a more thorough-going job next time round.


## WARTIME DISCUSSIONS ON LOCAL GOVERNMENT REFORM

At a very early stage in the war the government started to plan for the reconstruction that would eventually be required and, rightly, proposals began to take shape for building a better world than we had had before. As the war years passed plans were evolved in many fields in which local authorities operated. Some of these grew directly from the physical impact of war - the rebuilding of the blitzed cities, housing, town and country planning, the reorganisation of gas and electricity distribution - while others derived from the general war aims and the determination to improve on the social services when peace was re-established - a comprehensive health service, better educational facilities, a new system of national insurance.

The question immediately posed itself whether the structure of local government would be adequate for the expected strains of postwar reconstruction and expansion and in 1941 the Minister without Portfolio (Mr Arthur Greenwood) who was generally responsible for reconstruction plans invited Sir William Jowitt (then Solicitor General but underemployed in that capacity) to undertake a review of local government problems, and particularly to consider whether the regional arrangements established by the government for the co-ordination of civil defence could be of permanent value in solving some of these problems.

Sir William's review was not publicised, and his report was never published, but he consulted leading local government figures during the course of his work and it became generally known that local government reform was under consideration by the government. The topic was publicly debated in other quarters, too, as part of the general discussion of social reconstruction, particularly by those advocating regional government and the reorganisation of local government on regional lines.

Against this background all the four main local authority associations produced memoranda outlining their views. On some points they were all agreed. They were alarmed at the possible loss of functions from local to central government (local authority fire brigades had already been absorbed in the National Fire Service and there was talk of agricultural services being transferred too) and they combined in a vehement rejection of the idea that wartime regional arrangements should be retained after hostilities had ceased. Although these were accepted as a wartime expedient and a practical precaution in case of invasion, local authorities wanted to restore the situation in which they had direct access to ministers and their departments, instead of having to deal with a regional commissioner whose post bore some resemblance to that of a gauleiter.

The associations were also united in the view that the middle of the war was not the right time to embark upon schemes of local government reform – schemes which were bound to be controversial and would disrupt services at a time when authorities, with their staffs depleted, had more than enough to do already. Their views on reform were therefore statements of long-term aspirations rather than proposals which they expected (or wanted) to see implemented at that stage. Not unexpectedly these aspects of their memoranda rehearsed the views on which earlier evidence to the Onslow Commission had been based and displayed a fundamental divergence between the AMC and the other three associations. Predictably, the AMC advocated the general adoption of all-purpose authorities on the pattern of county boroughs.

> In regard to the type of authority which is likely to be best suited to the future needs of local government in this country, we suggest that the most satisfactory form of local government authority is, for most areas, a single authority invested with complete powers of local government within its area . . . and that any reorganisation of local government should be directed to achieving the object of setting up, wherever reasonably practicable, having regard to local circumstances, throughout the country, the type of authority referred to, which for convenience might be called a single all-purpose authority.[9]

The Association prudently reserved for further study what sort of area should suitably be administered by the all-purpose authorities they had in mind but saw no reason why it should not include rural as well as urban areas.

This approach was rejected by the other three associations, all of whom defended the *status quo* and the structure based on two tiers in the counties, with county boroughs as exceptions to this norm. The CCA made some positive suggestions with regard to the size of authorities, however, some of which foreshadowed later decisions. They proposed, for instance, that 100,000 should be accepted as the population prima facie needed to support a 'major local government authority'; in the case of counties with populations below this level the possibility of amalgamations should be explored by a Boundary Commission. Such a Commission should also consider the future of the smaller county boroughs; on this point the CCA suggested that county boroughs below 75,000 should be merged with their administrative counties and that the limit for the creation of any further county boroughs should be raised to 125,000. At the district level the Association favoured a complete reorganisation of all county districts with populations below 10,000; non-county boroughs and urban districts with populations under this figure, together with all rural districts (whatever their populations), should relinquish their separate styles, and should be regrouped and officially known as 'county districts'.[10]

Sir William Jowitt's report made no radical proposals, though he suggested some lines on which future developments might proceed. He was not persuaded that it would be desirable to retain the wartime regional arrangements after peace had been re-established. They were, in any case, a system of administrative decentralisation of central government functions to civil servants posted to regional offices, and thus had no lessons to teach on the regional organisation of local government. He was against plunging into radical schemes of reform while the country was at war (and pointed to the delays that would inevitably be involved if reform was preceded by another Royal Commission on local government or some other form of full dress inquiry). But Sir William had other doubts, too, about the wisdom of root-and-branch reform, and his remarks on this point were very much in line with the traditional British approach to constitutional change. 'The final test of the efficiency of any machine lies in the answer to the question "Does it work?" The answer to be given to this question must govern any recommendations to be made. So far as the machinery of local government is concerned I believe the answer to this question is a clear affirmative. In my view therefore it would be rash to abandon an organis-ation which has shown such versatility and resilience in favour of an untried paper scheme, which has the somewhat academic virtue of having no loose ends. I am convinced that the reorganisation and development of the local government system must take place through a gradual process of trial and error rather than any wholesale demolition of foundations.'[11]

In Sir William Jowitt's view, however, rejection of radical reform in the foreseeable future did not rule out the desirability of a revision of local government areas as soon as this was practicable, though this should take place within the county/county borough framework of the existing system. And – later in the war – this was the general line taken by the government when it was apparent that fighting would soon be over.

In August 1944 the Minister of Health (Mr Willink), when answering a question in Parliament, said that the government had considered the various proposals for local government reform put forward by the local authority associations and other bodies. 'It is clear from these that there is no general desire to disrupt the existing structure of local government or to abandon in favour of some form of regional government the main features of the county and county borough system; and the government do not consider that any case has been made out for so drastic a change. On the other hand, the government are satisfied that, within the general framework of the county and county borough system, there is need and scope for improvements, and in particular for amending the machinery of the Local Government Act 1933 relating to adjustments of status, boundaries and areas' (Commons Hansard, 3 August 1944, col. 1579). Proposals on these matters would be discussed with the local authority associations before being published in the form of a White Paper and then brought before Parliament in the form of legislation.

## THE LOCAL GOVERNMENT BOUNDARY COMMISSION 1945-9

The White Paper *Local Government in England and Wales during the Period of Reconstruction* (Cmd 6579, January 1945) fell into two main parts. The first reiterated the government's view that the reconstruction period after the war, when many social advances were planned, would not be the opportune moment for a general recasting of the local government system – even if there had been a desire for such a course and a consensus of opinion as to what changes should be made. In the light of this conclusion the second part explained the proposed new machinery for the adjustment of local government areas within the existing framework.

The then-current procedures, now contained in the 1933 Act, had two main drawbacks; these have already been referred to but changing ideas and conditions threw them into sharp relief. In the first place the procedures were different according to the type of local authorities affected. Quite apart from the possibility (the requirement, in some cases) of proceeding by private Bill, changes affecting counties, county boroughs and non-county boroughs involved ministerial orders which could be subject to the provisional order procedure with its scope for separate hearings before Select Committees of each House; changes restricted to urban and rural districts and parishes, however, were made by an order of the county council concerned, which became effective on confirmation by the

Minister of Health without any parliamentary proceedings at all. Secondly, the 1933 Act provided for the co-ordinated examination of areas only at the second-tier level. Even here, however, the achievements of the first reviews of the 1930s had been patchy because the initiative lay in the hands of sixty-one separate county councils (outside London) who had no clear guidance on the criteria they were to follow. There was no machinery for the systematic review of county and county borough boundaries; in such cases proposals could come forward at any time, each would be considered in isolation and there was no legal bar to a rejected application being revived again after only a short interval.

The principal objective of the government's proposals, therefore, was to devise a new piece of machinery which would command public confidence, which would work smoothly, expeditiously and cheaply (and this meant, among other things, reducing the number of formal stages through which proposals had to progress and the number of chances of appeal and modification) and which would ensure that all proposals were properly co-ordinated and not decided piecemeal.

To achieve these aims the Local Government Boundary Commission were established under the Local Government (Boundary Commission) Act 1945. The Commission were a small body consisting of a chairman, deputy chairman and three other (part-time) Commissioners. They had their own staff and power to appoint Assistant Commissioners, particularly for the purpose of holding public inquiries. The Commission combined the functions of the county councils (in the field of county district boundaries, though not parish boundaries) and of the Minister of Health (with regard to counties and county boroughs) and thus brought together responsibilities for boundary changes which had previously resided in many different hands. Indeed, in the substance of change their powers went further because they could consider the creation of new county boroughs (except in Middlesex) and the extension of existing ones – changes which since 1926 had been matters requiring private Bills. The power to proceed by private Bill was not withdrawn but it was left to be understood that such action would be strongly discouraged while the Boundary Commission were at work. The minimum population for the creation of a new county borough was raised, however, from 75,000 to 100,000 by section 3 of the Act.

In addition, the Commission could alter the boundaries of any county (except London), county borough or district, amalgamate such units, divide a county, urban district or rural district and redistribute the parts, constitute or demote a county borough. The only changes beyond their power were the creation of a new borough or the abolition of an existing borough by its absorption into an urban or a rural district; these exceptions were carried over from the limitation on the powers of county councils in carrying out county reviews and were founded on the sanctity of royal charters (see pp. 52–3 above).

A special problem arose in Middlesex where (on 1939 figures) there were no fewer than eight boroughs and urban districts with populations exceeding 100,000[12] and another three over 95,000.[13] Some at least of these authorities aspired to county borough status and others might wish to combine in order to reach the minimum qualifying population limit; but if any such claims were admitted it would be difficult not to allow them all. If that happened the county of Middlesex would be virtually destroyed, as effective county government would be impossible in what remained. The creation of county boroughs within the outer fringes of Greater London raised wider issues, too, as there were possible candidates in metropolitan Essex, Surrey and Kent; but Middlesex was by far the most serious problem. It was met - though only on a temporary basis - by prohibiting the Boundary Commission from creating any county boroughs in Middlesex (proviso to section 2 (1), Boundary Commission Act 1945).

The administrative county of London was excluded altogether from the Boundary Commission's jurisdiction but there were two urgent issues here demanding study. The first (which the government shelved) was whether the outer boundaries of the county should be extended. The difficulties of doing so were notorious. It would be bound to raise the most acute opposition from the adjoining counties, and have repercussions on the political balance within the new extended county. It could hardly be accomplished without a complete reorganisation of local government in London because the constitution of local authorities and the distribution of functions within the administrative county differed, for historical reasons, from the structure of local government in the areas which would be included in any extension of the metropolis. Just as the government had declined to contemplate upsetting the existing county/county borough basis of local government outside London at a time when postwar reconstruction was the major task in hand, so they also recoiled from the equally complex and controversial issues of the government of Greater London. 'Several county councils and other local authorities in and around London are at present engaged in recasting their educational services and will shortly be confronted with other similar tasks. It would, in the view of the government, be a mistake to interrupt those tasks by throwing into the melting pot the whole problem of London and the Home Counties' (Cmd 6579, p. 19).

The second issue in London (on which the government took action - though it came to nothing) was whether, even if the county boundary remained unchanged, the existing arrangements within the county should be modified; should the number of metropolitan boroughs be reduced? was the allocation of functions satisfactory? There was no statutory machinery for modifying the areas of the metropolitan boroughs or the City; none had been provided in the LGA 1888 or the London Government Act 1899. Changes could therefore be made only by local Act or by a new London Government Act. Legislation would therefore be needed and to pave the way an experienced committee, chaired by Lord Reading, was set up in 1945 charged with the task of examining the number, size and boundaries of the metropolitan boroughs and the distribution of functions between them and the City, on the one hand, and the London County Council on the other.

The investigation ran into the sand, however, as the LCC and the Metropolitan Boroughs Standing Joint Committee declined to submit other than factual information, on the grounds that the matters being examined by the Committee could not be divorced from wider aspects of local government in Greater London. The government were forced to accept the view that problems of areas and functions within the county of London would have to await 'an investigation into the wider problem, which must in turn await the settlement of the range of functions, old and new, which are to be entrusted to local authorities', and the Minister of Health (Mr Bevan) formally announced that the Reading Committee had been wound up (Commons Hansard, 24 October 1946, cols 1-2).

But the Boundary Commission had a formidable task, even though London was excluded. They were an executive, not an advisory, body and their decisions were to be embodied in orders made by the Commission themselves - not in orders made or confirmed by the minister on the recommendation of the Commission. When the Commission had reviewed an area they were required to set out their conclusions in the form of an order which might provide for change or which might maintain the *status quo*. The purpose of a 'negative' order - which made no changes - was twofold: it provided (in the case of orders subject to parliamentary proceedings) a decision which could be challenged, and it also defined the date, ten years later, when the issue could be reopened. One of the purposes of the new machinery was to ensure a degree of stability to local government affairs and section 3 (8) of the Act laid it down that when an order of the Boundary Commission had come into effect, whether to make any changes or to retain the *status quo* of any local government area, the possibility of any further changes to that area should not be reopened within ten years unless the Commission were satisfied that 'by reason of a substantial change in the distribution of the population or other exceptional circumstances' it was desirable to do so.

The question whether or not the Commission's orders should require ministerial confirmation was considered within government circles during the preparation of the Bill. Boundary changes could be politically sensitive issues but the Minister of Health resisted the suggestion. Such a power in the hands of the minister, and particularly the complementary power to modify or reject a Boundary Commission order, would have defeated one of the essential elements of the new machinery - which was to reduce the number of tribunals who had to consider boundary proposals. If the minister had power to confirm, reject or modify the Boundary Commission's conclusions then he would have to go over all the ground already traversed by the Commission and hear all the arguments of the parties; the minister would be open, once more, to all the pressures customarily brought to bear by MPs in the light of local issues, and the usefulness of an independent Commission would be greatly reduced.

Ministerial confirmation of individual boundary changes therefore found no place in the ultimate machinery but any possible charge that the Commission were being given too free a hand was met in two different ways: by retaining the requirement that major changes, that is, those affecting counties and county boroughs, should be subject to review by Parliament, and by laying certain obligations on the Commission to act within guidelines laid down by the government - guidelines which (in some circumstances) needed to be approved by Parliament.

Direct parliamentary involvement in Boundary Commission orders affecting counties and county boroughs (including 'negative' orders refusing to make a non-county borough into a county borough) does not require extended treatment because, in the event, no such orders were made. Suffice it to say that they would have been subject to the new Special Parliamentary Procedure contained in the Statutory Orders (Special Procedure) Act 1945. The Special Procedure was developed from the provisional order procedure and was devised specifically to meet the needs of the postwar reconstruction period; it has been retained in permanent use, however, for certain ministerial orders of an 'executive' character, that is, orders made for the local implementation of a line of policy approved by Parliament in the parent Act. The provisional order procedure still applies, however, to orders of a 'legislative' nature which could raise new issues, for example, orders under section 303 of the Public Health Act 1875. Under the Special Parliamentary Procedure petitions may be presented to Parliament but are examined in committee (a Joint Committee of both Houses, not a Select Committee of each House) only if they seek detailed amendments to an order; if a petition aims to defeat the order as a whole (and hence to challenge the general policy contained in the parent Act) it can be considered only on the floor of the House as a political rather than as a quasi-judicial matter. Although also of wider interest as part of the general development of parliamentary control over delegated legislation, the application of the Special Procedure to possible orders made by the Boundary Commission marks a further step away from the earlier situation in which Parliament retained absolute control over certain types of local government change and exercised this control through procedures of a judicial, rather than an administrative, character.

## Ministerial guidelines and the Commission's procedure

The Boundary Commission Act required the minister to make and to obtain parliamentary approval for regulations covering the procedure to be followed by the Boundary Commission, and the general principles to be observed by them when reaching conclusions. The Local Government (Boundary Commission) Regulations 1945 covered both aspects in the same document[14] and, in framing guidance for the Boundary Commission, deliberately avoided rigidity: there was no infallible test by which it was possible to determine that a particular change was 'desirable'; the Commission's discretion should not be fettered.

Some possible elements of the 'General Principles' had been mentioned in the White Paper, which said that the government had in mind formulating advice *inter alia* on the size of local authority areas, on the linking of town and country and on the considerations which should govern the creation and extension of county boroughs. But, even though the General Principles (which were set out in the schedule to the regulations) represented the most comprehensive attempt until that date to frame guidance on local authority areas, their lack of precision and their cautious tone reflected the fact that, in essence, the whole exercise was proceeding by agreement. The point has already been made that machinery and policy have to be considered together; in this case the policy was to go no further than was acceptable to the local authority associations - which was not very far. Gradually, during the course of the consultations, any proposed guidance to the Boundary Commission which appeared to contemplate too painful a departure from the *status quo* was whittled down and made more nebulous. A look at two of the individual principles illustrates this point.

The White Paper had contained a fairly substantial passage on linking town and country. It was felt that the time had come for a different approach to the subject because increasing mobility was breaking down the ancient barriers between urban and rural areas. Their interests were complementary, not opposed, and this should be recognised when adjusting local government boundaries. But the idea had raised a good deal of suspicion. On the one hand there were old towns which dreaded absorption into surrounding rural territories; on the other hand representatives of rural areas were apprehensive lest efficient rural district councils should be forced into unwelcome amalgamations with urban areas, either by being swallowed up by the expansion of a big town or in order to bolster up some weak urban unit. Presentationally it was necessary for the General Principles to avoid anything which could be construed as an encouragement to county borough extensions and the outcome was the following neutral formula, which was designed to leave the Commission with a free hand, but could not have been of much help:

The interests of an urban centre and surrounding countryside should not necessarily be regarded either as diverse or as complementary. All factors should be considered to discover whether on balance a blending of urban and rural territories is desirable.[15]

The paragraph on population figures is also worth quoting in full:

It is not intended that the discretion of the Commission shall be limited by reference to population figures but the following considerations are stated for the general guidance of the Commission:
a. an order reducing an existing county borough to the status of a non-county borough should not ordinarily be made unless the population of the county borough as estimated by the Registrar General is less than 60,000;
b. in the absence of substantial agreement an order uniting a county with another county should not ordinarily be made unless the population of the smaller county as so estimated is less than 100,000.[16]

Guidance on this topic had caused the most difficulty in the discussions with the associations; the final version was the result of considerable modification. Most of the associations would have preferred that the General Principles should say nothing at all on the question of population sizes, but complete silence on the point would have given the document an air of unreality. It is a moot point whether this danger was altogether removed by the little which was in fact said. Only on one point had there been general agreement - that counties should not be forced into amalgamations unless their populations were less than 100,000; this was the figure which had been suggested by the CCA itself.

The original version of this paragraph had advanced two propositions regarding county boroughs, however: that existing county boroughs should not ordinarily be demoted unless their populations were below 75,000 and that no new county borough should ordinarily be created unless its population exceeded 125,000. Both these figures had been suggested by the CCA (see p. 58 above). The AMC protested that the figure of 75,000 was too high and would place a number of ancient centres at risk which included Exeter, Bath, Lincoln and Carlisle (besides Doncaster - the most recent county borough). The withdrawal of county borough status from at least the smallest authorities in this class was generally expected, but it was difficult to prove that one figure was necessarily more accurate than another. On this point, therefore, the government yielded to pressure and substituted the figure of 60,000 as the point at which demotion should ordinarily commence, though without prejudice to the possibility that the Commission might find special circumstances either above or below this limit (there were in fact thirteen county boroughs with populations between 60,000 and 75,000 and ten below 60,000). In addition the reference was deleted to the figure of 125,000 for new county borough creations. The AMC pointed to the undeniable fact that the minimum had been laid down in the Act as 100,000. Against this it was argued that the statutory minimum gave no automatic right to county borough status at this level and that it would be right for applicants to show a special case for new creations under 125,000. The deletion of this point from the General Principles followed relatively painlessly, however, when it was realised that there was only one possible candidate (Walthamstow) in the 100,000–125,000 range.

More significant was the dropping of any population figures for county districts. The CCA had advocated amalgamations to ensure that no county district had a population under 10,000. Early drafts of the General Principles had not adopted this proposal but had in mind suggesting a minimum figure of 20,000 for new urban district creations. No comparable figure would be put forward for rural districts (where geographical variations made wide differences likely) and no figure was needed for boroughs, as the powers of the Boundary Commission did not include either the creation or abolition of this type of authority – though borough boundaries could be adjusted. The draft of the General Principles discussed with the local authority associations had in fact suggested that 'if the population of a county district is under 5,000 there is a prima facie case for considering an alteration of boundaries or a union of the district with some other area'. But this, too, was strongly criticised by the UDCA who pointed out that boroughs were immune from abolition, no matter how small their population, and that some thirty-five boroughs in England and Wales were under 5,000. The number of urban districts under 5,000 was much higher than this – about 150 – but it was argued that they must be at an adequate level of efficiency to have escaped de-urbanisation under the county reviews, and therefore should not now be placed at automatic risk. In the end, all reference to the size of county districts was abandoned partly because there was a genuine problem in fixing a minimum population for these authorities whose geographical circumstances might vary so greatly, but largely because the government wished to be able to report to Parliament that the proposed regulations had been agreed with the associations.

In addition to the two paragraphs mentioned above, the General Principles stressed that the overall aim was 'to ensure individually and collectively effective and convenient units of local government administration'.[17] Within this objective a number of specified matters were to be taken into account and given such weight as the Commission thought fit in the circumstances of the case – including the 'nine factors' which also figured in the work of the subsequent Local Government Commission under the LGA 1958. These exhorted the Commission when considering any area to take into account certain 'main factors' – community of interest, development or anticipated development, economic and industrial characteristics, financial resources, physical features, population, record of administration, shape and size of the area and the wishes of the inhabitants.[18] These factors were not invented in 1945, however. They clearly owed much to the considerations long taken into account by the Ministry of Health and the Local Government Board when dealing with applications for county borough extensions (see p. 37 above). But the Act of 1965 left it to the Commission to interpret the expression 'effective and convenient' units of administration and there was nothing in the General Principles, carefully qualified at all points, to inhibit individual authorities from pleading their own special case to be left undisturbed.

On this basis the regulations were approved by each House almost without discussion. The Commons spent only twenty-five minutes on the subject; in the Lords there was no debate at all and the brief statement of the government spokesman (the only speaker) occupies less than a column in Hansard. So an earlier forecast was falsified that the debate on the regulations would be much more important than the debate on the Bill itself. Why was this? Clearly because the guidance given by the General Principles was so vague and cautious that it aroused little apprehension among local authorities that any significant or painful changes were likely.

The Boundary Commission Regulations also covered publicity for proposals and the holding of inquiries; procedure was further elaborated by Practice Notes published by the Commission for the guidance of local authorities and others involved. When the Commission had decided to examine a particular area the 'investigation stage' commenced. This involved giving notice to all the local authorities which could be affected and then collecting the data and information which the Commission would need. The emphasis at this stage was on informality. Local conferences were held, usually conducted by an Assistant Commissioner who then reported back to the Commission on the facts and the issues involved; but it was no part of his function to recommend solutions to the problems which the investigation might reveal.

The next main stage was the publication of the Commission's draft proposals regarding boundaries or status, which the Commission supplemented with a letter to the local authorities affected explaining the reasons for their provisional conclusions. The Practice Notes emphasised that these were the Commission's own proposals; it could be that such proposals followed, in whole or in part, an application put to the Commission by a particular authority but where the Commission put forward proposals they did so because, in the light of the investigation stage, they had themselves reached the provisional conclusion that such changes were needed.

The penultimate stage was the holding of a public inquiry by the Commission where objections to the proposals had been lodged by a local authority affected or by any person whose views (in the Commission's opinion) merited an examination in this way. Because the proposals under consideration were the *Commission's* proposals there was no question, at such an inquiry, of regarding one authority as the plaintiff and the others as defendants. The public inquiry would also be held by an Assistant Commissioner but not by the same individual who had conducted the investigation stage. Finally, after considering the report of the inquiry, the Commission's conclusions would be embodied in an order.

*The Commission's programme and proposals*
Section 1 of the Act of 1945 required the Commission to review 'the circumstances of the areas into which England and Wales (exclusive of the administrative county of London) are divided for the purposes of local government'. Attention was therefore directed at the areas of individual counties and towns, rather than towards the complete pattern of authorities in a region or sub-region (as was the approach under the later Act of 1958). The expectation that the Commission would consider changes to particular authorities was reinforced by a statutory requirement that they should examine applications made to them by counties, county boroughs or by any borough seeking county borough status (section 3 (2) and (4)).

In practice the Commission planned their programme with the aim of catching up on local government problems caused by the war, and gave priority to applications from county boroughs which had large schemes of reconstruction in prospect (whether from war damage or other reasons) and to cases in which applications respecting boundaries or status had been made to Parliament – or, but for the war, would have been made. In the event very few applications in these special priority classes reached the Commission so, after writing to all the major authorities, they divided the counties and county boroughs into two categories – the more urgent and the less urgent – and this subdivision dictated the order in which they arranged their investigations.[19]

During the three years in which they were at work the Boundary Commission and their Assistant Commissioners held over 1,300 conferences with local authorities, so they became well acquainted with the problems facing authorities at all levels and all over the country. They were soon encountering problems created by the statute under which they worked. The ten-year rule, for instance (referred to at p. 62 above), was enacted with the reasonable objective of preventing boundary changes from being made too frequently; but it also inhibited urgent (and possibly agreed) boundary modifications to facilitate housing development, because such interim changes would then prevent further and more comprehensive adjustments for another decade. The Commission were also irked at the restriction which prevented them from altering the status, as distinct from the boundaries, of non-county boroughs and early recommended that the law should be changed on this point.[20]

Their main proposals, however, were set out in their Report for 1947, in which they outlined a scheme of reorganisation which went far beyond anything that could be achieved under the powers given them by the Act. In effect, they rejected the policy which underlay the machinery they had been brought into existence to operate, and denied the basic assumption that it would be practicable to achieve 'effective and convenient units of local government administration' merely by boundary alterations and without at the same time looking at the allocation of functions. As a result of their discussions with local authorities the Commission became increasingly impressed by the difficulty of taking individual decisions in isolation,[21] and were convinced that the structure needed a radical overhaul – though it should remain based on a mixture of one-tier and two-tier local government. Single-tier authorities should be restricted to those few big units which were large enough to meet the operational needs of postwar services, while being sufficiently compact to avoid the charge of being remote. The Commission went back to the objectives of the 1888 Act in thinking that there should be only a very few such single-tier units. They listed twenty in England but, as three of these (Croydon, East Ham and West Ham) were in the Greater London area, the list bore a marked resemblance to the original ten candidates for county borough status in the 1888 Bill. The seventeen 'one-tier new counties' outside the Greater London area included two new amalgamations, based on Stoke and Brighton, but the others were single county boroughs, many of which would have been granted substantial extensions to remove the seeds of future boundary alterations.

The broad aim, the Commission urged, should be to create one-tier units with populations between 200,000 and 500,000 and two-tier counties between 200,000 and 1 million. The map of two-tier counties would need to be considerably recast, though many would be based on existing counties. Proposals for forty-seven two-tier counties in England included several amalgamations such as Hereford/Worcester, Cambridge/Isle of Ely/ Huntingdon/Peterborough, East and West Suffolk, Leicester/Rutland as well as the creation of completely new counties in Merseyside, South Lancashire and South Yorkshire.

Within the two-tier counties the pattern of districts would need to be revised, and in this field the Commission proposed a distinction between the larger and smaller districts. The larger, with populations generally between 60,000 and 200,000, would be known as 'new county boroughs' and would have a wider range of functions, including education, the personal health services and the children's service, all of which would be county council services in the rest of the county. The proposed creation of these 'most-purpose authorities' between counties and districts was one of the most eye-taking features of the suggested structure, especially as Manchester and Liverpool would both have been 'most-purpose authorities', that is, second-tier authorities within their respective new counties.

The Commission's proposals were received by the government without enthusiasm. True, they had already accepted, as the Minister of Health (Mr Bevan) had said during the committee stage of the Local Government Bill 1948, that 'everyone who knows about local government feels that it is nonsense to talk about functions and boundaries separately. They have got to be taken together.'[22] But the Boundary Commission's proposals had produced mixed and generally hostile reactions in local government circles and offered no agreed basis for further legislation, even if there had been time for it during the remainder of the lifetime of that Parliament.

In this state of conflict between machinery and policy the government had a number of alternative courses open to them. They might direct the Commission to proceed with their task on the basis of the 1945 Act; but this would have been unsatisfactory, as the Commission considered that without any jurisdiction over functions they had inadequate powers to achieve a pattern of effective and convenient units. Alternatively, the government might direct the Commission to proceed on the assumption that legislation would in due course be introduced on the lines of their report. But this would be tantamount to saying that the government accepted these proposals - which would have been premature and (with an election not too far away) politically rash. Or the government could wind up the Boundary Commission and embark upon the wider review of local government structure and functions to which the Commission's activities had pointed.

After taking ample time to consider the Commission's reports (including their Report for 1948 - a brief document in which the Commission impatiently listed the matters on which they were waiting for some response) the government eventually chose the last course, and the Commission were dissolved, by the Local Government Boundary Commission (Dissolution) Act 1949, without their work having resulted in a single boundary alteration. The previous machinery for adjusting boundaries (contained in the LGA 1933) was revived, subject, however, to the retention of the Special Parliamentary Procedure for orders affecting counties and boroughs, which would previously have had to be considered through the provisional order procedure. The Boundary Commission Dissolution Bill, as originally presented to Parliament, would have retained the figure of 100,000 as the minimum population entitling a borough to seek county borough status by private Bill. But, wishing to appear conciliatory, the Minister of Health (Mr Bevan) agreed to go back to the lower figure of 75,000 which had been in force before 1945. This change to the Bill was made by government amendment - against all logic. No new county boroughs were in fact created before the passing of the LGA 1958 though the period 1949-58 saw many boundary alterations and the creation of four new districts - Crawley, Harlow and Kirkby UDs and Epping & Ongar RD.

## THE LOCAL GOVERNMENT COMMISSION FOR ENGLAND 1958-67

When faced with these various possible courses of action 'we came to the conclusion', said the Minister of Health (Mr Bevan), during the second reading debate on the Bill to abolish the Trustram Eve Commission, 'that the correct procedure was for the government themselves to accept the responsibility of examining the whole position, and of ultimately bringing forward their own proposals. That examination is now in being' (Commons Hansard, 2 November 1949, col. 516).

The results (if any) of the alleged examination by the government were not divulged. Instead it became clear from statements made by successive ministers that governments of both persuasions were placing greater weight on the outcome of discussions between the local authorities associations than upon any central initiative.[23] Such discussions had been taking place, though without promising any change of attitude, and the associations had fallen back on the positions adopted during the time of the Jowitt review, advocating the more general adoption of two-tier or unitary arrangements as the case may be. It was during this period, from 1950 to 1955, that county borough Bills promoted by Luton, Ealing, Ilford and Poole were either defeated or withdrawn because of opposition from the central government on the grounds that the creation of new county boroughs should not proceed piecemeal when a comprehensive measure of local government reorganisation was clearly needed and could not be indefinitely delayed.

The government initiative, when it came, was taken by Mr Sandys shortly after he became Minister of Housing and Local Government in the autumn of 1954. He then met representatives of the local authority associations and told them that it would not be fruitful to embark on any extensive reform of local government unless there existed some broad measure of agreement among the local authorities themselves. He also made it clear that, in his view, the existing system had not broken down and that he would not be prepared to eliminate either the two-tier system in the counties or the single-tier system in the big towns. In effect the government were prepared to consider legislation for improving the existing arrangements, provided the associations were all agreed on what should be done, but were not prepared to contemplate any more radical (or controversial) reform.

In the light of this statement of the government's attitude the associations agreed once more to seek an acceptable basis for adjustments within the existing system, and a series of meetings was held with the minister in the chair. The outcome was the concordat printed as the appendix to the White Paper *Local Government: Areas and Status of Local Authorities in England and Wales* (Cmd 9831, 1956), consisting of a set of proposals agreed between the five associations which the government broadly accepted.

Besides dealing with areas and status the concordat also referred to the exercise of functions in the counties by the larger county districts. The proposal was that certain county functions – though exactly which ones needed further examination – should be directly conferred on the councils of the bigger districts or compulsorily delegated to them by the county councils. The government's views on this subject were set out in a further White Paper, *Local Government: Functions of County Councils and County District Councils in England and Wales* (Cmnd 161, 1957); and a third White Paper appeared shortly afterwards, *Local Government Finance (England and Wales)* (Cmnd 209, 1957).

These White Papers formed the basis of the Local Government Act 1958, through which the government aimed to strengthen local government in three related ways – by removing the weaknesses of the existing structure and eliminating a large number of small authorities; by giving the larger district councils a greater share of responsibility for certain county services (health, welfare and education); and by increasing the financial independence of local authorities by strengthening the rating system, introducing the general grant and reducing authorities' dependence on percentage grants.

Part II of the Act dealt with the areas and status of authorities and the provisions had three main aspects in mind: the conurbations, the county/county borough pattern in the rest of the country and the county districts.

The machinery was once more an independent Commission, but this time separate Commissions were appointed for England and Wales. The work which the Commissions were to do was seen as a single one-off exercise to bring the system into line with modern conditions, after which the Commissions were to be dissolved by order. They were named the Local Government Commissions for England and for Wales to distinguish them from the former Boundary Commission and because (at any rate so far as the English Commission were concerned) their field of work in the conurbations extended to functions as well as boundaries. In each case the Commissions were small bodies – seven Commissioners in England and five in Wales – most of whose members served on a part-time basis. The essential objective – 'effective and convenient local government' – adopted these words from the Boundary Commission Regulations but this time the 1958 Act placed on the new Commission the duty of reviewing the *organisation* of local government (section 17 (1)). It thus avoided the reference to local government *units*, and when the Act said that the Commission should hold separate reviews for such areas as they may determine (section 21 (2)) it was implied that these would be substantial parts of the country, and that they would not proceed county by county (as had the Boundary Commission).

The treatment of the conurbations was the Act's most significant innovation. It gave statutory recognition to the need to consider each of the main conurbations as a single local government problem. Outside Greater London five such conurbations were identified by the Act - Tyneside, West Yorkshire, South-East Lancashire, Merseyside and the West Midlands - and in these 'special review areas' the English Commission were given special powers which were not available to them elsewhere. In the conurbations a great variety of local government units were jumbled together, as the outcome of historical circumstances - counties, county boroughs, non-county boroughs, urban districts and even rural districts - and, given the need to look at each of these conurbations as a whole, all these various authorities had to be comprehensively reviewed together. Hence, in the SRAs the English Commission had powers to recommend virtually any system they considered apt to the circumstances.[24] They could propose the retention of the traditional county borough/county/county district pattern but with adjusted boundaries and possibly the co-ordination of some services through joint boards; or a pattern consisting entirely of county boroughs; or the setting up of a new 'continuous county', that is, one containing districts but no county boroughs. In the last type of case, a two-tier solution, the Commission could recommend a new allocation of functions as between county and districts, and it did not necessarily follow that each district council should have exactly the same functions.

Greater London was excluded from the ambit of the Local Government Commission for England and on this point the Act departed from the White Paper on areas and status. The White Paper had proposed that the Commission should be excluded only from the county of London but should review the rest of Greater London, subject to the proviso that no county boroughs were to be created in Middlesex (Cmd 9831, paras 44-7). This was a thoroughly unsatisfactory approach to the problem of local government in Greater London which demanded to be looked at as a whole, on the same basis as the other conurbations. This need was accepted by the government when preparations for legislation were put in hand and the decision to appoint a Royal Commission on London Government was announced by the Minister of Housing and Local Government (Mr Brooke) during a two-day debate in July 1957 on the motion to take note of the three White Papers on areas and status, functions and finance (Commons Hansard, 29 July 1957, col. 918). Accordingly, the 1958 Act excluded the Local Government Commission from the metropolitan area which was defined in the Act in a way which coincided with the area named in the Royal Commission's terms of reference - the Metropolitan Police district together with certain fringe authorities. Four counties (Surrey, Kent, Essex and Hertfordshire) found themselves partly within the ambit of the Royal Commission on Greater London and partly subject to review by the Local Government Commission. But both Commissions were advisory bodies and as the implementation of any recommendations depended on action by the government there was no danger, in practice, of incompatible solutions.

Outside the SRAs and the metropolitan area the two Local Government Commissions had the task of reviewing the pattern of counties and county boroughs but not the county districts. So far as counties and county boroughs were concerned, the Commission's proposals could include all the changes open to the Boundary Commission in the way of boundary alterations, the splitting or the amalgamation of authorities and the creation or demotion of county boroughs, and the Act reinstated the figure of 100,000 at which the population of a town was deemed to be sufficient to support the functions of a county borough. This time, however, the Act (unlike the Boundary Commission Act) clearly ruled that it was not open to a local authority to seek county borough status or an alteration of its boundaries by way of local Act while the Local Government Commission were at work or for some time thereafter, as the promotion of a private Bill for such purposes was prohibited for fifteen years from the passing of the Act, that is, until 1973.

The Local Government Commissions were advisory, not executive, bodies; they reported to the minister and their proposals had no force unless given effect by ministerial order. The minister had power to accept the Commission's proposals, to reject them or to modify them and the department (not the Commission) prepared the necessary order. This had to be presented to Parliament along with the Commission's report on the review area and became subject to either affirmative or negative resolution, according to the substance of the order.

Orders which were confined to boundary alterations of counties or county boroughs were subject only to negative resolution, but the more substantial (and potentially more controversial) orders required affirmative resolution in each House, for example, any order dealing with a special review area, the creation or demotion of a county borough, the amalgamation or dismemberment of any counties and also any regulations made for the guidance of the Commissions in the exercise of their functions. The significant point to note here, however, is that, while Parliament continued to have the last say in proposals affecting the major local government units, this control was now exercised entirely on the floor of the House on a take-it-or-leave-it basis; Parliament had the option of accepting or rejecting an order but no longer had the power to examine petitions in committee or make detailed amendments, as would have been the case had either the provisional order or the Special Parliamentary Procedure been applied to orders following on the work of the Local Government Commissions.

The task of reviewing county districts, which had been within the jurisdiction of the Boundary Commission, was returned to the county councils, whose obligation arose when the Local Government Commission had finished their work in any area, that is, when the county pattern was regarded as settled. The Act laid down a number of procedural requirements and provided that the county council's final report on the review should be submitted to the minister. In certain circumstances the minister was obliged to hold a local inquiry and any order giving effect to changes proposed as the result of the review became subject to negative resolution. There was also a fall-back provision which would have allowed the minister to direct the Local Government Commission to carry out a fresh county review if he was not satisfied with the county council's proposals.

The concordat between the local authority associations had expressed their clear agreement that the review of county districts should once more become the responsibility of county councils, though this course was not without its critics. Some feared that the county councils would be too timid in proposing changes which would upset the *status quo*, or would be reluctant to make changes in favour of big districts which might have county borough aspirations. Others feared that county councils would lack sympathy for ancient traditions, especially those of the municipal corporations - a fear not unconnected with the fact that the Act took a further step towards placing non-county boroughs on the same footing as urban and rural districts as regards proposals affecting areas and status. This development was accepted by the AMC as part of the concordat, however, and received specific support in the White Paper (Cmd 9831, paras 51-2).

It had been one of the weaknesses of the first county reviews (and one again castigated by the Boundary Commission) that boroughs still retained a special position which prevented them from losing their status as a county district or from being absorbed by another type of unit. Even the 1958 Act made no provision for the compulsory abolition of a borough as a chartered corporation and if a borough was amalgamated with another borough, with an urban district or a rural district, the resultant unit still had to be a borough. But where a borough was so small as to resemble a village which elsewhere had only parish status it was now possible, as part of the county review, to include that borough in a rural district as a parish - though as a parish with special characteristics (section 28 (5) and schedule 7). The borough council lost its status as a county district and the local government functions which went with this, but it retained its status as a borough, though with some modifications appropriate to its now more modest role. It retained its charter rights, corporate property and regalia (though not its aldermen); it continued to be called a borough, its civic head still retained the style 'mayor' and its chief officer that of town clerk; it exercised all the powers of a parish council, plus any special powers given by its charter and preserved for the borough council by the county review order. It had long been clear that the very small boroughs, like other authorities of the same size and resources, were inadequately equipped to meet the demands of growing local government services and it was logical that some should (like many small urban districts) assume the role of parishes rather than county districts. But the concept of the chartered corporation, created by royal Prerogative, proved so tenacious that such corporations now existed at all levels in local government as county boroughs, non-county boroughs and rural boroughs (or, more accurately, 'boroughs included in rural districts').

## The Local Government Commission Regulations

The Local Government Commission Regulations,[25] like the earlier Boundary Commission Regulations, laid down guidelines applying both to the substance of the change which might be proposed and also to procedural requirements which the Commissions had to observe.

As regards the substantive guidance this was (as before) more in the nature of reminders about matters to be taken into account than specific rules or limitations. The Commissions had a wide discretion which the regulations did little to fetter. Their significance was more as a record of the discussions which had taken place between the government and the local authority associations, and as a description of the general objectives of the whole exercise.

Using almost the same words as before the new regulations reiterated the basic purpose of each of the reviews to be carried out by the Commissions; these were to be directed 'to effective and convenient local government throughout the whole of the review area and not merely in individual areas of local government'.[26] The nine factors which had been identified in the Boundary Commission Regulations (see pp. 66–7 above) were listed again.

Certain of the individual regulations (nos. 8, 9 and 10) dealt specifically with county boroughs. When considering whether to recommend the creation of a new county borough the Commissions were to take into account the probability of any increase or decrease in the population of the town; while the existence, or early prospect, of a population of 100,000 was not an indispensable requirement no new creation should be recommended below this figure unless the Commission involved were satisfied that there were 'special circumstances' which made that particular change desirable; and in every case of a new county borough proposal the Commission had to consider all related proposals affecting the town in question and the administrative county from which it would be withdrawn, and satisfy themselves 'that the change is on balance desirable'. The regulations which dealt with new county borough creations were, said the minister, 'carefully worded. I am not anxious to put any gloss on them' (Mr Henry Brooke, Commons Hansard, 9 December 1958, col. 266). This showed a wise caution.

Indeed, where the regulations attempted to be more specific – in connection with county borough extensions – they created a fruitful source of debate and contention in their application to individual cases. One of these, for instance (regulation 11), said that, when considering whether any part of a neighbouring county district should be included in a county borough, the Commission should examine not only whether the area in question was substantially a continuation of the town area of the existing (or proposed) county borough but also whether it 'has closer and more special links with it than those which necessarily arise from mere proximity'. The meaning of these words, inserted to reassure county councils and county districts and to counter any presumption that county borough boundaries should automatically include all the continuous built-up area, was argued at length at public inquiries.

Other regulations (nos. 12 to 18) dealt with the special review areas though without importing any novel thoughts that would not in any case have occurred to the English Commission. In each SRA local government needs had to be considered in relation to the area as a whole, and proposals for SRAs had to be co-ordinated with proposals for surrounding areas (especially where counties lay partly within an SRA and partly outside). If a pattern of county boroughs was recommended for any SRA the Commission were to consider the size of such boroughs and the need to avoid 'a multiplicity of autonomous local authorities'; and if a continuous county was recommended, and proposals made for a redistribution of functions, they should have regard to 'the desirability of securing an adequate range of responsibilities both to the county council and to the county district councils concerned'.

On the procedural side the regulations added some requirements to the provisions set out in the Act itself; the cumulative result of the Act and the regulations together laid down a formidable process which aimed at being flexible but turned out (in some instances) to be the reverse.

The first steps lay with the Commissions. They had to decide what areas they should adopt for the purpose of carrying out their reviews, and to which of these areas they should give priority. The English Commission had certain areas – the SRAs – defined for them in the Act, but they had to divide up the rest of the country into general review areas (and keep the minister informed as to their proposed programme in case he wished to issue any directions on the point – he never did).

When the English or Welsh Commission had decided to embark upon the review of a particular area (and the English Commission commenced with three related areas – the West Midlands SRA and the West Midlands and East Midlands general review areas) they had to give public notice of their intention. In addition they invited the authorities within the area to supply information and views about their own problems and about the review area in general, and they also invited views from a wide range of other public bodies. The submission of written statements was followed by meetings at which the Commissions discussed local government problems with representatives of individual authorities and with other bodies too.

The Commissions then published draft proposals for the areas under review and sent copies to all local authorities and interested bodies, accompanied - though this was not a statutory requirement - by a brief statement of the reasons for the Commission's provisional conclusions. These statements were sometimes criticised as being insufficiently detailed though chiefly, one suspects, by authorities who felt they could more easily pick holes in matters of detail than mount a case against broad conclusions. A period had to elapse for representations, which the Commissions were required to consider and then to 'confer with representatives of such of the authorities and bodies ... as desire to be represented' (section 21 (4)). These statutory conferences were a new part of the procedure for considering major changes, though conferences had had to be held between county councils and county district councils before county councils prepared their final proposals for the county reviews in the 1930s.[27] The aim was to permit representatives of local authorities to exchange views with the Commission and with each other in a relaxed atmosphere removed from the formality of a public inquiry. For practical reasons it was usually necessary to hold conferences for separate parts of review areas - even in the SRAs - because of the numbers of authorities and their representatives attending.

In the light of views expressed on their draft proposals the Commissions had to formulate their final recommendations and forward them to the minister, together with their report on the review area. So far as that review area was concerned the Commission's functions were then at an end.

The minister now had to publish the Commission's report and proposals and invite representations. If the minister intended to give effect to the Commission's proposals and if objections had been lodged, he was required to hold a public inquiry into such objections. An inquiry could be dispensed with if the minister was satisfied that he was sufficiently informed about the point at issue, but he could never dispense with an inquiry if the objection came from a local authority threatened with extinction or the loss of county borough status.

The minister was empowered to reject the Commission's proposals or to give effect to them by order with or without modification. But in certain circumstances the minister might wish to proceed in a way which could not properly be described as a 'modification' of the Commission's proposals: he might wish to adopt a diametrically opposed course to that recommended, or himself to propose changes where the Commission had suggested none. In such cases the minister had to consult with the local authorities in the review area concerned, then publicise his own proposals, receive representations and hold a public inquiry into objections as if the proposals had been made by the Commission (section 24).

Finally, any order made by the minister had to be laid before Parliament together with the Commission's report on the area, and the order was subject to either affirmative or negative resolution.

These were the stages of the procedure laid down in the Act and regulations but yet another possible stage was discovered to be embedded in one of the Standing Orders of the House of Lords.[28] The terms of reference of the Lords committee to which such orders are referred – at that time the Special Orders Committee, but now the Hybrid Instruments Committee – say that, where any such order contains provisions which (but for the terms of the parent Act under which the order was made) would have required a private Bill or a hybrid Bill, then persons who would have been entitled to petition against the private or hybrid Bill are entitled to petition the Special Orders Committee. That Committee, unless they are satisfied that the whole matter had been adequately investigated already, might recommend that the order be referred to a Select Committee who could go over the whole ground again and hear counsel, witnesses, and so on. And when the West Midlands Order was before Parliament a petition from eight authorities was in fact heard by the Special Orders Committee – though that Committee decided that there should be no further inquiry into the matter.

The possibility of petitioning the Special Orders Committee may have been a desirable safeguard in the case of some types of earlier orders but was hardly appropriate to orders affecting local government areas and status in view of the fact that, in the LGA 1958, Parliament had itself prescribed an elaborate procedure to ensure that interested parties had two separate opportunities of expressing their views before an order was made – at the statutory conferences and at the public inquiries. The House of Lords Committee on Procedure in fact recommended that the Standing Order should not apply to orders under the LGA 1958[29] but this recommendation was not accepted by the House (Lords Hansard, 15 July 1965, cols 249 ff.).

In a procedure which was to some extent experimental it was inevitable that some steps would raise controversy in operation. One of these was the form of the Commission's explanatory memoranda accompanying their draft proposals (p. 78 above). Another was the purpose of, and procedure at, the public inquiries held by the minister. The Act required that in certain circumstances the minister should hold a public inquiry into objections lodged with him regarding the Commission's final proposals. The inquiry, it should be noted, was into the objections not into the proposals and as the Commission were (as regards any review area) *functus officio* when they had delivered their final proposals and report, they played no part in the proceedings. This aroused great wrath on the part of those local authorities who disagreed with the Commission's proposals; they wanted the Commission to be represented at the inquiry to explain and to defend their report; they felt that the inquiry should investigate and pronounce on the merits of the proposals and of any alternatives which objectors might prefer. It was an additional source of grievance that the inspectors appointed to hold the inquiries refrained from coming to any conclusions or making any recommendations, even on the objections, and a number of local authorities in the Black Country, led by Wednesbury Borough Council, challenged (unsuccessfully) the validity of the inquiry. The court held that the inquiry was an administrative, not a judicial, one and dismissed the claim that it was invalid because the inspector had not pronounced on the merits of the case argued before him.[30]

## Progress under the Act of 1958

As the work of the English and Welsh Commissions went forward, the procedure laid down by and under the Act came under increasing criticism as being complex, cumbersome and unlikely ever to achieve any worthwhile improvement of the existing system. The history of the West Midlands reorganisation, although an extreme example, lent obvious support to critics of the procedure. The West Midlands SRA was one of the first three review areas to be tackled, along with the West Midlands and East Midlands general review areas. Work began in 1959. Preliminary discussions, the publication of draft proposals and the holding of statutory conferences occupied 1959 and 1960. The Commission's final report and proposals were presented to the minister in May 1961; the principal feature of these was the recasting of the mixed county borough/county/county district structure in the Black Country into five large county boroughs grouped round Dudley, Smethwick, Walsall, West Bromwich and Wolverhampton. A public inquiry into objections to the Commission's proposals was held by the minister and sat for fifty days between October 1961 and February 1962. In July 1962 the minister announced his decision to accept the Commission's recommendations in principle, and in November of that year a full statement of the minister's reasons for his decision was sent to the local authorities concerned, together with conclusions on the many detailed recommendations regarding the boundaries between the new authorities. Work proceeded within the department on the order needed to give effect to these decisions (work which had to embrace many consequential matters not considered by the Commission), but legal action challenging the validity of the procedure delayed its presentation to Parliament. The judgement of the Court of Appeal in this action (see above) was not given until October 1965, after earlier proceedings on crown privilege in respect of the inspector's terms of reference had been disposed of. Finally (after some further delay in the House of Lords while petitions were heard by the Special Orders Committee) the West Midlands Order[31] was approved by Parliament in December 1965 and came into effect on 1 April 1966 – seven years after the Commission had started their review of the area.

Proposals for another SRA – Tyneside – followed a course which protracted itself for different reasons. Local government on Tyneside had been the subject of investigation by the Scott Royal Commission in 1937 (Cmd 5402). The Trustram Eve Boundary Commission would have retained the City of Newcastle-upon-Tyne as a single-tier unit but would have included the other county boroughs in their respective geographical counties – Tynemouth in Northumberland, Gateshead and South Shields in Durham. The Local Government Commission tackled Tyneside and other northern review areas next in their programme after the midlands and commenced these reviews in 1960, continuing through 1961. Draft proposals for Tyneside were published in February 1962; after the statutory conference stage their final report and proposals appeared in July 1963. The Commission's proposed solution for Tyneside differed from both their predecessors' as they recommended the establishment of a 'continuous county' with four most-purpose districts based on the four existing county boroughs. At the local inquiry in 1964 the continuing lack of any Tyneside consensus was again demonstrated as yet further alternative possibilities were discussed, including the division of Tyneside between Northumberland and Durham, the establishment of four county boroughs and the creation of a single county borough for the whole area. The report of the public inquiry was published in July 1965 when the then minister (Mr Crossman) dismissed the two-county solution – which amounted to a denial that Tyneside needed to be considered as a single entity – and, after meeting with representatives of local authorities in the area, he announced his provisional view that the Commission's continuous county approach should also be rejected in favour of a single county borough. The Act required further consultations with the local authorities, however, before the minister could formally put forward his counter-proposal for a single Tyneside county borough, which he did in February 1966. Objections were duly lodged against this solution, too, and a second public inquiry was held in June/July 1966. By this time, however, the Redcliffe-Maud Royal Commission on Local Government in England had been appointed and as they (not unreasonably) felt unable, at that early stage in their work, to forecast how a single Tyneside authority might fit in with their ultimate recommendations, Mr Greenwood (Mr Crossman's successor as Minister of Housing and Local Government) decided in May 1967 not to proceed further in this area. Again a period of seven years had elapsed and this time there was nothing to show for it.

The Act had little effect on the pattern of authorities in Wales either. The Welsh Commission's draft proposals, covering the whole of the Principality, were published in May 1961 and, after the statutory conferences, their final report was published in December 1962. They proposed that the thirteen administrative counties in Wales and Monmouthshire should be reduced by amalgamations to a total of seven. Cardiff, Swansea and Newport should retain their county borough status, with extended boundaries, but Merthyr Tydfil should be demoted to become a non-county borough in Glamorgan. County borough claims by the boroughs of Rhondda and Wrexham were rejected. The Welsh Commission were not happy with their proposals, however, and they regretted their inability to consider functions as well as areas. Circumstances ranged from the sparsely populated areas of mid-Wales to the heavy concentration of population in the south and, had they been permitted, the Welsh Commission would have wished to consider the desirability of a special review area in south Wales. This was ruled out, however, because the government had bowed to pressure from Welsh MPs during the committee stage of the Local Government Bill and had accepted an amendment which precluded the establishment of any SRA in the Principality.[32]

After prolonged cogitation the government finally announced, in February 1964, that, while they would go ahead with public inquiries into objections to the county borough extensions (and. Cardiff and Newport were both extended by order), they would not proceed under the 1958 Act with the other recommendations of the Welsh Commission. The government shared the view of the Commission that the geographical circumstances of Wales differentiated it from England and that it was desirable to consider both areas and functions together. They therefore proposed to reconsider what pattern of local government might be appropriate in the special circumstances of Wales, and would publish their proposals in the form of a White Paper; any eventual reorganisation in Wales would be effected by separate legislation (Commons Hansard, 26 February 1964, cols 434–9).

The machinery set up by the 1958 Act ground on slowly and with friction. And (though this is not unusual) it all took much longer than had been originally hoped. When the English Commission was first set up it was thought that their work might be finished in five or six years. In practice it tailed off towards the end of 1965 when it became clear, following the speech of the minister (Mr Crossman) to the AMC Conference in September of that year, that the government contemplated a new and far more radical approach to reorganisation. By that time the Commission had completed their reviews and submitted final proposals for six out of the nine general review areas into which they had divided the country and three of the five SRAs. No final proposals were put forward for the Merseyside or South-East Lancashire SRAs or for the North-Western, Southern or South-Eastern general review areas.

After the Redcliffe-Maud Commission had been appointed the Local Government Commissions for England and Wales were formally dissolved by the Local Government (Termination of Reviews) Act 1967 and, of the outstanding proposals which had already been submitted to the minister, implementation was confined to boundary changes for which there was an immediate urgency based on housing needs.

In total, three new county boroughs had been created on the English Commission's recommendations (Luton, Solihull and Torbay) and three existing county boroughs had been absorbed in new and larger units;[33] twenty-four existing county boroughs had been extended; Cambridge and the Isle of Ely had been amalgamated to form a new county as had Huntingdonshire and the Soke of Peterborough, and a number of changes, usually of a minor and uncontroversial character, were made to county boundaries. In most cases the Commission's proposals had been accepted in substance, though in two major instances the government of the day had rejected the English Commission's proposals – over Tyneside (already mentioned) and the proposal to amalgamate Rutland and Leicestershire.

*County reviews under the LGA 1958*
The 1958 Act revived the obligation originally placed on county councils by the LGA 1929 to review county districts and rural parishes in their respective counties and, once more, the department were faced with the task of offering advice on the sort of result which county councils might aim to achieve. The circular which was eventually issued after lengthy exchanges with the local authority associations was not notably more explicit than the guidance issued under the 1929 Act. It quoted the nine factors from the Local Government Commission Regulations, and it placed emphasis on the need to support an adequate nucleus of qualified staff in order to provide services to modern standards. But in the absence of general agreement among the associations on any population figures the circular fell back on banal generalities:

> The Minister has considered whether he can offer any guidance on the minimum size desirable for county districts in terms of population. He has decided that he ought not to suggest a figure, recognising as he does that any one figure might, for geographical and other reasons, be too low for full effectiveness in some areas, and too high for convenience in others. But, in view of the responsibilities placed on him by the Act, the Minister thinks it right to indicate at this stage that he will not be prepared to endorse recommendations which, in his opinion, have. given too little weight to the importance of securing districts of sufficient size in population and resources to be fully effective.[34]

Six counties managed to complete county reviews in the wake of the Commission's activities and uncontroversial parts of these were implemented in the case of Shropshire, Cornwall, Worcestershire, Herefordshire and Bedfordshire. As in the 1930s these county reviews varied in the vigour of their approach but in total seven boroughs lost their status as county districts and became 'boroughs included in rural districts'.[35] In addition a large number of county district boundaries were amended in the period 1958–72 where there was an urgent need for change without waiting for the county review.

## MACHINERY AND POLICY DURING
## THE PERIOD OF LIMITED CHANGE

The point has already been made that machinery and policy go together. Machinery will operate successfully only if the changes to be brought about have been clearly defined and fully discussed, if they command sufficient support for their implementation to be politically practicable, and if the government have sufficient determination to carry through those changes even though they may encounter opposition in the process. Equally, the policy cannot be given effect unless the machinery is apt for the task; if it is too cumbersome, complicated or hedged around with opportunities for delay or appeal, the weight of the machinery may sink the policy. With these thoughts in mind what conclusions can be drawn as regards the interaction of machinery and policy during the period covered by this chapter?

An overall objective was common to the whole period: to retain the existing county/county borough system (outside London) but, within this framework, to create stronger authorities and to rationalise boundaries. Three successive efforts were made to improve the pattern of authorities but with very small success in relation to the labour involved. In retrospect the conclusion must be that the fault, at each stage, was shared between machinery and policy, though in differing proportions.

Very few counties managed a thorough-going reorganisation of districts in the 1930s; the results of the county reviews were patchy, and in some areas only nominal. One clear obstacle inhibited reform – the inability of the county councils to propose the abolition of any borough, however small or ineffective. This defect in the machinery was matched on the policy side by the lack of positive guidance from the centre, especially on the size of districts expressed in terms of either population or rateable value. This was partly due to the difficulty of reaching any agreement with the associations on minimum sizes, and this, in turn, was linked to the special position of the boroughs – the UDCA were bound to oppose any suggestion of a minimum population whether 20,000, 10,000 or even 5,000 while boroughs below these figures remained protected.

The setting up of the Trustram Eve Commission represented a far more ambitious effort at reform. It was a permanent body, its terms of reference embraced all the main operational authorities – counties, county boroughs and county districts – and it was an executive, not an advisory, body. The preliminary stages of their procedure leading up to the formulation of their final proposals included informal consultations and formal public inquiries; at the order-making stage (though this was never reached) the minister had no role to play because the Commission's orders, in so far as they needed confirmation, would have gone straight to Parliament. The Commission were subject to the same limitation as the county councils had been in that they could not abolish any borough, and they chafed under the ten-year rule, but the failure of this effort to reform the pattern of authorities chiefly resulted from the fact that machinery and policy parted company. It was true that the policy guidance, expressed in the Boundary Commission Regulations, was at best cautious and at worst nebulous because the government went no further than the (restricted) common ground to which all the four main associations were prepared to agree. But the problem which emerged was the disagreement of the chosen instrument - the Boundary Commission - with the fundamental basis of the whole exercise: that changes should be made to the areas and status of authorities without significantly altering the existing balance between counties and county boroughs, and without touching the allocation of functions.

Lastly, there was the Hancock Commission. Again the aim was to retain a system comprising both counties and county boroughs but there were important differences of machinery. The Commission's task was to carry out a single review of counties and county boroughs (but not county districts) and when this was complete they were to be wound up. The Commission were an advisory, not an executive, body and their conclusions were presented to the minister as a set of recommendations. If he decided to implement them, with or without modifications, he had to arrange public inquiries into objections before any order was laid before Parliament. The powers of the Hancock Commission were wider, however, in the conurbations - the special review areas - where their recommendations could embrace the whole structure of local government (including districts) and the allocation of functions, and it is worth recalling that the basic set-up in the metropolitan counties which resulted from the LGA 1972 could have been produced through the machinery of the Act of 1958.

In practice the Hancock Commission's efforts, though they produced some useful changes, could not achieve the general improvements hoped for, and the reasons must again be sought partly in machinery and partly in policy. The various stages laid down by the Act and regulations and, in particular, the requirement that the minister should substantially duplicate the work of the Commission by holding public inquiries to examine objections, added up to an impossibly cumbersome procedure which produced friction between authorities and allowed the maximum pressure to be exerted to prevent individual proposals from going through. On the policy side the ambivalent guidance contained (this time) in the Local Government Commission Regulations once again reflected the government's desire to proceed only on the basis of agreement with the associations.

This timidity was illustrated by the then government's loss of nerve when faced with the emotional campaign to prevent the abolition of Rutland as a separate county, notwithstanding that this particular change was one of the most obvious that the whole machinery had been designed to achieve. 'Determined though they are to carry through a thorough-going overhaul of local government, the government have decided there are grounds for treating Rutland's case as unique', said Sir Keith Joseph, the Minister of Housing and Local Government (Commons Hansard, 1 August 1963, col. 663).

The change of government in 1964 and the advent of a new minister (Mr Crossman) hastened the acceptance, as regards England and Wales, of two conclusions which emerged from this period of limited reform and which had already been acted on in the case of Greater London. First: the expanding scope of local government activities and the changing nature of services – especially in the fields of planning, transportation, education and the social services – made it impossible to cling any longer to the county/county borough framework on which the 1888 Act had been based. Radical change was required. Secondly: this must come from general legislation and must be carried through by the central government; major changes could not be effected through an independent body looking separately at different parts of the country.

## NOTES: CHAPTER 3

1   LGA 1888, section 57 and LGA 1894, section 36.
2   Onslow Commission Evidence, Pt IX, p. 1803 (Appendix CIII to Memorandum submitted on behalf of the Minister of Health by Sir Arthur Robinson).
3   ibid., Pt IX, p. 1716 (Sir Arthur Robinson's memorandum, para. 56).
4   ibid., Pt IX, p. 1774 (Sir Arthur Robinson's memorandum, particularly paras 233–322).
5   Ministry of Health Memorandum LGA 24 (September 1929) and LGA 42 (February 1931).
6   Memorandum LGA 24, para. 7.
7   Memorandum LGA 42, para. 4.
8   Ministry of Health Annual Report for 1938–9, Cmd 6089, p. 120.
9   AMC Memorandum on Reorganisation of Local Government, *Municipal Review*, August 1942.
10  Report on Local Government Reform adopted by the Executive Council of the CCA, *County Councils Gazette*, March 1942.
11  Ministry of Health file 91047/1/2 (PRO reference HLG 43/1094).
12  Ealing B, Edmonton B, Harrow UD, Hendon B, Heston & Isleworth B, Tottenham B, Wembley B and Willesden B.
13  Enfield UD, Hornsey B and Twickenham B.
14  SR & O 1945 No. 1569.
15  General Principles; schedule to the Boundary Commission Regulations (SR & O 1945 No. 1569), para. 3.
16  ibid., para. 7.

17   ibid., para. 1.
18   ibid., para. 2.
19   Local Government Boundary Commission's Report for 1946, paras 8 and 9.
20   ibid., para. 31.
21   Report for 1948, para. 11.
22   Commons Standing Committee B, 16 December 1947, col. 157.
23   Dr Dalton, during a general debate on local government (Commons Hansard, 17 July 1951, col. 1178) and Mr Macmillan, during the second reading debate on the Ealing Corporation Bill (Commons Hansard, 26 March 1952, col. 520).
24   By combination of any of the possible changes listed in sections 18, 19 and 26 of the LGA 1958.
25   SI 1958 No. 2115.
26   ibid., regulation 3.
27   LGA 1933, section 146.
28   House of Lords Standing Orders (Private Business), No. 216.
29   HOL 154 dated 23 June 1965.
30   *Wednesbury Corporation* v *Minister of Housing and Local Government* (No. 2) [1965] 3 All E.R. 571.
31   The West Midlands Order 1965, SI 1965 No. 2139.
32   Commons Standing Committee D, 11 March 1958, col. 732.
33   Smethwick into Warley (as part of the West Midlands reorganisation), Middlesborough into Teesside and West Hartlepool into Hartlepool.
34   MHLG circular No. 35/62, 2 October 1962.
35   Bishops Castle, Bridgnorth, Lostwithiel, Ludlow, Much Wenlock and Oswestry, as a result of county reviews and South Molton (Devon) as an *ad hoc* change under section 141, LGA 1933.

## Chapter 4

# Direct Government Action: London

## THE MAIN STAGES OF CENTRAL GOVERNMENT ACTION

The shape of the local government system is the product of central decisions, by Parliament and by the executive, though such decisions are taken within the whole framework of political action and after consultation with local government interests. Central decisions, also reflecting local government views, established the machinery for change and set in train the successive exercises, already described, for modifying local authority areas. But the point was reached when the whole structure of local government had to be reshaped; when tinkering with boundaries within the existing system was no longer an adequate response to the rapid social and political developments of the twentieth century.

The great expansion of governmental activity of all kinds and the growing involvement of central government in economic and social welfare have resulted in local administration becoming ever more closely bound up with national policies. Decisions about the local government system are therefore decisions about an important part of the machinery of government through which national programmes are implemented in the social field. Major reorganisation could be undertaken only through direct action by the central government but circumstances in the 1960s and 1970s were very different from those which faced the legislators of the nineteenth century. When London government was reformed in 1963-5, and when the rest of England, with Wales, was tackled in 1972-4, the governments of the day were faced with a formidably complex task in defining the changes to be made, anticipating their repercussions and organising the transition from the old system to the new with the minimum of disturbance to services.

The remainder of this study looks at the operation from the point of view of the central government. It does not set out to be a guide to the new system, either in Greater London or in the rest of the country, save in so far as some reference to the main changes are needed as background material. Still less does it aim to pass value judgements on the alternative courses advocated by a great variety of exponents. Its main aim is to describe the sort of matters which had to be considered and the kind of decisions which the central government had to make as each of the separate reorganisations proceeded.

In each case the exercise had to be planned as a whole. All aspects had to be related to all others within the timetable and the course of action adopted as regards any particular matter often depended on the time available before some inexorable deadline. For convenience the matters dealt with in this study are considered in four stages.

The first stage involved the absolutely essential decisions which the government had to take in order to set the operation in motion: whether to tackle reorganisation at all and, if so, what system to adopt and within what timetable. This stage had also to embrace broad conclusions about areas, functions and finance. In dealing with these aspects this chapter and the following one look at Greater London and at the rest of England and Wales separately, and pursue the question of areas in the context of the basic decisions.

The second stage (dealt with in Chapter 6) required the broad conclusions to be worked out in more detail, often in consultation with the local authority associations and other interested bodies. The constitution of the new authorities had to be settled and arrangements for their election; machinery devised for future boundary changes; general propositions on the main services had to be extended to minor functions; detailed decisions taken on financial matters such as rating, grants, accounts and audit.

The third stage (Chapter 7) involved the legislation itself; its drafting and passage through Parliament.

Finally, the Act, when passed, required a great amount of further detailed work either by subordinate legislation or by administrative action to ensure its implementation and the final changeover on the appointed day (Chapter 8).

## THE ROYAL COMMISSION ON LOCAL GOVERNMENT IN GREATER LONDON

London government has always been regarded as a special problem to be dealt with separately from local government in the rest of the country, but there had been no attempt to amend the boundaries of the administrative county of London or of the metropolitan boroughs since they were originally defined by or under the Acts of 1888 and 1899. The Royal Commission on London Government (the Ullswater Commission), appointed in 1921, had devoted their main attention (Cmd 1830, 1923) to examining certain proposals put forward by the LCC - proposals which prophetically urged the need for a single directly elected authority for the whole of Greater London, but which failed to gain support at that time. More recently the Reading Committee had been set up in 1945 to examine the number, size and boundaries of the metropolitan boroughs and the distribution of functions as between the LCC and the boroughs; but (as recorded at p. 62 above) they were unable to proceed with their work and the government agreed that in practice it was impossible to consider the county of London apart from the local government problems of the much wider area which now constituted Greater London. The LCC area had been excluded from the jurisdiction of the Local Government Boundary Commission in 1945 but no action had been taken following the dissolution of the Reading Committee until preparations were well ahead for setting up the Local Government Commissions in the Bill which became the Local Government Act 1958. The White Paper on areas and status (Cmd 9831) had proposed leaving the county of London untouched; the Local Government Commission would review the outer parts of Greater London but (as under the 1945 Act) no county boroughs should be created in Middlesex. It became increasingly apparent that this approach was inadequate to the problems of Greater London as a whole; and at the more local level it failed to meet the aspirations of the bigger boroughs and urban districts in Middlesex who were totally dissatisfied with the proposals for the compulsory delegation of certain services discussed in the White Paper on functions (Cmd 161).

A comprehensive study of local government in the whole of the Greater London area was needed and a review by an independent body clearly suggested itself in view of the complexity of the situation and the political sensitivity of the issues involved. The decision to appoint the Royal Commission was announced during the debate on local government in July 1957 (see p. 73 above).

The Royal Commission on Local Government in Greater London, chaired by Sir Edwin Herbert, were a small body of only seven members, none of whom had served in local government as a member or officer and none of whom were identified with any specific approach to local government problems. It differed, therefore, from the Onslow Royal Commission and the later Redcliffe-Maud Royal Commission, both of which were bigger and included people drawn from all the main types of local authorities. The terms of reference of the Herbert Commission required them to examine the existing system and working of local government in the Greater London area and to recommend such changes in the structure and distribution of functions as 'would better secure effective and convenient local government'. Greater London was defined for the Commission's purposes as the Metropolitan Police district together with certain fringe areas, thus aiming to include all the development that might conceivably be regarded as part of the continuous built-up area of Greater London. Police and water were excluded from the Commission's purview, however, as neither were to any significant extent the direct responsibility of local authorities in the review area.

The review area included the whole of two counties, London and Middlesex, and parts of four others – Surrey, Kent, Essex and Hertfordshire. Within the area were three county boroughs and about a hundred metropolitan boroughs, non-county boroughs and urban districts. This plethora of units were governed by three distinct systems of local government. In Croydon, East Ham and West Ham there was the one-tier system characteristic of county boroughs. In the counties other than London there was the normal two-tier system which obtained throughout the rest of the country. In the county of London a different two-tier system operated – one in which, for historical reasons, the LCC exercised more functions than county councils elsewhere (notably in the fields of education, the personal social services and housing) and the metropolitan boroughs had correspondingly fewer responsibilities.

Local authorities in Greater London faced the same kind of problems as those which confronted authorities generally but particularly urgent were those relating to planning, overspill, highways and traffic in this biggest of all the conurbations. The Abercrombie-Forshaw Plan for the county of London (commissioned by the LCC) and Sir Patrick Abercrombie's Greater London Plan drawn up in 1944 for the rest of the Greater London area, had provided a framework within which the separate planning authorities were broadly operating, but the shortcomings were obvious in an area divided between nine separate planning authorities at county and county borough level. The difficulties here, and in the administration of other services, were deployed by government departments in their written and oral evidence.

The Herbert Commission were unanimous in their conclusion that changes were needed, both from the view of administrative efficiency and the health of representative local government. Basic to their recommendations was the view they took that 'there is an entity which is so closely knit, so interdependent, so deeply influenced by the central area and so largely built-up, that it truly makes up the London of today' (Cmnd 1164, para. 895). London had grown outwards from the centre and was not, like other conurbations, a fusing of separate towns, though many individual towns had been absorbed in the process of London's expansion. To meet this situation it was essential that some services should be planned and administered for the area as a whole. For this purpose they proposed a directly elected Council for Greater London which would be responsible for overall planning, main roads, traffic, refuse disposal and the fire and ambulance services, and for certain concurrent and supplementary functions in connection with main sewerage, sewage disposal, housing, open spaces and entertainments. They also proposed that the GLC should have overall responsibility for educational policy and finance, though not for the management or maintenance of individual schools.

At the borough level the Commission proposed a reduction in the number of authorities to form a pattern of boroughs with a population range generally between 100,000 and 250,000. These authorities would exercise as many functions as possible – all those which did not absolutely demand to be dealt with for the Greater London area as a whole. The Commission saw the boroughs as the primary units of local government, and the need to concentrate responsibilities at the more local level was crucial, in their view, to the maintenance of the health of local government in the metropolis; only in this way would public interest be maintained and able men and women attracted to serve as members and officers. The London boroughs would thus be responsible for health and welfare and for the children's service and the library service; they would be the primary housing authorities and would have local responsibility for planning, highways and sewerage; in addition they would share the educational service with the GLC and would be responsible for the running of schools within the broad policy and financial limits laid down by the GLC.

As regards areas, the Commission proposed a slightly smaller area for Greater London than had been defined in their terms of reference. They considered each of the authorities round the fringe of the review area (Cmnd 1164, chapter XVI) and attempted to gauge the extent to which it was an independent unit, to assess the strength of its links with the centre, and to reach some conclusion as to whether it looked outwards towards the country rather than inwards towards London. They looked at complete local government units in order to minimise administrative problems and, on the basis of their examination of individual areas, they proposed the exclusion of Dartford UD in Kent, Waltham Holy Cross UD in Essex, Potters Bar UD in Middlesex and a number of authorities in south-east Hertfordshire. Within the area which they regarded as constituting the predominantly built-up entity of Greater London they made tentative proposals for a pattern of fifty-two London boroughs (including the City which the Commission thought should be left undisturbed in boundaries and status but should have the same functions as the London boroughs). The report emphasised, however, that the borough groupings were only provisional as the Commission had taken no evidence on this aspect.

## THE GOVERNMENT'S REACTIONS

The Herbert Commission reported in October 1960 and the Minister of Housing and Local Government (Mr Brooke) invited comments from local authorities and other bodies. In general, consultations on London government were conducted with each of the local authorities concerned and not through the local authority associations. The associations were kept in the picture but the issues were more usually regarded as special to Greater

London and to the individual authorities in this area, rather than as having implications for the country as a whole.

The consultation letter from MHLG[1] urged authorities not to get bogged down on boundary problems affecting the outer boundary of Greater London or the borough groupings; the Commission's proposals had been no more than tentative and there would be separate consultations on areas when issues of principle had been decided. Then, in order to concentrate minds on the main issues, authorities were invited to comment in particular on the essential elements of the Commission's approach – the primacy of the boroughs in the proposed new set-up, the need for certain functions to be planned and administered over the whole of Greater London, the creation of a directly elected Council for Greater London, the suggested division of functions, the financial implications and the arguments for and against including the metropolitan parts of Surrey, Kent, Essex and Hertfordshire in the Greater London area.

Meantime, while waiting for local authority reactions, the government were digesting the Commission's report and each department considering the implications for particular services. The form of the evidence given by departments to the Royal Commission had been influenced by the letter written by the chairman to the permanent secretaries involved, in which departments were asked a number of specific questions about the way in which individual services operated, with attention especially concentrated on education, the environmental health services, housing, personal health and welfare, town and country planning and traffic. Largely for this reason, no doubt, government departments offered no views, either separately or collectively, about the overall structure of local government in Greater London as distinct from the needs of particular services. Indeed this point was commented on by the Commission in their report:

> The thing which came out most clearly from the evidence of government departments was that they have in general, with the exception of the Ministry of Housing and Local Government, very little concern with the well-being and efficiency of the system of local government taken as a whole. They are mainly concerned with ends to which local authorities are one possible means among others; that is to say, their main function is to ensure that certain national services, which are in part administered by local authorities, are properly performed in accordance with national standards. The Ministries therefore could tell us a great deal about standards and techniques in (for instance) education, the personal health services and the welfare services, and about the relative success or failure of different local authorities. But they have reflected little (if at all) on the place of each service in the system of local government, or on the effect upon the metropolitan boroughs and county districts of the gradual erosion of their powers,

and they were in general not in a position to help us with the most difficult part of our task. (Cmnd 1164, para. 199)

At all events there was no prefabricated Whitehall plan for London government at variance with the Commission's proposals; instead there were several elements in the situation which were favourable to the acceptance of the Commission's report and its implementation, notwithstanding the understandable reluctance of any government to embark on a major measure of local government reorganisation.

In the first place the physical problems of Greater London connected with planning, housing, overspill, redevelopment and traffic were real and urgent, and had been getting worse not better. The Commission's proposals for dealing with these problems on an all-London basis offered a hopeful approach to matters which had particularly prompted the Commission's appointment and one which fitted in with the evidence given by departments on these functions. A new administrative structure would not by itself solve these problems but it was an essential preliminary.

Secondly, the publication of the Commission's report – especially (as was here the case) a report which was clearly and forcefully written and backed by the unanimous support of all the Commissioners – had created an atmosphere in which change was accepted as inevitable and in which government action was expected. In the rest of the country the special review areas were to be considered by the recently established Local Government Commission for England and it was impossible to contemplate the indefinite continuation in Greater London of the shortcomings which had been spelled out again in the Royal Commission's report.

Thirdly, when local authority reactions to the Commission's proposals were available they were (in part) favourable and (in part) not unfavourable. There was very widespread support for the Commission's thesis that the boroughs and urban districts in the Greater London area should be regrouped to form a stronger pattern of London boroughs and that these should be the primary units of local government. There was general support, too, for the proposition that for some purposes Greater London needed to be treated as a single entity with certain functions dealt with by an overall authority within the local government structure.

Here the consensus stopped, however, as there was no general agreement on the form of the overall authority. But the alternative to the proposed GLC was the revival of a scheme put before (and rejected by) the Royal Commission and then further elaborated in the light of the Commission's report. This proposal, supported by the London, Middlesex, Surrey, Kent and Essex County Councils, would have involved the retention of the existing county councils and county boroughs and the establishment of an indirectly elected joint board for an area substantially bigger than that proposed by the Herbert Commission and extending beyond the Green

Belt. The joint board would lay down the broad lines of planning development and draw up a master plan covering such matters as employment
policy, population targets and densities, communications and the Green
Belt; the board would determine the main road pattern and the main considerations for dealing with traffic management; it would plan and co-
ordinate refuse disposal, determine and co-ordinate a programme for overspill and maintain a statistical and intelligence unit for the whole area. The
board would not be an executive body but its activities would not be
merely advisory and consultative; when approved by the appropriate
minister, its plans would have binding force over the separate local
authorities in the Greater London area.

As a realistic alternative to the Herbert Commission's proposals the
'Home Counties Plan' (also known as the 'Surrey Plan') was a non-starter
and was abruptly dismissed in the subsequent White Paper: 'the government believe that a plan on these lines would not begin to meet the needs
of the situation'. In effect, therefore, there was no strong or credible
alternative to the Commission's proposals for a directly elected Greater
London Council and to this extent the dissenting voices in local government carried comparatively little weight.

Furthermore, and no government can be oblivious to the political
reactions, the Commission's proposals were broadly supported by Conservative authorities and by Conservative opinion in local government –
and broadly condemned by Labour authorities and Labour groups. This
generalisation was not universally true as, in individual instances, a local
authority's reactions would inevitably be coloured by the way in which
that particular authority was likely to be affected by the proposed changes.
This was obviously so in the case of the county councils supporting the
'Home Counties Plan'.

Finally, in favour of acceptance of the Herbert Commission's proposals –
though this was not openly argued and might be regarded as rationalisation
with the wisdom of hindsight – the Commission's solution had historical
precedent in its favour; it was in the tradition of earlier approaches to
London government. In essence it proposed a single authority for the
whole area of Greater London, coupled with a strengthening of the more
local tier of authorities which were to be reduced in number. These had
been the main ingredients of the reorganisation of London government
in 1888 and 1899 and earlier under the Metropolis Management Act
1855.

But while these arguments were favourable to the government's acceptance of the Commission's report there were points on which they had
reservations and these emerged when their conclusions were published as a
White Paper, *London Government: Government Proposals for Reorganisation* (Cmnd 1562, November 1961). That these reservations must have
been substantial is to be inferred from the fact that the best part of a

year passed between the date when local authority reactions were received and the time when the White Paper finally appeared – only just in time to permit the timetable of implementation which it then announced.

One of the government's reservations related to the size of the London boroughs. The Commission had proposed a population range of 100,000 – 250,000. This fitted in with the minimum population for the creation of new county boroughs in the rest of the country, which had been raised to 100,000 by the LGA 1958, but in truth this figure was now out of date. The expanding personal and social services required (in the view of the practitioners) a substantially bigger base for these increasingly specialised and expensive functions; the Ministry of Health, the Home Office and the Ministry of Education had, in their oral evidence, favoured units which were substantially larger – more of the order of 250,000 – 500,000. Larger units were (in their view) desirable in themselves, and additionally so if these functions were to be moved downwards to the London boroughs and not (like planning or the fire service) upwards to the GLC. Education, the health and welfare services and the children's service were all county and county borough responsibilities and there were nine such authorities at this level in Greater London. To follow the Commission's proposals would involve reallocating these services so that they would be run by fifty-two authorities, most of them much smaller than the existing ones. Larger London boroughs would mean fewer of them and would therefore slightly mitigate what the specialists were bound to see as a disadvantage. Indeed the Ministry of Education had included in their written evidence a remark which was often quoted during the subsequent proceedings when they said (a propos the arrangements being studied by the Royal Commission), 'There is no part of the area in which the present system of educational administration does not work at least tolerably well'.[2] From this point of view the creation of a larger number of smaller education authorities appeared to be a retrograde step.

Nor did the proposed division of education between the GLC and the London boroughs commend itself to the department which in 1944 had been responsible for concentrating the administration of education into the hands of county councils and terminating the previous arrangements under which responsibility for the educational service was shared between the county councils and the Part III authorities.

And in the LCC area there was a special problem. The metropolitan boroughs had never exercised education functions; education had been entirely in the hands of the LCC since 1903 and before then of the School Board for London. The LCC was the largest local education authority in the country and stood in very high esteem. The Ministry of Education were resolutely opposed to the break-up of the LCC education department and pointed, in addition, to the fact that schools in the county of London had been sited without regard to borough boundaries; to an extent not found anywhere else pupils, especially at secondary school level, crossed borough boundaries on their way to school.

As the main local government function and the most costly single service, education figured very prominently in the government's consideration of the Herbert Commission's proposals and on the two points referred to above the Ministry of Education view prevailed: the proposed division of responsibility between the GLC and the boroughs was rejected and the White Paper announced the government's intention to retain a single education authority for 'a central area with a population of the order of 2 million'. The boundaries of the area it would run were left over for further consideration in the light of the final pattern of the new boroughs (Cmnd 1562, paras 41-2).

Health, welfare and the children's service would all be borough functions in this central area and (along with education) throughout the rest of Greater London too. But, largely in deference to the needs of these services, the London boroughs were to be bigger (and fewer) than the Commission had proposed. Instead of a lower limit of 100,000 the government said that a higher minimum would be practicable and preferable in a closely knit area such as London, and their conclusion was that 'it would be desirable to aim at a minimum population of around 200,000 wherever possible. Some boroughs might be substantially larger than this' (Cmnd 1562, para. 20).

The constitution of the education authority for the central area was also left open at the White Paper stage. The area was to comprise 'several boroughs' so it can easily be conjectured that one possibility discussed within government circles was a joint board for this service. By extension it can equally be assumed that joint boards were mooted for other areas too, as a way of ensuring education authorities bigger than those offered by boroughs of the size suggested by the Commission. Such a solution was rightly rejected however. Joint boards lack the direct accountability of elected authorities. The joint board concept had received a dusty answer when put forward in the 'Home Counties Plan' and it would have been unthinkable to propose a pattern of primary authorities which, from the start, were inadequate to run the most important local government service.

## REORGANISATION IN LONDON: THE ESSENTIAL DECISIONS

The White Paper was published in November 1961 and announced the government's acceptance of the Herbert Commission's main proposals, subject to the two reservations already discussed - that there should be fewer and larger boroughs and that education should be a borough function everywhere save in the central area, where a single education authority would be responsible for this service in a group of London boroughs. While it was not possible to say when the necessary Bill would be presented to Parliament, 'the aim will be to make it possible for the new authorities to be elected in the autumn of 1964 and to take over from the existing authorities in April 1965' (Cmnd 1562, para. 55).

The White Paper therefore amounted to a commitment to proceed with a scheme for reorganising London government and indicated the timetable. A great many practical considerations had to be taken into account in arriving at these decisions – considerations which can be itemised separately but which necessarily interacted on each other and affected the ultimate conclusions.

The first question was: how and by what stages should the new system be brought into being? Could (or should) the Greater London Council be established in advance of the reorganisation at borough level – as had happened when the LCC came into existence in 1889 and when the reorganisation of the metropolitan boroughs took effect ten years later? But circumstances had changed so much and the proposed reform was so much more complex that a two-stage exercise would have created impossible problems. The area of Greater London could not be separated from the pattern of London boroughs and both had to be settled together. Functions – which had been so greatly expanded since the beginning of the century – were to be reallocated at each level and it would be impossible to do this unless all the new authorities were in being at the same time. In Middlesex, for instance, education, the personal social services and the children's service were county functions but after reorganisation would be borough responsibilities; it would not be practicable to transfer these functions to the existing boroughs and urban districts in Middlesex, some of which were too small, and it would be equally impracticable for the GLC to take over these services on an interim basis with a view to transferring them once again when the new boroughs were defined. Clearly the GLC and the London borough councils all had to become fully operational at the same time.

What is more, the authorities for the new areas needed to come into existence in advance of the date when they would formally become responsible for services in their areas. This followed from the complexity of the operation and the danger to the efficient maintenance of services unless the changeover was preceded by the longest possible period of planning and preparation (which had to include the internal organisation of each authority, the appointment of key officers, the preparation of financial estimates for the first year after reorganisation and the transfer of staff and property).

Even where a new London borough was territorially identical with an existing borough or urban district (which, in the end, happened only in the case of Harrow) there would be problems connected with transferred functions. Where a new authority was to be formed by the amalgamation of two or more complete units it would (subject to the reallocation of some functions) need to take over and unify the staff and assets of its predecessors. And when local authorities were to be divided territorially as well as functionally – as was the case with the county councils which operated partly within and partly outside Greater London – the problems were more complicated still. These considerations dictated the proposal that the new authorities should be elected in the autumn before taking over the following spring, and led, later, to the timetable for the elections being advanced so as to allow an even longer overlap period for preparations.

Many detailed matters connected with the constitution of the new authorities, the administration of functions and transitional arrangements were left over for further consideration after the White Paper was published but, inevitably, attention immediately concentrated on questions relating to areas and boundaries. The White Paper repeated the undertaking in the ministry's earlier consultation letter that there would be consultations on the borough pattern and, by implication, that such consultations would include the definition of the outer boundary of Greater London. Claims from some of the fringe authorities to be excluded from the new metropolitan area promised to be pressed with special vigour.

A complementary aspect of these consultations, and very relevant to the procedure to be adopted, was whether the new areas should be defined in the legislation and, if so, in what detail. New units composed of the straight amalgamation of existing boroughs and urban districts would make for ease of definition, would simplify the subsequent transitional problems and would also justify a broad approach to the subject that would be appropriate to the enactment of the new areas in the proposed statute. On the other hand, if it was intended to divide existing administrative areas with any degree of meticulous detail and to draw new boundaries in the process, the exercise would be bound to take longer and would attract demands for public local inquiries. A compromise between these two might have borrowed from the London Government Act 1899 in which the main elements of the new metropolitan boroughs were listed in a schedule and Commissioners were appointed to settle final details of boundaries and wards in schemes which were given force by Order in Council. The Local Government Commission (the Hancock Commission) were in existence in 1961 and one possibility would have been to ask them to define the outer boundary of Greater London, even if they were not given the task of settling the borough groupings within it.

The government's decision, however, was to settle all the new areas in the Bill itself. This necessarily meant that they would be defined mainly by reference to existing administrative areas, with only a minimal number of departures from established boundaries. It also meant that parliamentary discussions would be conducted as part of the ordinary stages of a public

Bill and would not include hearings with petitioners and witnesses. There can be no doubt that this approach was the most effective; it treated the initial establishment of the whole new pattern of areas as a political act, not one of administrative detail to be considered piecemeal, and by including the areas in the Bill itself it made sure that all boundary arguments were settled within a predetermined timetable.

Another essential element in the preliminary calculations was the election of the new authorities and the definition of the wards on the basis of which the first elections would be held. The new wards could not be settled until the borough boundaries had been finalised, but thereafter decisions on wards would have to follow speedily if the first elections were to be held in time for the new authorities to prepare for the takeover. Here again the procedure for considering wards was related to the time available, and to the most practicable way of achieving a quick though equitable result.

All these elements were relevant to the overall timetable for legislation and implementation, which affected Parliament and the central government as well as the local authorities. In the event, the new units were brought into being in three stages. The new territorial areas – the boroughs and Greater London – came into existence as soon as the Bill was passed. The new councils existed as local authorities from the date of their first election for the purpose of making preliminary arrangements, though at that stage they were authorities without responsibility for any local government functions. Finally, they took over their full functions on the changeover date.

Once the White Paper had been published, with a government commitment to legislation and implementation, all the arguments were in favour of pushing on as fast as possible. Existing authorities could not plan sensibly for the future when they had only a limited expectation of life; staff were naturally unsettled by uncertainties as to how the changes might affect them and recruitment to vacancies would be affected in some fields.

The central government's calculations were somewhat different but also pointed towards the speediest practicable timetable. When the White Paper was published in November 1961 the then Conservative government had a maximum of another three years in office as the next election could not be delayed after October 1964. Ideally it would be desirable for the whole process of legislation and implementation to be complete before the next general election, partly because it was a controversial subject in Greater London and would best be out of the way before the election campaign commenced in earnest, and partly to minimise the risk that if the Labour Party won the next election they would delay or reverse the proposed changes – to which they were vehemently opposed.

Complete implementation within this time-scale was not possible, however. For strong practical reasons all local government changes have, for many years, become effective at the beginning of the financial year on 1 April. As the White Paper did not appear until the close of 1961 the legislation could not follow until the 1962/3 session, which would allow elections to the new authorities in 1964 and the changeover on 1 April 1965. Even this timetable required many short cuts, such as the discussion of warding proposals before the borough pattern was complete, and any more elaborate approach to the definition of areas and boundaries would have extended the timetable. It was likely therefore, on the timetable briefly announced in the White Paper, that the elections to the new local authorities would be held before the next general election but it was clear that the final changeover would come after that election. Any delay in the introduction of the Bill to 1963/4 would have postponed the local government elections into the next Parliament, which would have given a different government a much better chance of halting the whole operation. So, although the White Paper was careful not to anticipate the Queen's Speech by announcing legislation in 1962/3, there can be little doubt that this had been accepted as the only politically practicable option.

Two other aspects of the timetable were also considered – its implications for elections to the existing authorities and its timing in relation to the review of parliamentary constituencies. The metropolitan borough council elections fell in the spring of 1962 but there were no elections to the LCC or other county councils due until 1964. If elections to these authorities had fallen in 1963 they would have chimed awkwardly with the Bill, which would then have been before Parliament. A Bill in 1962/3 could (and did) cancel the 1964 elections to the London and Middlesex County Councils, however, and postponed those for Surrey, Kent and Essex until 1965 when special elections were held on the basis of the new and reduced counties (the Hertfordshire County Council elections went ahead on the normal date in 1964 as the county was very little affected by the final changes).

There is no automatic connection between local government boundaries and the boundaries of parliamentary constituencies but the Parliamentary Boundary Commissioners are required to have regard to local government boundaries, so far as this is practicable and it is a reasonable assumption that major local government changes will in due course have some effect on parliamentary constituency boundaries. This naturally gives MPs a personal, as well as a public, interest in local government boundary alterations and in the London context ten ministers, including the Prime Minister, sat for constituencies wholly or partly within Greater London. Under the House of Commons (Redistribution of Seats) Act 1949 the Parliamentary Boundary Commission for England were required to review constituencies between the autumn of 1964 and the autumn of 1969, and the new local government areas in Greater London would then be taken into account. But while, to this extent, the reorganisation of London government would be relevant to parliamentary constituencies, there could be no repercussions to affect the next general election which was due not later than October 1964.

## THE NEW AREAS

The White Paper announced the government's conclusion that the boroughs should generally be larger than the Herbert Commission had proposed and that it would be desirable to aim at a minimum population of around 200,000 wherever possible. It added that the government 'propose shortly to circulate, as a basis for consultation with the local authorities, an illustration of how larger boroughs might work out'(Cmnd 1562, para. 20).

The procedure adopted for settling the new boroughs was necessarily related to the timetable and to the general considerations already mentioned. The new areas had to be settled in the Bill itself which (it was assumed) would become law in July 1963 before the summer recess. For this reason all the promised consultations on areas had to take place between the publication of the White Paper, in November 1961, and the summer of 1962. If the consultative process had not been completed by then it could not have been resumed until after the holiday period, in September 1962, which would have been too late for a Bill which, because of its complexity and controversial nature, clearly needed to be introduced at the beginning of the 1962/3 session, that is, in November 1962.

Necessarily, therefore, the consultations had to be kept tightly in the government's hands and they were launched by the promulgation of the government's own proposals for the new borough groups. These were published a fortnight after the White Paper in a circular to which was annexed a map of 'possible groupings'.[3] In addition to the City of London the map suggested thirty-three new boroughs and said that 'in drawing up this map regard has been had to present and past associations, to the location and areas of influence of service centres, to lines of communication and patterns of development. The relative weight given to these factors necessarily varies from place to place; but the groupings shown on the map represent an effort to reconcile them as far as possible.' Local authorities were invited to comment on the suggested groups, and the circular also said that the minister 'would be glad to know the views of any peripheral authority about its inclusion in or exclusion from the London area'. The implication of these final words was that the outer boundary would be settled as part of a single exercise – a logical approach if the London boroughs were regarded as the prime units of local government, Greater London being defined as the sum total of the London boroughs.

This map of possible groupings was the outcome of many alternatives considered by departments and by ministers, and purported to be no more than proposals which would be the basis of discussions in the spring of 1962. The general considerations taken into account in drawing up the proposed groupings were mentioned in the circular, but others had their influence, too. The reference to 'present and past associations', for instance, embraced a feature of the groupings – that in only one or two unavoidable instances did a proposed new borough cross an existing county boundary and, in particular, the group of inner London boroughs were all contained within the boundary of the LCC area.

This meant that, in the great majority of cases, each new borough had to negotiate with only one of the existing county councils in making transitional arrangements and (except Newham, in relation to a very small part of Woolwich north of the Thames) no new London borough had to cope with an inheritance derived partly from the special two-tier arrangements in the county of London and partly from the more usual two-tier systems elsewhere.

There were very few proposals, either, for departures from the existing local government boundaries; wherever possible the new groups consisted of amalgamations of complete existing units and new boundaries were proposed only where there appeared to be a very strong case for transferring part of an existing authority during the process of establishing the initial pattern of London boroughs. Regard was also had to the tentative proposals of the Herbert Commission; notwithstanding that the Commission had taken no specific evidence on this aspect their suggestions came from a body of influential people whose work had given them a deep knowledge of circumstances in the area. Finally, it can be assumed that the department's map anticipated some of the later decisions on the outer boundary, and made some guesses as to which of the fringe authorities might ultimately be excluded. Such considerations would help to explain, for instance, proposals for two exceptionally long boroughs – one which would have stretched from Tottenham to Cheshunt and the other from Brentford & Chiswick to Staines and Sunbury-on-Thames. It was no doubt expected that the fringe components of these two boroughs would ultimately be lopped off, so as to leave the remainder as more manageable units.

The circular which covered the map of possible groupings had referred to discussions on areas to be held with the London authorities in the spring of 1962, and this reference was elaborated when the government proposed a series of conferences, each covering several of the proposed borough groupings. The conferences, it was suggested, would permit the discussion of problems connected with both the outer boundary and the borough groups. They would be presided over by a number of town clerks from towns outside Greater London, who would hold the conferences on the minister's behalf so that he would be fully informed before deciding what proposals to lay before Parliament. 'They are not visualised as occasions for a forensic procedure involving the examination of witnesses and the like. They should, the Minister thinks, be on the pattern of the conferences held by the Local Government Commissions following the publication of their draft proposals for an area.'[4]

The proposal to seek the assistance of serving local government officers had been borrowed from the practice of the Trustram Eve Commission and town clerks were suggested as being officials most clearly experienced in the problems of borough government. The consultation letter also put forward some draft terms of reference and these included the task of making recommendations 'whether any existing county district or part of a district should be added to or left out of the suggested area for purposes of the Greater London Council, it being understood that Greater London is to include, as far as possible, the whole of the continuously developed area of London'.

These proposals attracted criticism on a number of counts. The county councils in Greater London claimed, for instance, that county council officials would be just as suitable as town clerks, and would indeed know more about the organisation of the county services which were to be reallocated to the London boroughs. Surrey thought poorly of the whole idea of informal conferences and wanted draft proposals from the town clerks to be followed by objections and public inquiries along lines similar to those contained in the later stages of the procedure prescribed by the Local Government Act 1958. Other suggestions were that, in anticipation of the conferences, the Ministry of Housing and Local Government should publish a detailed justification of the government's proposed groupings, and that a spokesman from the department should then attend at each conference to explain the reasoning behind the proposals.

None of these suggestions was followed but on two points criticism was much more widespread and, on these, the government spokesman (Mr Macleod, then Chancellor of the Duchy of Lancaster) gave specific assurances during the two-day debate on the White Paper in February 1962 (Commons Hansard, 20 February 1962, col 324–34).

First he referred to the suggestion, in the draft terms of reference proposed for the town clerks, that consideration should be given to the possibility of adding further districts to the Greater London area. This had been covered in the draft only for the sake of logical completeness as a point to be considered when the outer boundary was being finally reviewed but the government accepted that it was, in practice, not possible to *extend* the area of Greater London as proposed by the Royal Commission and to add any further district unless (and they left open this somewhat improbable eventuality) 'it is clear that it is the wish of its inhabitants that it is added'.

Secondly he dealt with the strongly held view that town clerks from provincial towns, however sagacious they might be, were not the right people to make recommendations regarding the outer boundary of Greater London and whether or not particular areas should be included. Town clerks, it was felt, would be too much inclined to see things in terms of the built-up area and to favour the inclusion of localities which others would regard as more properly left within their existing parent counties. The government accepted the strength of feeling on this particular point, and it was agreed that the Minister of Housing would himself hear and decide on representations regarding the fringe areas as a preliminary exercise, and would reach and announce his conclusions on the outer boundary before considering the borough groupings for the outer areas.

This second assurance - that the outer boundary and the borough groups would be dealt with separately - posed further timetable complications. Logically (and some authorities argued to this effect) the conferences to be held by the town clerks should be postponed until the outer boundary had been settled. But the time available did not permit this and consideration of the two aspects went forward simultaneously.

A number of applications were made by peripheral authorities, asking to be excluded from Greater London, and it was decided to handle these in two stages. In the first stage representatives of the authorities concerned met officials of the department and made their case for exclusion. Discussion centred especially on the location of development, on the extent to which that development was continuous with the main built-up mass of London, on communications and on links with the centre as against affinities looking outwards from London. The object, as Mr Macleod had said in the White Paper debate, would be 'to include within the London system the whole of the continuous town but no more than that'. He also referred to another principle which had carried weight - that as far as possible local authorities should not be divided.

On the assumption that the government would want to apply these criteria with reasonable flexibility six peripheral areas were strong candidates for exclusion - Cheshunt (Herts), Walton & Weybridge, Caterham & Warlingham, and Banstead (Surrey), Staines and Sunbury-on-Thames (Middlesex), while three areas, Chigwell (Essex), Esher, and Epsom & Ewell (Surrey), included some of the continuous development although the area was otherwise substantially separate from Greater London. In addition, representations were received from authorities who could have had little expectation of their applications being accepted.[5]

Following the meetings with officials the minister announced that Caterham & Warlingham UD, Banstead UD and Walton & Weybridge UD would definitely be excluded and that he would personally meet representatives of other areas, on which he had yet to reach a final decision. As a result of these further meetings Cheshunt UD, Esher UD, Staines UD and Sunbury-on-Thames UD were also excluded, as well as the greater part of Epsom & Ewell B and of Chigwell UD; in the last two cases it was decided

that the areas should be divided to leave small areas of continuous development in the Greater London area (though even this proposal was later
rejected by the House of Lords in the case of Epsom & Ewell and the
whole of that borough was excluded from Greater London).

The discussions on the outer boundary took place in April and May 1962
and the final decisions on this aspect were announced on 17 May. Meanwhile the town clerks° who had agreed to advise on the borough groupings
has proceeded with their conferences. They were able to take account of
the decisions on the outer boundary when drawing up their final
recommendations.

The town clerks' conferences covered groups of proposed boroughs and
these groups were suggested by the boundaries of the existing counties.
Two conferences were needed for London boroughs in that part of the
administrative county of London north of the Thames, and one of those
south of the Thames. Two conferences considered new boroughs comprised
of existing authorities in Middlesex and other conferences similarly covered
authorities in Essex, Kent and Surrey. Except for the conference dealing
with that part of the LCC area south of the Thames (which was notable
for the hostility displayed to the whole basis of local government reorganisation in London) the conferences were brief and businesslike, and all of
them were concluded in a single day.

The town clerks' report was by no means a rubber stamping of the
government's proposals.[7] A number of proposed boroughs round the
Greater London boundaries had been reduced in size and population by
reason of the government's decision to exclude the areas already mentioned.
These exclusions did not of themselves require other alterations to the
pattern of new boroughs within the reduced area of Greater London,
though one of the peripheral boroughs (Kingston upon Thames) now fell
significantly short of the government's preferred population minimum of
200,000 (in the end five of the thirty-two London boroughs had populations below this figure). For other reasons, however, and in the light of
arguments advanced at the conferences, a number of significant changes to
the government's map were proposed. The suggestion was dropped, for
instance, of a new London borough which might be created by subdividing
the metropolitan borough of Wandsworth; Wandsworth was indeed divided
but by transferring Clapham and Streatham to the new London borough
of Lambeth. In Kent the urban district of Chislehurst & Sidcup was divided
(an exceptional case, thought justified in this instance). In Essex the
borough of Wanstead & Woodford was joined with Ilford and not with
Walthamstow and Leyton; in Middlesex the proposed new London
boroughs comprising Enfield/Edmonton/Southgate and Tottenham/Wood
Green/Hornsey differed completely from the government's proposals.

The revised pattern of thirty-two London boroughs (excluding the City)
as recommended by the four town clerks was accepted by the government

in its entirety and was set out as schedule 1 to the Bill. In a few places it involved departing from existing administrative boundaries. In these cases – half a dozen in all – the new line was described in part II of schedule 1 either in full detail or by a more general description, which was later given final definition by order.[8]

## NOTES: CHAPTER 4

1   Dated 28 November 1960 and addressed to all local authorities wholly or partly within Greater London.
2   Herbert Commission Written Evidence: Memorandum of Evidence from the Ministry of Education, para. 34.
3   MHLG circular No. 56/61, 16 December 1961.
4   Consultation letter from MHLG to the London authorities, 26 February 1962.
5   Yiewsley & West Drayton UD (Middlesex), Carshalton UD, Coulsdon & Purley UD (Surrey), Romford B (Essex) and Barnet UD (Herts).
6   Mr S. Lloyd Jones (Plymouth), Mr F. D. Littlewood (Cheltenham), Mr Harry Plowman (Oxford) and Mr R. S. Young (South Shields).
7   *London Government: The London Boroughs* (HMSO, 1962).
8   The London Boroughs (Boundaries) Order 1963, SI 1963, No. 2031.

## Chapter 5

# Reorganisation in England:
# Essential Decisions

## THE REDCLIFFE-MAUD ROYAL COMMISSION

The decision, in 1957, to appoint the Royal Commission on Local Government in Greater London – the Herbert Commission – seems, in retrospect, to have been a natural, indeed an inevitable, one in the prevailing circumstances. Preparations were going ahead to set up the Local Government Commission who were to review the areas and status of authorities in the rest of England. Something had to be done about Greater London, which constituted an entity in whose local administration the central government could not fail to be closely involved. The failure of the Reading Committee had underlined the need to consider the area as a whole and, in the absence of some positive move by the government, the tangle in Greater London threatened to get worse with several big Middlesex boroughs seeking county borough status. The need to give special attention to the provincial conurbations had been accepted but it would have been asking too much of the Local Government Commission to take on such a vast problem as Greater London as an incidental appendage to their work in the remainder of the country.

But circumstances in 1965 did not so clearly point towards the need for a Royal Commission to review local government throughout England. An elaborate mechanism had been brought into existence for reviewing the major authorities and the Hancock Commission were more than halfway through their programme. A process of reorganisation was actually in train, on the basis of principles agreed with the local authority associations. A more radical and comprehensive approach would need to be based on a general conviction that the work of the Local Government Commission was proving inadequate to the needs of the times. The decision to take such an initiative was one for the government, but it was not one to be taken regardless of the climate of opinion in local government circles. Had there been a significant shift of local government opinion since the concordat of 1956, when the associations had reiterated their support for the basic essentials of the county/county borough framework? Three factors, taken together, suggested there had.

That period, between 1956 and 1966, had seen the steady pressure of long-term influences (outlined in Chapter 1 above) tending towards the need for bigger units of administration. These affected all local government services and they included, for instance, the reduction in the number of separate water undertakings in England (from 884 to 259) as a result of the active policy of amalgamations launched by the Minister of Housing and Local Government,[1] and the Home Secretary's proposals for reducing the number of separate police forces by regrouping county and county borough forces under powers contained in the Police Act 1964.

In the second place, pressures were particularly strong, in the fields of planning and transport, for action based on areas defined on principles which took no account of the local government map. During this period regional planning was given much greater emphasis, and regional studies for several areas were put in hand in the 1960s in co-operative efforts between central and local government; one of the best known - *The South East Study* - was published in 1964, but others included the North-West and the West Midlands. Regional planning was given an institutional background when the Regional Economic Planning Councils and Boards were set up in 1965 and, although their primary aim was to provide machinery for regional *economic* planning, the development stirred up fears that, in the long run, the establishment of regional bodies would lead to the transfer of functions from the existing local authorities. The Barlow Commission in 1940 had said 'Regionalism, as usually understood, involves primarily issues relating to the reform of local government in Great Britain'[2] and the two strands have always been close. The Crowther Steering Group, which directed the Buchanan study, *Traffic in Towns*, had touched this chord by proposing regional development agencies with executive powers.[3] In short, a number of moves and studies were emphasising the desirability of planning, and perhaps action, on a regional basis; the danger of regional bodies and/or the central government taking functions away from local authorities was obviously greater while interdependent areas remained separate within the boundaries of counties and county boroughs.

A third factor helping to create a new climate of opinion towards a more radical approach to local government was disillusionment with progress under the 1958 Act. The Hancock Commission were working steadily round the country, but far more slowly than had been hoped; an immense amount of work and friction was created and (most important) it was becoming clear that the resultant improvements, although locally worthwhile, would still leave the local government system essentially unchanged since 1888.

Mr Crossman, when he became Minister of Housing and Local

Government in October 1964, was faced with a number of proposals coming forward from the Local Government Commission and he became increasingly convinced of the need for a thorough overhaul of the whole system. When addressing the Town Planning Institute in April 1965 and again, to the CCA in the following month, he spoke of the intractability of planning problems when powers were in the hands of some 150 counties and county boroughs between whom existed a permanent cold war. But, on both occasions, he dismissed the early likelihood of any radical reorganisation of local government. The political difficulties of such a venture made reorganisation practicable only if a government was willing to tackle it during the first session of a new Parliament; reform would (in his view) make so many enemies that the government would need to carry it through early, so as to give time for grievances to be forgotten before the next election. But by the autumn of that year Mr Crossman had decided that perhaps the nettle might be grasped after all. At the AMC's conference in September 1965 he referred to the poor image of local government and to the extent to which this was attributable to the fact that the structure was out of date.

As Mr Crossman saw it, there were two main problems: first, the relation of size and function in local government under modern conditions, and secondly, and equally important, the way to resolve the conflict between local democracy (which is inherently small) and efficiency (which is sometimes big). In the absence of any existing agreement on first principles an authoritative analysis of these two problems might be produced by a committee so powerful and so impartial that its report would be accepted by both sides and would contain firm principles of action.[4]

Mr Crossman's kite was well received, and the government were persuaded to set in motion the cumbersome machinery that eventually led to reorganisation. The first formal step was the appointment of the Royal Commission on Local Government in England in May 1966, but a number of preliminary matters had to be settled before then.

Mr Crossman had, for instance, proposed an influential committee to settle first principles of reform. These would then be applied in detail by a subsequent operation - possibly (though he did not specify as much) by a new Commission which would supersede the Local Government Commission and would take the committee's report on first principles as their terms of reference. This approach was (quite rightly) not pursued. It would not have been practicable to separate principles from application without encountering the same problems inherent in the guidance given by earlier ministers to the Boundary Commission and then to the Local Government Commissions. If principles were in general terms then considerable discretion would have to be left to the body responsible for detailed implementation. This was tolerable so long as no drastic changes were contemplated but would not have worked when the whole object of the exercise was to create a radically new structure. In addition, the time-table would have stretched forward interminably, with two or three years to produce the first principles and an unspecified subsequent period in which to put them into effect. As soon as it became apparent that the idea of a more thorough-going reorganisation had sufficient support in principle such a method of proceeding was dropped in favour of a Royal Commission which would be charged with producing a fully worked-out scheme.

The unfinished work of the Local Government Commission for England presented a further problem. A number of final proposals were with the minister awaiting his decision and implementation. Draft proposals had been published in some areas, notably the Merseyside and South-East Lancashire SRAs and the North-West GRA. But the Commission's final reports had still to be delivered in these areas. No work had been done at all in the Southern and South-East GRAs. There was something to be said for allowing the Commission to complete its programme – or at any rate to complete its work in the North-West. But this would have meant making a number of changes in the Commission itself as the chairman (Sir Henry Hancock) had died and the deputy chairman (Mr Michael Rowe) had been appointed President of the Lands Tribunal. More important, however, was the fact that any delay in appointing the Royal Commission would have meant a loss of impetus towards that more drastic reform which would, it was to be supposed, in any case supersede any marginal improvements that the Local Government Commission could accomplish in the meantime. It was therefore decided to wind up the Boundary Commission with its work unfinished but to implement those proposals already with the minister for which a case could be made on the grounds of urgency (see pp. 82–3 above).

Finally, consideration of a Royal Commission for England involved parallel consideration of what should be done in Wales and Scotland. The position in the former was that the proposals of the Local Government Commission for Wales had proved unacceptable (see p. 82 above) and the Secretary of State for Wales had set up an interdepartmental working party to help him examine problems of both areas and functions. Work (it was said) was well advanced towards producing revised proposals for Wales; it was therefore left that these should proceed separately, and that there should be a White Paper in due course on local government reorganisation in Wales. In Scotland a White Paper had been published by the Conservative administration in June 1963 (*The Modernisation of Local Government in Scotland*, Cmnd 2067, 1963) which had made suggestions for recasting the existing system. A steering committee of elected councillors, and a working party of central and local government officials, had been set up to make further recommendations and elaborate the details. Two years of activity had failed to produce agreement but, nevertheless, there was wide acceptance of the need for reform, so the situation was not dissimilar to that in England. The differences between the geography and local government system of England and Scotland pointed to separate Royal Commissions for each country, however, and the decision to appoint two Royal Commissions was contained in one announcement (Commons Hansard, 10 February 1966, cols 638–44). The Royal Commission on Local Government in Scotland was established under the chairmanship of Lord Wheatley.

Although no undue significance should be attached to the point, the terms of reference of the Redcliffe-Maud Royal Commission, unlike those of other postwar Commissions, dropped the use of the expression 'effective and convenient local government'. Instead they reflected more explicitly the twin problems already referred to by Mr Crossman in his address to the AMC. The Commission were required to consider the existing functions of local government, outside Greater London, and make recommendations for authorities and boundaries 'having regard to the size and character of areas in which these [functions] can be most effectively exercised and the need to sustain a viable system of local democracy'. The reference to areas and boundaries made it clear that the Royal Commission were expected to produce a detailed scheme of territorial reform, and not merely a set of principles for subsequent application. But in other respects the Commission's activities were to be restricted (expressly or impliedly) in ways which attracted criticism - at any rate from people outside local government. The concentration on the existing functions of local government was intended to head off the danger of a wide-ranging review of government functions in general, and the possibility of reallocating services as between central and local government. There are, after all, limits to what can be usefully considered in any one operation - though the Commission did not feel themselves inhibited from discussing the possibility of unifying responsibility for the various branches of the NHS within a reformed structure of local government (see p. 174 below). Finance was not specifically mentioned in the terms of reference, as would have been natural if the Commission's views were expected on this vital aspect of local government; the position here was that, although the Commission were not positively discouraged from considering changes in local government finance, it was clear (for example, from the nature of the evidence given by government departments) that the Commission were not expected to spend much time on financial recommendations of a radical nature - on discovering new sources of revenue, for instance.

## The evidence given to the Commission

The Commission reported widespread agreement, among those who gave evidence, on the need for fewer and stronger units of local government and on the need for the organisation of local government to reflect the links between services. These two strands of thought were related, and both follow from the expansion of local authority functions.

In the light of the material placed before them the Commission identified two main groups of services which should be administered together: the services concerned with the physical environment (planning, transport and major development) and the personal services (education, the personal social services, health and housing). On the need to keep the personal services together, the Royal Commission came to the same conclusion as the Seebohm Committee whose report was published while the Royal Commission were at work (Cmnd 3703, 1968; see p. 7 above).

As regards the environmental services, witnesses all agreed on the need for wide areas combining both town and country, and the MHLG argued in favour of adopting the city region as a planning unit of the future. On this the department's written evidence said: 'In many parts of the country the pattern of settlement now consists of a conurbation of one or more cities or big towns surrounded by a number of lesser towns and villages set in rural areas, the whole tied together by an intricate and closely meshed system of relationships and communications, and providing a wide range of employment and services. The more specialised and sophisticated services of these wide areas are characteristically to be found in the main urban core, but their economic base is provided by the population of the area as a whole. It is these wide areas which are becoming the most important communities of the second half of the twentieth century – and for which the expression "city regions" has been coined.'[5] In the department's view, if this concept was accepted the country could not be divided into more than, say, thirty to forty units without dividing areas which are entities for planning purposes.[6]

In the field of the personal services the sizes of authorities were expressed in terms of the population needed to support and justify these increasingly specialised services. The Department of Education and Science thought that an education authority should normally have a population of at least 500,000, though they were prepared to accept 300,000 in the more sparsely populated areas. The Ministry of Health said that local health and welfare authorities should have a minimum population of around 200,000, and considerably more where possible. The Home Office favoured a population of at least 250,000 for the children's service. These departments, along with others who gave evidence, agreed that thirty to forty city regions on the lines suggested by MHLG would suit their services, too.

On city regions, the Commission's report said 'government departments left us with the impression that, were it not for democratic considerations, they would really like a system of 30 to 40 all-purpose authorities' (Cmnd 4040, para. 158). The MHLG would have accepted such a pattern for the services for which they were responsible but were forced to admit that 'a local government structure consisting solely of 30–40 all-purpose units would reduce the opportunities for local participation in government, and for people to bring their problems to local elected representatives. It would, for example, drastically reduce the number of elected members of authorities. It could also be argued that no arrangements made by these authorities to decentralise their administration and to keep in touch with local opinion could be an adequate substitute for local government of the type to which this country has become accustomed. These considerations suggest that these main units of local government should be supplemented by a second tier of elected authorities entrusted with appropriate executive functions.'[7] But the list of possible functions which might (in the department's view) be exercised by second-tier authorities amounted to a very unexciting package, with nothing in the planning field and only unimportant aspects of housing and highways, to be eked out with the provision of parks, cemeteries, bus shelters and public clocks.

The city region concept, of which MHLG was the principal (though not the only) exponent, was the first of the three main types of structure which according to the Commission could be distinguished in the evidence (Cmnd 4040, para. 157). The other two were:

(a) a two-tier system, with geographical counties (singly or in combination) at the upper tier and much enlarged districts, including the then-existing county boroughs, at the second tier. The CCA were among those favouring this approach; they thought England could be divided on these lines into forty to fifty first-tier areas with a population of at least 500,000 each. The minimum for second-tier authorities should be 40,000;

(b) authorities responsible for most of the functions of local government (most-purpose authorities), with provincial authorities above them for functions requiring very wide areas. Several witnesses advocated this approach including the AMC. That association did not suggest any particular size for their most-purpose authorities, though they clearly had in mind more and smaller units than the thirty to forty city regions; the area of each of their main units would be based on the town which was its natural centre and, within its boundaries, there would be a proper bringing together of town and country which would recognise community of interest and acknowledge their interdependence.

Prima facie, all the three main types of structure put to the Royal Commission were two-tier structures but in practice they contained strong echoes of the county/county borough debate which had characterised the whole period since 1888. The CCA approach was the traditional county viewpoint, with first-tier authorities based on the existing counties and with all county boroughs included in a strengthened pattern of second-tier units. As against this, the MHLG's city regions and the AMC's most-purpose authorities were, in essence, based on the strengths of unitary authorities as exemplified by county boroughs.

It is true that the AMC had at last (and reluctantly) departed from their historic adherence to the unitary principle and admitted that, for some purposes such as town and country planning and highways, strategic plans should be drawn up on a regional basis, but executive functions would still remain concentrated in units which were based on big towns. Equally reluctantly the MHLG accepted that thirty to forty all-purpose authorities would probably not be politically acceptable, but their evidence suggested that only minor functions should be exercised at the second tier within the city region; the main services should all be concentrated in the city region authority, who might also exercise a substantial degree of financial control over the lower-tier authorities. The Royal Commission summed up the affinities between the two approaches thus: 'The difference between the AMC and the Ministry lay not in their underlying concept of how local government areas should be determined but in the scale on which they applied it' (Cmnd 4040, para. 171).

*The Redcliffe-Maud Commission's recommendations*
With the evidence of witnesses supplemented (though not very conclusively) by various research studies, the Commission based their detailed proposals on certain general principles. First was the need to get away from the artificial distinction between town and country, so that the local government structure could reflect their interdependence rather than their differences. Next was the need to allocate functions so that linked services were in the hands of the same authority. The two main groups of services identified by the Commission have already been mentioned – the environmental services and the personal services – but the Commission also stressed that these were not two self-contained and separate groups. To an ever-increasing extent they interacted on each other; planning and transportation are necessarily linked to housing and other forms of development, the whole physical environment affects people's lives and the services, including the personal services, that are required. From this point of view the best solution would be to concentrate responsibility for all local government services in the same authority – a solution which would not only permit all administrative decisions and financial priorities to be settled within a coherent plan for the needs of the area in question, but would also have the clear advantage of comprehensible local government; attention and local interest would be concentrated on *the* authority in whom responsibility for local services clearly resided.

The extent to which this ideal solution would be practicable depended on the operational requirements of services and the extent to which these could be made to fit into a single pattern of authorities. On the planning and transportation side the Commission found it possible to accept the city region concept in many areas, but not for the country as a whole; some suggested city regions would have to be so big that a second tier of authorities would be needed if local government was not to be too remote from its electors. For the personal services the Commission thought DES's minimum of 500,000 for education authorities was unnecessarily high and took the view that a minimum population of 250,000 would suit the health and welfare services, the children's service and education as well, with an upper limit of 1 million or thereabouts (though the idea of an upper limit was more flexible).

Lastly, and still in the realm of what might be practicable as distinct from theoretically desirable, there was the need for new units to be founded on the existing areas and authorities. 'We wish to maintain wherever possible the momentum of the present local government system. It is a going concern on a large scale, supported by long tradition and many loyalties. We have therefore preferred, where we could, to form new units out of existing local government areas rather than draw completely new boundaries' (Cmnd 4040, para. 279).

With these principles in mind the Commission examined how far it would be possible to divide the country into units which needed to be planned as a whole and which fell broadly within the population range 250,000–1,000,000. In such areas their preference was for a 'unitary' authority, responsible for all local government services.

They were prepared to separate the environmental from the personal services and allocate these to separate tiers only where the area needing to be planned as a whole was so big that a single authority would be too remote – but then only providing that the second-tier units within such an area could all be defined so as to result in coherent and democratically manageable units broadly within the 250,000–1,000,000 population range needed for the personal services. These conditions were to be found only in the conurbations.

The Commission's proposals for the main authorities are well known. They recommended that England, outside Greater London, should contain fifty-eight unitary areas in each of which one authority should be responsible for executive functions. In three conurbations or 'metropolitan areas' round Liverpool, Manchester and Birmingham (which the Commission named Merseyside, Selnec and West Midlands respectively) a two-tier pattern should be established with the environmental services at the upper level and the personal services in the hands of a total of twenty metropolitan districts each with a minimum population of 250,000 or thereabouts.

While the unitary authorities or (in the conurbations) the metropolitan authorities and districts should be responsible for all local government services, these main authorities needed to be supplemented both above and below. At the provincial level, and for areas roughly corresponding to the eight economic planning regions, there should be indirectly elected provincial councils whose main function would be to make and keep up-to-date a strategic plan for the future development of the province; such plans should be subject to ministerial approval, when they would become the binding framework within which the unitary and metropolitan authorities would make their own plans.

And below the main authorities the Commission proposed that there should be local councils, elected (although perhaps only optionally in the metropolitan districts) for the areas of each of the existing county boroughs, boroughs, urban districts and for those parishes which had parish councils. Such local councils would not be responsible for any services, though they should have a general power to spend money for the benefit of their areas and for improving the amenity and convenience of life there, and (outside the metropolitan areas) they might undertake minor works with the agreement of the unitary authority concerned. Their most important function – and indeed the only duty to be positively placed on a local council – would be to make known the views of the local community on any matter affecting it. For their part, the main authorities should consult the local councils on any matter of importance in their area.

So far as the main executive responsibility for local government services was concerned, therefore, the Redcliffe-Maud Commission were convinced that the all-purpose authority was both desirable and practicable. Their leaning towards the county borough as the model was clearly expressed in their report: 'there is great strength in the all-purpose authority; and this has been shown in the county borough councils. Not all of them have exploited their potential strength to the full, partly because their areas have been inadequate, partly because their organisation has been fragmented. But where a county borough council under strong leadership has co-ordinated its services and set out to achieve objectives through the use of all its powers, it has been the most effective local government unit we have known' (Cmnd 4040, para. 252).

### Reactions to Redcliffe-Maud

Inherent in the Commission's approach were a number of points on which discussion was bound to concentrate: was it in fact feasible to adopt the county borough form of administration (which had so far been restricted to big towns) for the administration of local government in areas of very different character in (say) Devon or Cumberland? At what point, and in what local circumstances, does the advantage of unitary administration outweigh the problems of conscripting a variety of local authority functions within a single area, which may be too small for some services and too big for others? At what point does the administrative advantage of a small number of big authorities outweigh the greater possibilities of participation offered by a larger number of units? Is it correct to rule out the possibility of second-tier authorities unless they are big enough and compact enough to be responsible for the personal services, including education; or, in other words, might not the democratic case for the local administration of some functions outweigh the administrative advantages of unified administration of all services by a single larger authority? These were, of course, the questions which had been raised over the years in the debate between all-purpose authorities as against a two-tier system, between county boroughs and counties.

The need for decisions was urgent because, like the Herbert Commission on Greater London, the Redcliffe-Maud report raised expectations of change in local government and this necessarily created a climate of uncertainty. Many matters connected with reorganisation had to be taken into account by the government in reaching conclusions, however. The first of these were naturally the reactions to the Commission's recommendations.

Consultations were opened immediately on the publication of the Commission's report, when the local authority associations were invited to comment on the proposed new structure as a whole and its principal components – unitary authorities, two-tier arrangements in the metropolitan areas, local councils and provincial councils. More detailed aspects, including boundaries and matters affecting staff interests, would be the subject of separate and subsequent consultations. All local authorities were individually concerned, however, and a general invitation to comment was sent to them in addition to the specific invitations addressed to the associations; later in 1969 ministers met representatives of each of the main associations.

Inevitably reactions were mixed, but there was general agreement on the need for change and no one advocated the retention of the *status quo*; the end of the county borough on the 1888 pattern – as a town completely separate from its hinterland – appeared to be generally accepted. But there were major differences on the system which should be adopted instead. Initially, reactions of the associations fell into two main groups. The CCA and the AMC both accepted the proposals for two tiers in the conurbations and the concept of unitary authorities elsewhere; the UDCA and the RDCA rejected unitary authorities altogether and wanted two tiers everywhere.

But while the CCA and the AMC both supported unitary authorities in principle they differed in the application of the concept. The AMC, whose membership included many medium-sized and small boroughs, wanted more (and smaller) units than the Royal Commission had proposed; the CCA wanted fewer and larger, with populations of at least 500,000.

The initial support of the CCA for unitary authorities was influenced by the fact that a number of the units proposed by the Redcliffe-Maud report would have been closely based on existing counties, and the county councils concerned saw themselves becoming the sole executive authority for the whole area. But from the beginning the association was deeply split between these councils and the others, who adhered to the two-tier approach which the association had consistently advocated. Before the end of 1969 the CCA abandoned their support for unitary authorities and reached broad agreement with the UDCA and RDCA on a common approach to reorganisation. The structure they proposed would have involved two tiers everywhere but with a distinction between the conurbations and other parts of the country. Within the conurbations the structure proposed by the Royal Commission was broadly accepted but, in the associations' views, there should be other metropolitan areas in, for example, West Yorkshire, Hampshire and parts of south-east England; the boundaries of the metropolitan areas should not be so widely drawn as those proposed by Redcliffe-Maud for Merseyside, Selnec and the West Midlands, and education should be a top-tier function. Elsewhere, outside the conurbations, there should be a second tier of districts with populations of, say, 60,000–100,000 (and possibly higher in some areas); the functions of these new districts should be somewhat less than in the metropolitan areas and, in particular, they would not be responsible for the personal social services.

The Royal Commission's proposals were very much in line with the main suggestions from government departments, both as regards the number and size of the main authorities and the concentration of responsibilities within the unitary areas. It is true that MHLG had foreseen the need for a second-tier of authorities on democratic grounds, but the Commission suspected that the department's real preference would be for all-purpose authorities within each city region. On the other hand the Commission's final proposals would have resulted in rather more – and hence smaller – units than the thirty to forty which departments had generally favoured. In the planning and transportation field the Royal Commission proposed a total of sixty-one responsible authorities – fifty-eight unitary authorities and three metropolitan authorities. For education the Royal Commission had rejected the need for authorities with at least 500,000 population (as urged by DES) and had proposed a total of seventy-eight local education authorities (fifty-eight unitary and twenty metropolitan district authorities).

Assuming that the main elements of the Redcliffe-Maud structure were acceptable there were various ways in which the proposals could be brought more closely into line with departmental evidence on these functions. The first would be to redraw the map of unitary authorities and metropolitan districts so as to produce fewer and larger units than the Commission had proposed. A note of reservation from Mr Jack Longland would have done just this, and with education very much in mind. His proposals would have resulted in a total of fifty planning authorities (as against the Commission's sixty-one) and sixty-three education authorities (as against seventy-eight) and would clearly have carried much weight in

DES. On the other hand, the Commission's pattern of areas was the result of prolonged study and there were obvious reasons for adopting it as the basis of further consultations, if other aspects of the new structure were broadly acceptable.

The second possibility would be to make education a top-tier function in the conurbations, instead of a district function. This would have been an improvement from the point of view of those who advocated as few and as large education authorities as possible, but it would have run counter to the recommendations of both the Royal Commission and the Seebohm Committee on the desirability of education being the responsibility of the same local authority as the other personal services.

The third possibility would be to adopt additional metropolitan areas besides the three recommended by Redcliffe-Maud. From the White Paper (Cmnd 4276) and the statement made, when it was published, by Mr Crosland (who had taken personal charge of the consideration of the Redcliffe-Maud report following his appointment as Secretary of State for Local Government and Regional Planning in October 1969), it transpired that the government had considered a number of possible extra metropolitan areas including West Yorkshire, South Hampshire, Central Lancashire, Tyneside and Nottinghamshire/Derbyshire (Commons Hansard, 4 February 1970, cols 430–42). Such a move would have reduced the number of planning authorities by identifying larger areas which needed to be planned as single units; but the adoption of extra areas of two-tier local government would have made it less easy to withstand pressures for two tiers everywhere, and would have eroded the administrative advantages to be gained by the general establishment of unitary authorities.

As discussion of the Royal Commission's proposals proceeded it became clear that this last point was the most controversial. The general structure proposed for the metropolitan areas was likely to be acceptable – it was closely modelled on the system already adopted and operating in Greater London. It was also agreed in principle that there should be fewer and bigger authorities for major functions elsewhere, and that the county borough, as hitherto known, should disappear. It was further agreed that, whatever major authorities finally emerged, they would need to be complemented by some kind of more local grass-roots bodies. The crucial question was whether such bodies should be responsible for any statutory services.

The Royal Commission had proposed that they should not. In their suggested system local councils would have the primarily representational role of making known the views of their inhabitants to the unitary authorities, coupled with a general power to improve the local environment; only the larger ones might take part in certain services (for example, housing, highway improvements) and then only with the consent of the unitary authorities.

This concept had few adherents. Taking into account the existing parishes with parish councils there would have been something like 7,000–8,000 local councils, and the great majority would have been very small and weak. This was far too many to permit effective and regular two-way consultations between local councils and unitary authorities. On the other hand, it was argued, where a local council replaced a former county borough, borough or urban district council its lack of functions would be unlikely to attract worthwhile members. And, looking at the new structure as a whole, the concentration of all services in the hands of the unitary authorities would result in a drastic reduction in the total number of elected members responsible for executive functions in local government. There were about 32,000 councillors sitting on county, county borough and county district councils in England, outside Greater London (not counting some 3,500 aldermen), whereas the Royal Commission's proposals would have meant a total of about 6,000 councillors, at most, sitting on the main authorities.

## OTHER CURRENT PROPOSALS

In the debate about unitary authorities or two-tier arrangements in England the government had also to take account of other proposals which favoured two-tier systems of one kind or another. The first of these was Mr Derek Senior's Memorandum of Dissent, in which he set out his own proposals as an alternative to those recommended by his fellow Commissioners. Mr Senior adopted a very similar division of functions into two groups – the environmental and the personal services (though he thought education should be administered by the authorities responsible for the former group, and he rejected the need for it to be associated with the personal services). He also agreed that where the functional needs of the two groups coincided they should be administered by the same authority. He differed from his colleagues, however, in thinking that this coincidence could be discovered in more than a very small minority of areas; in most cases the functional requirements of the two groups were so different that the services could not be effectively discharged in a single pattern of all-purpose authorities. He proposed a predominantly two-level system for the main services, with thirty-five regional authorities responsible for the environmental services and education, and 148 district authorities for the personal services and other functions appropriate to smaller areas. In four areas the regional authority and the district authority would be the same.

Mr Senior's two levels of executive authorities would have been complemented by five appointed provincial councils for strategic planning, and by elected common councils at grass-roots level for parishes, towns or parts of towns. He also proposed the articulation of the operational authorities by delegation from regional authorities to district officers, responsible for areas corresponding to the districts, and by joint arrangements which would embrace all the districts within each region. It was a closely argued memorandum but it would be fair to say that, although much admired in those academic circles where socio-geography is more important than the practical aspects of political life, his approach never got off the ground as a possible model for reorganisation.

More potentially awkward, from the government's point of view, was the situation on Welsh reorganisation. The proposals current when the report of the Redcliffe-Maud Commission was under consideration were for a conventional county/county borough approach which included two tiers in the counties; these proposals had been published by the government themselves in the form of a White Paper, *Local Government in Wales* (Cmnd 3340). This had appeared in 1967, while the Redcliffe-Maud and Wheatley Commissions were still at work, and was the outcome of the activities of the interdepartmental working party set up to develop the proposals of the Local Government Commission for Wales, coupled with consultations with local government interests. The Welsh White Paper contemplated the retention of three of the four Welsh county boroughs (Cardiff, Newport and Swansea) and a two-tier structure of counties and county districts elsewhere, though with a rationalisation of areas by amalgamation – the thirteen counties of Wales and Monmouthshire would be reduced to five and the 164 county districts, together with Merthyr Tydfil, reduced to a total of thirty-six new districts.

After the publication of the Redcliffe-Maud report the Secretary of State for Wales held further consultations with Welsh local authorities and their associations, and decided to undertake another review of the situation in the geographical counties of Glamorgan and Monmouth. The aim would be to fall into line with England so far as the imminent abolition of county boroughs was concerned, and to achieve the amalgamation of town and country in south Wales. There was no question of abandoning the two-tier approach in the rest of the country, and the Secretary of State for Wales gave public assurances to this effect to the Welsh authorities. In the central and northern parts of Wales it was, of course, always possible for the government to differentiate these sparsely populated areas from the conditions generally found in England. So, when announcing the further review of local government in Glamorgan and Monmouthshire, during the debate on the Address in October 1969, the Prime Minister (Mr Wilson) added that 'we all recognise the undesirability of seeking to impose a single type of solution on the various and very differing parts of Britain' (Commons Hansard, 28 October 1969, col. 32).

The Prime Minister would also have had in mind the report of the Royal Commission on Local Government in Scotland, as this had been published in September 1969 (Cmnd 4150), and the Minister without

Portfolio (Mr George Thomson) had been asked to co-ordinate the government's consideration of the reports of the two Royal Commissions. The Wheatley Commission had proposed a two-tier system for Scotland, too, with seven regional authorities and thirty-seven district authorities and had specifically rejected a single level of all-purpose authorities. Whereas it could be argued that unitary authorities would, in any case, be inappropriate to the sparsely populated Highlands, seven-tenths of the total population of Scotland (about 3·5 million out of 5 million) live in the central lowlands, where population densities were comparable to those in the proposed English unitary areas. In events the government did not complete their consultations on the Wheatley report in time to announce their conclusions on local government in Scotland before the general election in June 1970.

Yet another consideration relevant to the future structure of local government was the existence of the Commission on the Constitution. They had been appointed in February 1969 under the chairmanship of Lord Crowther (on whose death Lord Kilbrandon became chairman in March 1972) with Scotland and Wales particularly in mind, but their terms of reference specifically included regions within the United Kingdom. Admittedly the Commission were required to direct their attention to 'the present functions of the central legislature and government' but it would be impossible to consider regional devolution of central government functions without regard to the organisation of local government, especially if regional bodies might also be set up as part of a reformed system of local authorities. Indeed, the Constitutional Commission were required to consider (*inter alia*) developments in local government. When referring to the proposal to establish the Commission on the Constitution, during the debate on the Address in October 1968, the Prime Minister mentioned the expected reports of the Royal Commissions on Local Government in England and in Scotland and said 'action to be taken following these reports ought not to have to wait until the Constitutional Commission has finished its work. On the other hand decisions taken following Maud and Wheatley may well have some bearing on the Commission's consideration of some of the central issues referred to it and may help it in its thinking.' So it was acknowledged that proposals affecting the regional organisation of functions could not be kept in watertight central and local government compartments, though local government reorganisation was not to be held up while waiting for the report of the Commission on the Constitution. Whether the Redcliffe-Maud Commission had been consulted on, or informed about, the intention to establish the Commission on the Constitution is not revealed in the Redcliffe-Maud report which made only a passing reference to the subject in a paragraph which records their view that the province would not be the right area for the operation of local government services (Cmnd 4040, para. 439) – a view, incidentally, which was specifically endorsed by Mr Crosland (Secretary of State for Local

Government and Regional Planning) when the government's White Paper was published (Commons Hansard, 4 February 1970, col. 441).

The government also had to take account of the possible repercussions of the Redcliffe-Maud report – and also of the Kilbrandon Commission's report (when it came) – on the machinery for regional economic planning. The Regional Economic Planning Councils were established as appointed bodies who would assist the formulation of regional strategies and advise the central government on regional aspects of national policies. Their field of activity was primarily that of economic planning but there was an area of common interest (though not an overlap of responsibility) between the Planning Councils and local planning authorities.

In addition to these various sets of proposals, extant or expected, relevant to the structure of local government, the central government also had in mind developments affecting some of the major local government functions such as police, the health service and water.

The programme of amalgamation of police forces under the Police Act 1964 had been going ahead while the Redcliffe-Maud Commission were at work and was expected to result in a total of forty-one forces in England outside Greater London.[8] Some further changes would be needed to adjust police organisation to the Commission's sixty-one unitary and metropolitan areas.

Organisational changes in the health services had been foreshadowed in the 1968 Green Paper on the National Health Service.[9] This outlined the need for the unified administration of the three branches of the service – the hospital services (then the responsibility of the Regional Hospital Boards and Boards of Governors), the general practitioner services (under Executive Councils) and a number of personal health services administered by local authorities, such as home nursing and midwifery, maternity and child care, health centres, health visiting and the ambulance service. That Green Paper expressly kept open the possibility of the unified health service being administered within a reorganised local government system after the Redcliffe-Maud Commission had reported, but the then Minister of Health (Mr Kenneth Robinson) included discreet warning words in his preface about the financial problems that such a solution would raise, as the greatest part of the cost would still have to be found by the central government. On the other hand, the transfer away from local authorities of the local health services left in their hands by the National Health Service Act 1946 would also cause severe organisational difficulties, in view of the close operational links between them and the welfare services for which local authorities would in any case continue to be responsible. As had already been noted (p. 112 above), the terms of reference of the Redcliffe-Maud Commission, which restricted them to the existing functions of local government, did not prevent them from suggesting that ways could be found round the problems of financial responsibility so as to permit the administration of the NHS by reorganised local authorities (see p. 174 below), and Mr Senior's Memorandum of Dissent urged this solution even more strongly. In any case (said the Royal Commission) local government services and the health services should be organised on the basis of the same operational areas because of the very strong links between them.

Another main function under consideration by the government at this time was water – which general term included all the activities of the river authorities (conservation, land drainage, fisheries and the prevention of pollution), water undertakers (local authorities, joint boards and water companies) and local sewerage authorities (county boroughs, county districts and joint boards). Increasing demands on the country's water resources led the Minister of HLG to reconstitute the Central Advisory Water Committee (which had been in abeyance) in September 1969, specifically to give further consideration to the administration of water functions in the light of the Redcliffe-Maud report. The ministry's evidence to the Royal Commission had treated water supply and sewerage as functions which they expected to remain in local government hands but the parliamentary secretary to the ministry (Lord Kennet) had told a congress on 'The Future of Rivers', even before the Royal Commission had reported, that the CAWC would probably be reconvened to review the whole question.

## LABOUR PARTY REACTIONS TO THE REDCLIFFE-MAUD REPORT

The National Executive Committee of the Labour Party organised eight regional conferences to discuss local reactions to the Redcliffe-Maud report. These showed that there was widespread acceptance within the party of the general approach, with two-tier arrangements in metropolitan areas and unitary authorities elsewhere. The outcome of consideration within the Labour Party was summarised in the NEC's pamphlet *Principles for Local Government Reform in England* published in December 1969. There was a cautiously worded recommendation to the government that 'consideration be given to the possibility of creating additional metropolitan areas' and Tyneside, Teesside, South Hampshire, Leeds/Bradford and Sheffield were mentioned, along with the possibility of two metropolitan areas in the West Midlands instead of only one (with one centred on Birmingham and the other embracing the five county boroughs of the Black Country). Within the metropolitan areas education should be a metropolitan, not a district, function. The possibility was also mooted of 'a very few more unitary authorities'.

The NEC reported lack of enthusiasm for local councils, and forecast confusion between the old and the new authorities if local councils were retained for the areas of former authorities; this would hinder the final emergence of the unitary authorities. Rather than follow the proposal for local councils for all former county boroughs, boroughs and urban districts, therefore, the NEC suggested that community councils, with powers similar to those of parish councils, should be set up outside the metropolitan areas – but only in those places where people wanted them.

### THE TIMETABLE

In his statement to Parliament on the publication of the Redcliffe-Maud report the Prime Minister (Mr Wilson) said that the government intended to press ahead quickly with a view to bringing a Bill before Parliament 'as soon as possible' (Commons Hansard, 11 June 1969, cols 1460–75). According to Mr Crossman's Diaries, the Prime Minister favoured instant moves towards accepting and implementing the Redcliffe-Maud proposals because, *inter alia*, impending changes in local government boundaries would provide a reason for shelving the recommendations of the Parliamentary Boundary Commission – whose Second Periodical Report (dated 21 April 1969) proposed changes thought to be disadvantageous to the Labour Party.[10] If true, Mr Crossman's record might help to explain why the Prime Minister, in his statement to Parliament, said, among other things, 'I can say at once that the government accept in principle the main recommendations of the report, which state that a major rationalisation of local government is called for, that there should be a very marked reduction in the number of units with executive responsibility and that the anachronistic division between town and country should be ended'. These were not, in fact, recommendations of the Redcliffe-Maud Commission; they were the reasons why the Commission were set up.

Be this as it may, consultations on the main principles of the report were needed with the local authority associations and other interested bodies, and it was obvious that government decisions could not properly be taken before the end of 1969 or early in 1970. Separate consultations would also be needed on areas, and these would necessarily involve many hundreds of local authorities. So it would clearly be impracticable to introduce the necessary legislation (which was bound to be complicated) before the 1971/2 session; on the pattern of events in Greater London this would allow elections to any new authorities in 1973 and final implementation in 1974. The later stages of any such timetable were problematical at that date in 1969, however, because the government, having been elected in March 1966, were bound to go to the country at latest in the spring of 1971. In fact the general election was held in June 1970, only a few months after the government had announced their conclusions on local government in England in the White Paper referred to below.

## THE LABOUR GOVERNMENT'S CONCLUSIONS

The government's White Paper *Reform of Local Government in England* (Cmnd 4276) was published in February 1970, and announced the conclusion that the government agreed with the main features of the Redcliffe-Maud proposals with two-tier government in the conurbations but unitary authorities elsewhere. In the main debate on the general adoption of unitary authorities or two tiers (outside the metropolitan areas) the government came down in favour of the Redcliffe-Maud unitary approach, though without any illusions that this would be a generally acceptable solution. 'There is no "right solution" to the problems of reorganisation' (said the White Paper). 'Whatever solution is chosen must sacrifice some things in the interest of others; and further changes will be needed from time to time to match the changing pattern of work, life, settlements and society . . . In the government's judgment, the Commission's analysis is sound in its broad essentials and their proposals provide the best basis for reorganisation' (Cmnd 4276, para. 9).

The government thought that unitary authorities of about the size recommended by the Royal Commission would be right, but they disagreed with two of the proposals for the metropolitan areas: education should be a top-tier and not a district function, and there should be additional metropolitan areas – in West Yorkshire and in South Hampshire. Each of these areas should, in the government's view, be planned as single unit but it is permissible to infer that the government saw other advantages too; a metropolitan structure for West Yorkshire, with education at the top tier, would preserve – and indeed enlarge – the West Riding of Yorkshire education service, while a similar structure for South Hampshire would make it possible for the Isle of Wight to retain substantial local government functions as a metropolitan district (the Redcliffe-Maud proposals would have included the Isle of Wight in a unitary authority based on Portsmouth, so that all services would have been run from the mainland, and there would have been no elected authorities operating on the island other than a group of local councils).

The acceptability of local councils as the grass-roots bodies within unitary areas clearly worried the government, who devoted a whole chapter of the White Paper to this subject. On one point they thought the Royal Commission had gone too far in trying to find functions for local councils, and they disagreed with the proposal that the larger of such councils might play some part in the running of statutory services – even with the agreement of the unitary authorities concerned. Such arrangements, they thought, would lead to a division of responsibility which could only cause confusion and be harmful to services. On this point the government adhered more closely to the unitary principle than did the Royal Commission, but they sought an alternative way in which local councillors could be associated with the administration of significant functions – through arrangements which would result in local councils appointing members to serve on area committees of unitary authorities, which would be responsible for the decentralised administration of statutory services. The details of this suggestion were left for further consultations.

The Redcliffe-Maud proposals on provinces were deferred for further consideration after the Commission on the Constitution had reported and meanwhile the Regional Economic Planning Councils were retained, and reassuring noises were made about the value of their work. A White Paper on local government in Scotland was promised and a reference included to the further review of Glamorgan and Monmouthshire, where it would be impossible to preserve the division between counties and county boroughs any longer. This review by the Secretary of State for Wales resulted in the publication, two months later, of a White Paper, *Local Government Reorganisation in Glamorgan and Monmouthshire*, proposing that three unitary areas on the Redcliffe-Maud pattern should be defined, based on Cardiff, Newport and Swansea (Cmnd 4310, March 1970: this White Paper had a very hostile reception when it was debated in the Welsh Grand Committee in May 1970). But complete reconciliation between the proposals for England, Wales and Scotland was apparently not expected as the English White Paper was careful to repeat the substance of the Prime Minister's earlier warning: 'differences in the geography and history of the three countries make it inappropriate to try to force the structure of local government into the same mould for each' (Cmnd 4276, para. 14).

A further Green Paper on the National Health Service[11] was published immediately afterwards, also in February 1970, but the local government White Paper had anticipated this to the extent of announcing the government's firm conclusion that the NHS would be reorganised outside, and not within, the reformed local government system, though agreeing that the health services and the local authority personal social services would have to be closely co-ordinated. The Green Paper developed this theme by announcing that the unified health service would be administered by area health authorities which would operate within the same territorial boundaries as the local authorities responsible for the social work services, that is, the unitary authorities and the metropolitan districts (outside Greater London), and that these local authorities would each appoint a proportion of the members of the AHAs. The National Health Service would also have a tier of regional health authorities, though these would operate within areas small than the proposed Redcliffe-Maud provinces and would have only advisory functions.

The White Paper confirmed the proposed timetable outlined above (p. 126), with legislation in 1971/2, elections in 1973 and the final change-over in 1974. It indicated that the new areas would be defined in the Bill itself and not left to any subsequent stage or separate body of Com-missioners. It also adopted the Redcliffe-Maud boundaries as the basis for consultations on areas (with the suggested unitary authorities as the initial districts within the two additional metropolitan areas of West Yorkshire and South Hampshire).

Consultations on areas and boundaries were initiated by a circular addressed to all local authorities in England (outside Greater London)[12] after the publication of the government's main conclusions. The circular underlined two points already stressed by the White Paper (Cmnd 4276, para. 91). First: there was much to be done within the proposed timetable; consultations must be full and thorough, but lengthy inquiries based on forensic procedures would not be appropriate; consultations would include public conferences but they should not be excessively formal. Secondly, the consultations on boundaries between areas would not be the occasion for reopening arguments on the main structure of local government, on which the White Paper was the starting-point for the next stage.

The circular allowed just over four months for comments on areas and boundaries, and asked that these should reach the ministry by the end of July 1970. It also stressed that any alternative proposals needed to be looked at in relation to the pattern of units as a whole and added, for good measure, that authorities would 'of course wish to discuss such matters with their neighbours'. Attempts to discourage individual authorities from making *ex parte* boundary proposals had been a recurring feature of post-war reorganisation. These consultations were under way when Parliament was dissolved in preparation for the general election held in June.

## THE SITUATION IN JUNE 1970

The situation at the time of the general election could not be other than confusing for anyone seeking a coherent approach to local government in England, Wales and Scotland. Government decisions had accepted the view that in some areas (the metropolitan areas in England) the patterns of development had produced areas which, while requiring to be treated as a whole for planning and transportation, contained too many people for a single authority effectively to administer the personal and other local government services; in these areas two-tier government was needed. In other areas (mid- and north Wales, for example) development was scattered and population densities much less, and these conditions also justified two-tier local government. In between these areas of high density and low density it would seem that unitary authorities would be appropriate (for example, in most of England and in south Wales). But in the central lowlands of Scotland, where densities were similar, unitary authorities had been rejected by the Wheatley Commission who had proposed two tiers, and there was no evidence to suggest that the government would disagree with the Wheatley Commission on this aspect. Indeed, when the Conservative government's White Paper *Reform of Local Government in Scotland* (Cmnd 4583), based on the Wheatley report, was later debated in the Lords, Lord Hughes for the Labour Party indicated that it was on the same lines as would have been followed by his party had they remained in office (Lords Hansard, 23 March 1971, cols 815–16).

In this situation it was perhaps not surprising that the Labour Party manifesto for the 1970 election did not go into details, and merely said, 'We shall carry through in the next Parliament a major reorganisation of local government. Strong units of local government will make possible much more effective town and country planning.'[13]

## THE CONSERVATIVE GOVERNMENT'S APPROACH 1970–4

The general election in June 1970 brought the Conservative Party back into office and they came with a pre-announced commitment to the principle of two tiers in local government. Like the Labour Party, the Conservatives had organised regional consultations on the Redcliffe-Maud report but results were very different; Conservative reactions were strongly against the unitary solution.

Although many details remained to be filled in, Mr Peter Walker's speech during the Commons debate on the Labour government's White Paper had contained a number of pointers indicating the direction in which the Conservative Party would be likely to move if returned to office. In that speech when dealing with structure he referred to the problem of the 'bottom tier' or local councils, as proposed by the Redcliffe-Maud Commission. The dilemma had already been pinpointed by the Commission themselves when summarising the MHLG evidence: while aware of the democratic case for another level of local government below city regions, the department were reluctant to see the lower tier given responsibility for any important functions but were uncertain whether they would be worthwhile bodies without it (Cmnd 4040, para. 160). On this, said Mr Walker, 'I come down on the side of saying that we must ensure that the bottom tier has worthwhile functions to perform, and I reject the concept of local councils' as envisaged by the Royal Commission (Commons Hansard, 18 February 1970, col. 449).

On the alternative approaches of unitary and two-tier systems, Mr Walker pointed out that, in the structure envisaged by the Labour Party's White Paper, the unitary arrangements would still affect only a little over half the population of England (58 per cent) while the remaining 42 per cent would live in areas for which two levels were thought right; and two-tier systems were also proposed for Wales and Scotland. 'The government have said they are showing flexibility by providing two-tier government in one part of the country and one-tier government in the other. We believe that there should be a similar pattern all over the country' (col. 454). This was repeated in the election manifesto: 'We will bring forward a sensible measure of local government reform which will involve a genuine devolution of power from the central government and will provide for the existence of a two-tier structure.'[14] Government departments therefore had ample warning of the change of direction that might be needed and time to consider alternative possibilities.

As the general election came at a time when local government reorganisation was already under way an early statement was needed from the new government to reduce, if not to remove, the inevitable uncertainty produced by the change of administration. The two main questions requiring to be answered (for each of the three countries of Great Britain) were: what type of two-tier system did the government favour and what would be the timetable of change?

The Queen's Speech said only that proposals would be worked out for England, Scotland and Wales in full consultation with all concerned. A brief circular to local authorities in England[15] reiterated the intention to hold further consultations and, in the meantime, asked that any authorities which had formulated their views on the areas adopted by the previous government[16] should send them in, though authorities would not be in any way committed by such comments in relation to any fresh structural proposals which the new government might put forward.

The promised consultations on reorganisation were conducted in writing but produced little that was new. The AMC published a restatement of the proposals which they had made to the Redcliffe-Maud Commission under the sub-title 'Proposals for a Dual System'[17] in which the primary units would be most-purpose authorities complemented by provincial councils. The scheme was further developed in two directions. First, the provincial councils were given much more extended treatment (possibly with an eye to influencing the Commission on the Constitution) and their role expanded to include not only some planning and co-ordinating functions but also executive responsibility for police, fire, water supplies and regional aspects of the health service. Secondly, at the operational level, the association tackled the problem which prudence had hitherto deterred them from attempting – to suggest how their proposals might work out on the map. The result (which the association were careful to stress was only for purposes of illustration) produced fourteen regions and 132 most-purpose units compared with the eight Redcliffe-Maud provinces and seventy-eight unitary authorities and metropolitan districts; not unexpectedly sixty-one of these 132 most-purpose authorities would have had populations below the 250,000 which the Redcliffe-Maud Commission had adopted as the desirable minimum. The criticism levelled against

Redcliffe-Maud was even more relevant here – that the main units would be too small for many services while still being too big for really local functions.

The CCA, for their part, reiterated their support for the tripartite agreement which they had reached with the UDCA and RDCA in 1969 in response to the Redcliffe-Maud report, with a system resembling the Royal Commission's proposals for the metropolitan areas but with a more traditional type of county/district units in the rest of the country (see p. 119 above).

As Mr Senior's two-tier proposals had never attracted any support as a solution which could be implemented, the alternative systems advocated by the main local authority associations were the front runners and it should have caused little surprise when the government, being committed to two tiers, preferred the more evolutionary approach to the one based on most-purpose authorities set out (most recently) in the AMCs' dual system.

The government's solution was for two levels of authorities each exercising substantial functions, but with recognition of the special position of the conurbations. This last element had been a feature of much postwar thinking; it led to the definition of the SRAs in the Local Government Act 1958 and to the Redcliffe-Maud metropolitan areas; and Mr Walker, during the debate on the Labour government's White Paper, had conceded the need to define metropolitan areas and to give reality to the boundaries of the major conurbations. Outside the metropolitan areas it was inherently likely that the Conservative Party would wish to adhere more closely to the existing county pattern and structure, rather than to a structure which would attract the controversies attaching to the unitary authorities and local councils.

The Conservative White Paper (*Local Government in England: Government Proposals for Reorganisation*) therefore came down in favour of two tiers everywhere, but with a different set-up in the conurbations. The rationale here was based on Redcliffe-Maud – the existence of areas which required to be treated as entities for the environmental functions, especially planning and transportation, but which were sufficiently populous and compact for all the districts to have populations big enough to support the personal group of services, including education. (By retaining education as a district service in the metropolitan counties the Conservative Party followed Redcliffe-Maud; both the Labour Party White Paper and the CCA/UDCA/RDCA tripartite agreement would have allocated education to the top tier in the metropolitan areas.) On this basis six metropolitan counties were proposed, in Merseyside, Greater Manchester, the West Midlands, West Yorkshire, South Yorkshire and Tyne and Wear. While not saying so in explicit words it was clear that the metropolitan areas would not be so widely drawn as in the Redcliffe-Maud proposals. In a carefully worded paragraph the White Paper said: 'The boundaries of these areas should include all the main area, or areas, of continuous development and any adjacent area into which continuous development will extend. It may be right to include closely related built-up areas, too. But none of these proposed metropolitan counties can practicably contain the solution of all the planning problems of the conurbations and, where it is impossible to meet all housing and redevelopment needs within the county boundaries, the answer will lie in development well outside the metropolitan area, in accordance with a carefully worked-out regional plan' (Cmnd 4584, para. 32).

Outside the metropolitan areas there would be some substantial districts but population densities were much more varied. The rationalisation of the areas of county boroughs and county districts would reduce the existing disparity in the size of second-tier units (and 40,000 was mentioned as the lowest desirable size) but big differences in population pointed, in these counties, to the education and personal social services being county functions. The main district functions (outside the metropolitan areas) would be, according to the White Paper, housing, planning control, refuse collection and amenities but not libraries, highways or refuse disposal.

Other matters were deferred. Regional arrangements would have to await the report of the Commission on the Constitution and water services would need consideration in the light of the imminent report of the Central Advisory Water Committee.[18] The Secretary of State for Social Services (Sir Keith Joseph) had already announced in Parliament that the new government, like their predecessors, proposed to unify the NHS outside local government but that modified proposals on the administration of the health services would be made (Commons Hansard, 5 November 1970, cols 437-9); the reorganisation of the NHS would need to become effective at the same time as local government reorganisation, and the new health authorities would need to work closely with the local authorities responsible for the personal social services and the public health services (Cmnd 5055, August 1972).

With the adoption of two levels of local authorities generally throughout England the clash of principle between unitary authorities in England and two tiers in Scotland and Wales disappeared. The publication of the English White Paper was matched by virtually simultaneous publication of the government's proposals for those countries too.[19]

## STRATEGY OF IMPLEMENTATION

The White Paper setting out the government's proposals for England thus briefly defined the type of solution to which they intended to give effect and, with the complementary documents on Scotland and Wales, set the framework for local government organisation in all three countries. But local government and the NHS, with water in the offing – and they all had to be considered together – added up to a very formidable package for Parliament and the central departments to cope with, so the government were faced with the preliminary organisational problem of deciding how and when to tackle these interrelated changes.

The main subject of this study is local government in England and on this part of the package it was natural for the Department of the Environment, into which the Ministry of Housing and Local Government had been merged in October 1970 and which now had overall responsibility for local government, to look back to the reorganisation of London government in 1963–5. The procedures and timetable of London reorganisation provided a starting-point for the calculations. After the Herbert Commission had reported the then government's White Paper had been published in November 1961. The London Government Bill had been introduced twelve months later, in November 1962, and passed by the summer of 1963. The new authorities had been elected in the spring of 1964 and had taken over on 1 April 1965, a total of just under three-and-a-half years between the White Paper and final implementation.

A parallel timetable for the rest of England would require a White Paper by the end of 1970 (or as soon after as possible), a Bill in 1971/2, election of the new authorities in 1973 and final implementation in April 1974.

There were strong reasons for favouring this timetable, if it could be achieved. In the first place it was the quickest practicable and for this reason would be supported by people in local government.

Secondly, this timetable would fit in with the likely life of that Parliament. As the general election had been held in June 1970 the next election could not be later than the summer of 1975 and might come in (say) 1974. There would be advantages in completing the process of reorganisation, so that it was not hanging around as a piece of unfinished business at the next election. This had happened when the 1964 election fell during the last few months of the London reorganisation, and it had produced an additional element of uncertainty.

Thirdly – though this was less immediately urgent – it would fit in with the next review of parliamentary constituencies. Under the House of Commons (Redistribution of Seats) Acts, a further review of constituencies was timed for completion by 1979 – ten years after the Parliamentary Boundary Commission's previous report.[20] Such a review would need to start in 1975, and preparatory work in 1974. Constituency boundaries are related to local government boundaries and it would be desirable for any new local government areas to be defined by then so that the constituency review could start on time.

But it was not possible to consider legislation on English local government in isolation. A decision would also be needed on whether English and Welsh reorganisation should be dealt with in the same Bill. And a commitment to local government reorganisation would require dovetailed legislation and administrative action to synchronise the reorganisation of the NHS and (probably) water as well. Parallel legislation and action would also be needed in Scotland. From the point of view of parliamentary business, therefore, these related measures would pre-empt a substantial amount of time in two, or possibly three, sessions; they would need to be weighed against other legislative candidates such as the Bill on Britain's membership of the EEC.

Moreover, local government reorganisation in the rest of England was a bigger and more complex task than in London. Greater London contained no local government parishes and the London proposals were uncomplicated by provincial considerations. With different arrangements for the metropolitan and non-metropolitan counties, the allocation of functions in the new exercise would be more complicated and the whole Bill would take longer to draft. In particular, more new areas needed to be defined – some 400 instead of only thirty-three – and electoral divisions devised within each for purposes of the first election.

The practical problems of defining areas and electoral divisions were a major preoccupation throughout the early stages of the reorganisation exercise and it was against this somewhat crowded background that the department examined four possible ways of approaching reorganisation. Underlying the whole study of alternative courses was the desirability, as far as was practicable, of Parliament itself settling the major areas in the Bill, in order to define the framework of the new structure.

The first possible course was to tackle reorganisation in two stages. The new counties would be defined in a Bill in 1971/2, would be elected in 1973 and take over their functions in 1974, leaving reorganisation at district level until a second and later stage. This was broadly what had happened in the Local Government Acts of 1888 and 1894; the first of these had dealt with counties and the second with districts and parishes.

The similarity stopped there, however, and this kind of two-stage operation would now have been impossible. Quite apart from the fact that it would have prolonged the final reorganisation process to some undefined ultimate date, the new counties (unlike those adopted in 1888) would frequently have new boundaries, thus making necessary some modification of the district pattern even in the first stage. Moreover (and the same problem had arisen in the alternative possibilities for London reorganisation – see p. 98 above) some functions would have to undergo a double upheaval in the metropolitan areas where education, the social services and libraries could not be administered at district level until the new districts had been defined and their councils elected; these services would therefore have had to become county services on a temporary basis, and transferred back to the districts when the latter had been reorganised at the second stage.

The second possible course was therefore to define the counties and metropolitan districts in the 1971/2 Bill, leaving only the non-metropolitan districts to a subsequent stage - possibly placing on each new county council the task of reviewing the district pattern within their area. This course would have avoided the double disorganisation of functions in the metropolitan areas, but again it had the disadvantage of prolonging the exercise to an indefinite date without avoiding some immediate adjustment at district level where new county boundaries were drawn.

The third possibility studied was to delay the whole exercise for a year. The time thus gained could be used to draw up proposals for both counties and districts so that all the new areas, at both levels, could be included in a 1972/3 Bill. This course had one apparent advantage - it would allow all the county areas and all the district areas to be considered together. But the dangers far outweighed this advantage. The year's delay would mean a loss of momentum. The resulting Bill with some 400 new authorities in England alone (quite apart from Wales, if the same Bill covered both countries) would have made impossible demands on parliamentary time.[21] Finally, it would have delayed the ultimate implementation until April 1975, which would almost certainly be after the next general election.

The fourth possibility reverted to the scheme for a Bill in 1971/2 which would define the counties and metropolitan districts. It would, however, hive off the non-metropolitan pattern to a separate exercise, though one to be completed in time for the whole of the new system to come into full operation in April 1974. DOE might perhaps have been responsible for this exercise too, but there would be considerable advantages in entrusting it to an independent body. To carry out the necessary consultations, therefore, and to prepare proposals for the non-metropolitan districts, a Boundary Commission would be set up which would, in addition, become a permanent piece of machinery for reviewing not only local government status and boundaries but also electoral divisions. Their proposals for the non-metropolitan districts would be embodied in an order which would need to come into effect in time for the definition of electoral divisions before the first district elections.

This fourth possibility was the one adopted by the government and outlined in the White Paper, with as firm a commitment to legislation in 1971/2 as is thought constitutionally proper in advance of the Queen's Speech (Cmnd 4584, paras 53–8). In a complex situation it was obviously essential to have the main stages of the whole operation worked out well in advance. It was equally important to announce the timetable, partly in order to reduce uncertainty among local authorities and their staffs and partly because a number of procedural short-cuts would be needed which could be justified and explained only if the tightness of the timetable was fully appreciated from the start. In particular, consultations about counties and districts would have to overlap with the result that district patterns were considered before the county boundaries were firm; and in both counties and districts the arrangements for electoral areas would need to be considered before the local government boundaries were finally settled.

This timetable for local government reorganisation in England also allowed time for the legislation on the NHS during the 1972/3 session (the National Health Service Reorganisation Act 1973) and, in the event, on water too (the Water Act 1973), so that all the changes came into operation together on 1 April 1974.

## AREAS: THE COUNTIES AND METROPOLITAN DISTRICTS

On the same day as the White Paper was published the Department of the Environment sent a circular to all local authorities in England, accompanied by a map illustrating the government's proposals for the new counties and metropolitan districts.[22] In drawing up these revised boundary proposals the government were able to build on the consultations which had been started by their predecessors (and which they themselves had kept going – see p. 131 above) on the basis of the Redcliffe-Maud areas, and a number of the proposed new counties were wholly or substantially the same as unitary areas recommended by the Royal Commission. Elsewhere there were a number of departures from the Redcliffe-Maud map, however. Not only did the government propose six metropolitan counties instead of three but also drew the boundaries of Merseyside, Selnec and the West Midlands much more tightly. Outside the conurbations the aim was to produce a pattern of fewer major authorities than had been proposed by Redcliffe-Maud and, in doing so, to follow the existing county pattern unless there were very good reasons for departing from existing boundaries (such departures included the proposed new counties which became Avon, Cleveland and Cumbria).

The new pattern proposed at this stage would have produced forty-four counties (one fewer than the existing number of forty-five administrative counties) and thirty-four metropolitan districts; but all the counties would have had populations exceeding the desired minimum of 250,000 (though only just in the case of Northumberland) whereas eleven of the metropolitan districts were below this figure (and three were below 200,000).

. The department's circular was followed by another in the summer,[23] and together they defined the procedures which the government intended to follow in consultations before reaching conclusions on the proposals for areas to be included in the Bill. In the first place comments were invited in writing; alternative suggestions would be welcomed, provided they were within the general framework of two-level government with a desired minimum population of 250,000 for authorities responsible for education and the personal social services. To emphasise the impossibility of looking at individual areas in isolation, however, authorities making new suggestions were asked to follow through all the consequential changes that would be needed in other areas and to discuss these with the authorities affected. But one line of suggestion was discouraged in advance: on the basis of the criteria laid down in the White Paper the government had already reached the conclusion that the metropolitan pattern was suited only to the six areas they named, and to no others.[24]

The response was heavy. Nearly all counties, county boroughs and county districts commented on the proposals and over 300 modifications were suggested, varying from the major to the minuscule. A number of these had been expected and needed to be considered more fully. It would have been impracticable, in the time available before November 1971 when the Bill had to be presented, to hold conferences throughout the country to consider every area, so the Conservative government's White Paper had not repeated the general undertaking on this point given by their predecessors (Cmnd 4276, para 91). But some conferences were clearly required, and these were arranged in July and September 1971, before and after the summer holiday period. They were held by Mr Graham Page (the Minister for Local Government and Development within DOE) and Mr Michael Heseltine (the parliamentary secretary on the local government side of DOE) who, separately, presided over a series of conferences in those parts of the country where proposed change (or lack of change) raised special controversy. The department's circular had indicated that the secretary of state would take the initiative in arranging these conferences where they were needed to supplement the information already available, and that only a very limited number would be required.[25] In fact they included all the conurbations and the proposed new counties round Teesside and Bristol, as well as other areas such as Plymouth, South Hampshire and north-east Essex, where strong feelings had been aroused.

The nature of these conferences was similar to that of the statutory conferences held by the Local Government Commissions under the LGA 1958 and the conferences held by the four town clerks who advised on the grouping of the London boroughs, save in this case they were held by ministers and not by separate bodies acting in an advisory capacity. Their purpose was to enable ministers to assess the strength and balance of local feeling, to emphasise to the local authorities themselves (who despite departmental exhortation were not always in close touch with each other) that there are two sides to every boundary, and also to strengthen the hands of ministers who, when they came to defend the controversial proposals in Parliament, could speak with personal knowledge gained from meeting the authorities concerned and visiting and inspecting the disputed areas. The atmosphere was informal and the 'forensic procedures' characteristic of earlier methods were absent.

In the light of these conferences and inspections, and the written comments in other areas, the government's final conclusions on the counties and metropolitan districts were included in the Bill. A large number of modifications were made at this stage to the government's original proposals but a great many others (especially minor matters of detail) were left to be dealt with under the permanent machinery for subsequent boundary adjustments. The major development at this stage, which became apparent when the Bill was published, was the proposal to create a new county straddling the Humber, by amalgamating the East Riding of Yorkshire with the northern part of Lincolnshire to form the new county of Humberside.

Further amendments to the pattern of authorities were made during the passage of the Bill and it is convenient to refer to them here. This aspect of the Bill took up more parliamentary time than any other and it was also the aspect which caused the most apprehension in DOE. The historical precedent of the 1888 Act loomed constantly in the background. On that occasion the government of the day had originally proposed the creation of only ten county boroughs, all with populations of about 150,000 or above; as the result of pressures during the passage of the Bill through Parliament changes were made which led to the creation of sixty-one county boroughs – several with populations under 50,000 – thus undermining the new structure before it was established (see p. 14 above). As matters turned out, however, the modifications made during the parliamentary consideration of the Local Government Bill in 1972 were confined to changes which could be accepted without altering the essential pattern of areas, weakening the structure or creating precedents which could be quoted at subsequent stages of the Bill's progress.

A number of proposed amendments to the Bill were prompted by the desire of county boroughs to retain as many functions as possible – and at any rate the additional functions of education, the personal social services and libraries that would be exercised by metropolitan, as against non-metropolitan, districts. Hence the proposals for additonal metropolitan counties in central Lancashire (with districts based on Blackpool, Preston, Blackburn and Burnley), in Hampshire (with districts based, *inter alia*, on Southampton and Portsmouth), for Humberside (Kingston-upon-Hull) and Thameside (which would have embraced both sides of the estuary, with districts including Southend and the Medway towns).

None of these proposals met the government's guidelines, however, because although some of the proposed metropolitan districts would have had populations of 250,000 or more, in no case did the proposed county divide sensibly into districts which all met this criterion. Some of the districts would either have been too small in population to form effective education authorities, or would have been unacceptably extensive and scattered from a geographical point of view.

Other major proposals derived from the natural desire of existing authorities to retain their identities within the new system. Some of these took the form of proposing new metropolitan districts which would keep separate certain authorities which the government's proposals would have amalgamated, for example, Bury and Rochdale in Greater Manchester, and St Helens and Huyton-with-Roby in Merseyside. These two changes were agreed because the metropolitan districts thus created substantially met the population criteria which the government had adopted. On the other hand the proposed separation of Warley from West Bromwich and Sutton Coldfield from Birmingham were both resisted as, in each case, the change would have meant creating metropolitan districts with populations unacceptably short of the desired minimum.

Other proposals took the form of suggested new counties in which particular urban centres would have had a more dominant position than under the pattern in the Bill, for example, the creation of a separate county for North Staffordshire based on Stoke-on-Trent, and a county of Tamar based on Plymouth.

In two cases existing counties fought hard to retain their separate identity - Hereford and the Isle of Wight. The government resisted both proposals on the grounds that the population in each case was too far below the proposed lower limit for education and the social services. They eventually accepted the special case for the Isle of Wight, however, but only during the final stages of the Bill in the second House when it was too late for the precedent to be quoted in favour of further amendments.

## AREAS: THE NON-METROPOLITAN DISTRICTS

The White Paper had announced the government's decision to set up a Boundary Commission, whose first task would be to make recommendations for the initial pattern of districts outside the metropolitan areas. The proposed pattern of new districts would be debated in Parliament and given effect by order at about the end of 1972, so as to leave time for the electoral divisions to be settled and elections held in 1973 (Cmnd 4584, para. 56). The White Paper envisaged the first elections to the non-metropolitan district councils being held in November 1973 but ways were later devised to permit this date to be advanced (see pp. 206–8 below).

The date by which the non-metropolitan district pattern had to be settled was thus determined by the need to fit in with the overall timetable leading up to 1 April 1974. Formally the Boundary Commission (for which provision would be needed in the Bill) could not be appointed until the Bill had received Royal Assent, but as this could not be before July 1972 - and in fact was much later - virtually the whole of the process of considering the new district pattern had to take place before the

Commission had any official existence and while county boundaries were still being considered in Parliament.

The Boundary Commission was established on an informal basis as the 'Local Government Boundary Commission for England – Designate' in November 1971, as soon as the Bill had been given a second reading in the Commons. The Commission thus had about twelve months in which to formulate their proposals but this would not have been long enough to deal with the regrouping of more than 900 existing boroughs and districts had the process not started even earlier.

The first moves towards drawing a new pattern of districts were taken in the White Paper itself and in the circular on areas issued at the same time. These set out the general approach and, while accepting the need for the new districts to vary considerably in size, said 'the government would expect them to have populations ranging upwards from 40,000 save in sparsely populated areas' (Cmnd 4584, para. 34). Within this framework the government wanted the exercise to be based as far as possible on plans worked out by the existing authorities themselves and were 'determined to offer local authorities, communities and interests the greatest opportunity for local initiatives in drawing up proposals for the new pattern of districts'. In preparing their recommendations the Boundary Commission would take account of local proposals and would consult fully with the local authorities concerned (Cmnd 4584, para. 56 and circular 8/71, para. 13).

The timetable made it necessary for local authorities to start thinking of the future district pattern before the Boundary Commission could be appointed, even on an informal basis, and while the government were themselves carrying out consultations on county boundaries. This process – the simultaneous consideration of both counties and districts – continued until the end of 1972, and was practicable because local authorities now generally accepted that reorganisation would take place on the lines adopted by the government, and co-operated in working towards implementation. In many areas, where there was little or no dispute over county units, these simultaneous consultations at both levels caused little practical difficulty; last-minute amendments to the county pattern, when the Bill was in the Lords, affected the Isle of Wight and the boundary between Hampshire and Dorset, and had repercussions at district level, but these (and earlier changes as the county pattern was gradually finalised) were surmounted with the help of the local authorities concerned.

But if county, county borough and county district councils were to draw up preliminary proposals for consideration by the Boundary Commission they needed to be told as soon as possible what the Commission's terms of reference would be. The government drafted these in consultation with the local authority associations, and they were set out in the second circular on areas issued in July 1971.[26] This asked any existing authority wishing to make proposals to do so on the basis of the guidelines within which the Boundary Commission would later operate (and which were set out at an annexe to the circular) and to send these proposals to DOE by the end of October 1971 so that they could be waiting for the Boundary Commission when they started their 'designate' existence.

These guidelines elaborated very significantly on the reference to population in the White Paper, which had spoken only of an expected minimum of 40,000, and they now emphasised that in most cases districts should be much larger than this. Hence the guidelines said that 'Except in sparsely populated areas the aim should be to define districts with current populations generally within the range of about 75,000–100,000'.[27] As usual these figures, too, were accompanied by saving clauses to the effect that they were not absolute limits and that regard should also be had to 'the desirability of producing in each county a pattern of districts which are broadly comparable in population and conducive to effective and convenient local government throughout the county as a whole', but they clearly indicated – and in far more definite terms than had ever been used before in connection with (say) the county reviews or the work of the postwar Commissions – the general scale of the amalgamations which the government desired to achieve.

The guidelines did not reproduce the nine factors which figured in the earlier regulations for the Trustram Eve and Hancock Commissions but substituted a general direction to weigh all relevant considerations in the light of local government reorganisation, as set out in the White Paper, and required the Commission, among other things, to have particular regard to the wishes of the local inhabitants, the pattern of community life and the effective operation of local government services.

For the first time parliamentary constituencies openly appeared in guidelines for local government boundaries, though admittedly in a phrase of delphic neutrality. The possible ultimate repercussions of local government boundary changes on constituency boundaries have already been noted. In the past political apprehensions had been raised more by county borough extensions than other types of boundary alterations; county constituencies, which often embraced a number of small districts, could usually reckon on being left relatively undisturbed by modifications to district boundaries. But the creation of a completely new pattern of districts, with a population norm very similar to that of a parliamentary constituency, was a different matter and might cut drastically across the way in which counties were already divided for the purposes of parliamentary representation. The difficulty of instructing the Boundary Commission on exactly how much weight should be given to this aspect was avoided by the use of a time-honoured parliamentary phrase, and the relevant guideline said 'The Commission will also wish to take note of the pattern of Parliamentary constituencies in each county'.[28] In practice –

and no doubt because parliamentary constituencies are subject to periodic reviews – this guideline appears to have made only a minor contribution to the Commission's thinking.

Finally, on procedure, the guidelines directed the Commission to consider suggestions and proposals put to them by local authorities and other bodies, and then to publish their own draft proposals as the basis for further consultations. This followed the precedents of the Acts of 1945 and 1958 in that the draft proposals were to be those of the Commission, not of any particular authority or group of authorities, but the subsequent processes were, of course, left much more flexible. The Commission were enjoined to carry out 'the fullest practicable' consultations on their draft proposals but to submit their recommendations in time for them to be debated in Parliament in the autumn of 1972 and the boundaries of the new districts to be established by order before the end of that year.

## THE BOUNDARY COMMISSION'S REVIEW OF NON-METROPOLITAN DISTRICTS

The setting up of the Boundary Commission designate was announced in November 1971, a few days after the Commons had approved the government's proposals in principle by giving the Bill its second reading. The Commission inherited, via DOE, representations from nearly all the existing authorities (sent in response to the invitation contained in circular 58/71) and from many other sources as well. The draft proposals for all the non-metropolitan districts, except those in Cleveland (on which the government issued separate guidance), took account of these suggestions and were published on 25 April 1972.[29]

A special problem arose in Cleveland. The guidelines for the Boundary Commission included one which read, 'The identity of large towns should be maintained'.[30] This had been included to reassure the big boroughs that they would generally remain undisturbed as local government entities. But Teesside, formed in 1968 by the amalgamation of (*inter alia*) Middlesbrough CB, Stockton-on-Tees B, Redcar B, Thornaby-on-Tees B and Billingham UD, would have accounted for two-thirds of the population of the new county of Cleveland. The dominant position of Teesside would have resembled that of Peterborough in the former Soke and would have made it impossible to establish a sensible pattern of districts. The Boundary Commission were therefore specially directed to ignore this guideline so that Teesside could be split up again and the new county divided into not fewer than four districts.

In total the Commission's draft proposals would have reduced the 949 existing county boroughs and county districts outside the metropolitan counties to a total of 278 new districts, none of which would have had populations below 40,000. Initially, comments were requested in writing and the Commission's circular letter poured cold water in advance on any alternative proposals that did not claim a substantial measure of agreement among the local authorities concerned. It was not to be expected that the Commission's draft proposals, even though they were generally based on local initiatives, would command complete acceptance. In the event, however, some three-quarters of the existing authorities accepted the draft proposals, and even those who objected (said the Commission) generally adopted a practical and realistic approach and a readiness to offer alternatives. These consultations identified the areas of continuing difficulty and, in these cases, the Commission held meetings locally with the authorities involved. The procedure was similar to the conferences held by ministers on the county and metropolitan district proposals in that they were informal in character, only a comparatively few were thought necessary, and these were arranged on the initiative of the Commission not of the authorities themselves.

The Local Government Bill was given Royal Assent in October 1972 which permitted the Local Government Boundary Commission for England to be formally appointed and then immediately to present their final recommendations (Cmnd 5148, November 1972). These reflected the consultations with local authorities, in the light of which a number of changes had been made to the draft proposals. The Commission now recommended the formation of 296 (instead of 278) non-metropolitan districts to replace the 949 county boroughs and county districts outside the metropolitan counties. Of the 278 districts defined in the draft proposals 212 remained unchanged, forty-one had been modified to a minor extent and forty-three had been significantly altered, often by being subdivided. Of the final total about one-third (104 out of 296) fell within the range recommended in the guidelines between 75,000 and 100,000, 82 were above this range and 111 below it.

Fourteen of the new districts were below 40,000. The Commission had drawn up their draft proposals so that no district fell short of the suggested minimum and they were criticised by local authorities for an undue emphasis on arithmetic to the disregard of other considerations. The Commission answered this point in their report when they explained that they had thought it desirable to test the feasibility of large districts in all areas before concluding, in the light of representations (as they now did in several instances), that special circumstances - usually sparsity of population - justified a district with a lower population.

The other general point on which the Commission's proposals disappointed some authorities was in respect of the boundaries of the large towns, that is, those with populations within or above the 75,000–100,000 range. Under the guidelines these retained their identity (see p. 143 above) and generally this meant that former county boroughs became new districts on their own without being amalgamated with neighbouring authorities. But in many cases the boundaries of these towns were out-of-date and the borough councils concerned put forward claims for extensions. These, the Commission decided, would have to wait to be dealt with later, through the permanent machinery for boundary adjustments contained in the Bill; boundary extensions were proposed by the Commission only in those cases where they were needed to include the whole of the designated area of a new town or an area defined for town development in a single new district. This course was dictated by the tightness of the timetable; boundary alterations of this type - especially at a time when arguments would turn on the working of a new system that had not yet come into operation - were likely to be contentious and time-consuming, and could not be pursued in detail when the main aim was to get the essentials of the new pattern settled within the deadline of the end of 1972.

Even with the modifications to their draft proposals the Commission's final recommendations still left some authorities dissatisfied. This was inevitable but the great majority of authorities accepted the view that, within the framework of reorganisation now agreed by Parliament, the Commission's proposals were the best practicable. The government had another and more general reason for inclining towards their acceptance and it was bound up with the long-term role of the Boundary Commission. If this body was to establish itself as the independent organ of adaptation - in the field of electoral divisions as well as local government areas - it was desirable to act on the assumption that the Commission's proposals were normally accepted, and that only in quite exceptional circumstances should the government of the day depart from the Commission's advice.

For all these reasons the government adopted the Boundary Commission's proposals for the initial pattern of the non-metropolitan districts and the order was approved by affirmative resolution in each House in December 1972 - just within the deadline laid down in the White Paper.[31]

One possible procedural stage might have delayed the order. As it represented the final completion of the new pattern of operational authorities the order was regarded as sufficiently important to require affirmative, instead of only negative, resolution. But an affirmative resolution order (as already noted, p. 79 above) came within Standing Order 216 affecting private business in the House of Lords and might be petitioned against if it dealt with a matter that would otherwise have required to be enacted by a private or hybrid Bill. A single general order, dealing with all the non-metropolitan districts, would probably not fall within this category but it could not be guaranteed in advance that the pattern of districts would be dealt with in only one order, or that an amending order might not be needed (for some unforeseen reason) dealing with only one or a few non-metropolitan districts. If this had happened the order might be delayed by petitions, which would have been inappropriate in the light of the nature of the exercise carried out by an independent body established by Parliament for the purpose. To guard against this situation the Bill prevented the operation of the Standing Order in question and the hearing of petitions; this is the effect of paragraph 1 (3) of schedule 3 to the LGA 1972.

## NOTES: CHAPTER 5

1   Redcliffe-Maud Commission Written Evidence: Memorandum by MHLG, Pt I, para. 160.
2   Royal Commission on the Distribution of the Industrial Population, Cmd 6153, 1940, para. 371.
3   Ministry of Transport, *Traffic in Towns* (HMSO, 1963); Report of the Steering Group, paras 49–52.
4   *Municipal Review*, November 1965.
5   Redcliffe-Maud Commission Written Evidence: Memorandum by MHLG, Pt II, para. 10.
6   ibid., para. 36.
7   ibid., para. 81.
8   Redcliffe-Maud Commission Written Evidence: Memorandum from the Home Office and Cmnd 4040, para. 347.
9   *National Health Service: The Administrative Structure of the Medical and Related Services in England and Wales* (HMSO, 1968).
10  Richard Crossman, *The Diaries of a Cabinet Minister*, Vol. 3 (London: Hamilton and Cape, 1977), pp. 509 and 516.
11  *National Health Service: The Future Structure of the National Health Service* (HMSO, 1970).
12  MHLG circular No. 21/70, 24 March 1970.
13  *Now Britain's strong let's make it great to live in* (The Labour Party, 1970), p. 17.
14  *A Better Tomorrow* (The Conservative Central Office, 1970), p. 25.
15  MHLG circular No. 59/70, 9 July 1970.
16  Set out in MHLG circular No. 21/70.
17  *Municipal Review* Supplement, December 1970.
18  Published later in 1971: *The Future Management of Water in England and Wales* (HMSO, 1971).
19  *The Reform of Local Government in Wales – Consultative Document* (HMSO, 1971) and *Reform of Local Government in Scotland* (Cmnd 4583, 1971).
20  Boundary Commission for England: Second Periodical Report, Cmnd 4084, 1969.
21  The Welsh districts were in fact all defined in the Bill. But this was practicable partly because there were only thirty-seven new districts in Wales (as against some 300 in England) and partly because the proposals for second-tier amalgamations had been under discussion in Wales for some years.
22  DOE circular No. 8/71, 6 February 1971.
23  DOE circular No. 58/71, 22 July 1971.
24  Circular 8/71, para. 7.
25  Circular 58/71, para. 4.
26  ibid., paras 9–15 and Annexe.
27  ibid., Annexe, para. 2.
28  ibid., Annexe, para. 7.

29 Local Government Boundary Commission for England – Designate: *Memorandum on Draft Proposals for New Districts in the English Non-Metropolitan Counties proposed in the Local Government Bill* (HMSO, 1972).

30 Circular 58/71, Annexe, para. 3.

31 The English Non-Metropolitan Districts (Definition) Order 1972, SI 1972 No. 2039.

## Chapter 6

# Subsidiary Issues

## FURTHER DECISIONS IN LONDON AND THE REST OF ENGLAND

The two preceding chapters have outlined the basic decisions which the government of the day had to take, first in relation to Greater London and then for the rest of England. These set the broad framework of the government's conclusions as regards the nature of the new system to be established, the areas in which the new authorities would operate and the timetable and strategy of the operation. Within this framework, however, many details had to be filled in and it is convenient, from now on, to consider Greater London and the rest of England together; a number of the matters which arose were common to both these two major reorganisations.

The topics to be dealt with in this chapter have been chosen on a severely selective basis to illustrate some of the fields in which government decisions had to be taken in connection with the completion of the structure of local authorities, the retention of ancient dignities, the machinery for future change and the exercise of functions. This is no more than a sample and certainly not a comprehensive catalogue of all the details which had to be settled. Nor would it be correct to give the impression that the government's conclusions on such matters were all cut-and-dried before the respective Bills were introduced; on some, further or modified decisions were taken as the parliamentary stages progressed.

## COMPLETING THE NEW STRUCTURE

The initial decisions on local authorities naturally concentrated on the main operational authorities who would be responsible for the statutory services. Throughout most of England and Wales these were to be the counties and the districts. Within Greater London they were to be the London boroughs and the GLC, but special problems among the operational authorities were raised by the City of London and the Temples and these are referred to below.

On the other hand, the reorganisation of London government was not complicated by considerations of authorities above or below the main operational units. The question of provinces and provincial authorities was not generally under discussion in 1963-5, and in any case could not have been raised in the context of a measure applying only to London and not to the country as a whole. But the Redcliffe-Maud recommendations had included provincial councils and the whole topic was very much to the fore when decisions were being taken on the structure of the rest of the country in 1971 - though by that time the Commission on the Constitution were at work and, in events, the further elaboration of this element in the structure was deferred (see p. 133 above).

Parishes could not be ignored, however. Although they presented no problems in London (as the Greater London area contained no rural districts and hence no parishes as local government units) they demanded a substantial amount of attention as part of the arrangements for the rest of the country and these, too, are dealt with below.

*The City of London* is unique and, as a local authority, it is a complete anomaly. Its area of 677 acres has remained almost unchanged since the Norman conquest. It is a borough by prescription, a county of a city and has its own lieutenancy. Its constitution differs from that of other local authorities and may be amended by the corporation itself (save where this power of amendment has been expressly limited by statute).

In some fields the City exercise the same or similar functions as other boroughs in London and pay for these from the rates in the usual way, for example, housing, planning and environmental health. As part of the administrative county of London between 1888 and 1965 the City contributed through the county precept to the cost of services provided by the LCC in the City as well as in the rest of the county, for example, education, the personal social services, highways and the fire service.

But in other respects the City is uniquely different from the generality of local authorities. It has its own police force, is the health authority for the whole of the port of London, and maintains four of the London bridges, certain important markets and extensive open spaces outside the City at Epping Forest, Burnham Beeches and other places.

Further: the City is in a class by itself when it comes to financial resources in relation to population. As part of the central core of London the City contains an enormous concentration of rateable value though the benefit of this (like the rateable value of Westminster and other wealthy central boroughs) was and is spread more widely through London rate equalisation schemes. And, in addition to the rates, the corporation have a substantial income known as the City's Cash (which includes income from corporate property and market rents and tolls) from which the cost of a number of functions special to the City - including ceremonial - is defrayed.

Finally, the anomalous position of the City stands out in the contrast between the established position of the authority and the size of its resident population. At the time the Herbert Commission were sitting fewer than 5,000 people lived permanently within the City, though some

350,000 came in for work each day. This gave a figure of about £2,800 as the rateable value per head of resident population as against £238 for Westminster (the next on the list) and £15 as the average for the country as a whole. But despite such rate resources, when expressed in this way, the population of 5,000-odd hardly qualified the City to rank among the London boroughs, for which the Royal Commission had proposed a minimum population of 100;000 (and still less under the government's proposals for boroughs with minimum populations of 200,000).

This point was fully accepted by the Herbert Commission who nevertheless proposed that the City should remain as a separate entity within its existing boundaries, and that it should have all the statutory powers exercised by the London boroughs. This recommendation was based only to a small extent on local government grounds (because, on all the criteria otherwise applied to local authorities in Greater London, the City is indefensible) but rather on the grounds that the City is a national, rather than a local, institution supported by the indefinable – and non-transferable – charisma derived from centuries of history and tradition.

The Conservative government of the day had little difficulty in accepting the Commission's conclusions. Nor did the opposition challenge it seriously in the context of the London Government Bill. Lord Morrison of Lambeth delivered a predictable diatribe against the City, having (as the government spokesman put it) 'his bit of fun', and amendments were moved in committee to include the City in a big new central borough,[1] in borough No. 1 (with Westminster, Paddington and St Marylebone),[2] or in a completely new, if somewhat improbable, grouping in which the other components would have been Finsbury, Shoreditch, Stepney and Southwark.[3] But success for these amendments could hardly have been expected and, although the City continues to be the target for attack from some quarters, the fact remains that if ever the City is abolished it will be as a result of a political decision having little to do with local government.

*The Temples* offer a good example of a recurring event in all legislation – a matter of minor significance in the operation as a whole but one which takes up a disproportionate amount of time for those involved in preparing the Bill and ensuring its implementation.

The Herbert Commission, having heard no evidence on the subject, were able to dismiss it in a single short paragraph under the heading of 'The Inns of Court': 'Some of these have a special position which should be preserved. They stimulate a sense of antiquity without standing in the way of efficient local government.'

The Inner and Middle Temples were the last of the 'places' in London which stood outside the general system of local government because they did not fall within any parish. The Extra-Parochial Places Act 1857 had also referred to Gray's Inn and Charterhouse but these had since been absorbed into what were, by 1963, the metropolitan boroughs of Holborn and Finsbury respectively. The Temples, however, were not within any metropolitan borough or the City, though they formed part of the administrative county of London.

The Act of 1857 designated the chief officers of the two Honourable Societies – the Sub-Treasurer of the Inner Temple and the Under Treasurer of the Middle Temple – as overseers of the poor within their respective areas and, in this capacity, they became rating authorities and also inherited certain other local government functions, chiefly in connection with public health. The small area involved – only a few acres – and the limited number of residents in the Temples meant that desperate local government problems did not often arise, but various arrangements had been made over the years to make sure that services were provided as necessary. Apart from the functions exercised by the Inns themselves some services were provided by the City (for example, police) while the LCC were of course responsible in the Temples, as in the rest of the county, for education, the personal social services, the children's service, the fire service, main drainage, and so on. Highway functions had not been a problem because, apart from the Victoria Embankment (which was an LCC responsibility), there were no public highways in the Temples[4] and the question of exercising functions under the Housing Acts never arose because the Honourable Societies own all the properties. For this reason they did not levy a separate rate in order to raise the sums they paid to the City and to the LCC as their contribution towards the cost of the services provided by these two bodies.

The situation was anomalous (and far more obscure than might be inferred from the brief outline given above) and, prima facie, the London Government Bill offered an opportunity for a minor piece of administrative rationalisation by including the Temples within the City. This course would have been strongly resisted by the Temples, however, who had no desire to lose their special status and, as the two Inns could call upon powerful voices to urge their case, the government decided to accept the Herbert Commission's recommendation and leave well alone. The Bill promised to be sufficiently controversial without provoking unnecessary quarrels.

No essential changes were made by the Bill, therefore. The two Treasurers remained the rating authorities within the Temples, and responsible for the same local government functions as before. Arrangements between the Temples and the City were left undisturbed. And the GLC provided for the Temples, as for the rest of Greater London, those services it took over from the LCC.

Problems arose, however, in connection with those functions which had previously been exercised by the LCC but which were now to be transferred to the London boroughs and to the City, especially the children's service, the personal social services and local aspects of planning. Clearly the

Temples could not be placed on an equal footing with the London boroughs as authorities responsible for these services but on the other hand the two Societies did not want the Bill to be drafted so as to give even the impression that the City had responsibilities within the Temples. Nor, for their part, did the government want the Temples to figure prominently in the Bill at all; it would have created confusion and derision in Parliament if references to the Temples had kept on cropping up in clause after clause.

The London Government Act 1963 therefore made only minimal references to the Temples as part of the territorial area of Greater London and provided, in section 82, for the exercise of most local government functions in the Temples to be regulated in detail by Order in Council.

This order[5] was not finally made until six years after the London government reorganisation had become effective, when it made special provision for the exercise of planning functions in the Temples and provided, *inter alia* (but less obtrusively than if it had been set out in the Act itself), that the Common Council should be the authority responsible for health and welfare and children's services in the Temples, as well as in the City. This did not necessarily mean, however, that the City would provide the services themselves. Section 5 (2) of the London Government Act specifically allowed the City to agree with any adjacent London borough that the latter should exercise functions on behalf of the City – and such agreements could cover any service which the City was responsible for providing in the Temples.

*Parishes* as units of local government were reformed by the LGA 1894 and were subdivisions of rural districts. There were no rural districts and hence no local government parishes in the area adopted for Greater London, but they were an integral part of the structure in the rest of the country. The situation in the 1960s was usefully reviewed by the Redcliffe-Maud Commission whose proposed local councils would have taken the place of parish councils in rural areas.[6] There were then some 10,000 rural parishes in England. About 43 per cent of these had fewer than 300 inhabitants and nearly 80 per cent were under 1,000. Only forty-nine parishes (0·5 per cent of the total) had populations over 10,000. All parishes have to hold an annual parish meeting and about 7,000 parishes had a parish council as well. The present position on this point is now governed by section 9, LGA 1972: a parish is required to elect a parish council if the population includes more than 200 local government electors; if the number is smaller than this the parish may still resolve to elect a parish council but the district council must also agree if the figure is less than 150.

Parishes have certain statutory powers, some of which are also available to district councils; they have no statutory duties. The review carried out for the Royal Commission showed that more than half the money spent by parishes on revenue account went on the public lighting of streets and footpaths and on parks and recreation grounds. Smaller amounts were spent in connection with burials, highways and allotments. Parish councils also have power to spend modest sums for the general good of the area and many make imaginative use of this power. Very few parishes employ any full-time officials; they rely very heavily on part-time or unpaid help and have been described as a species of do-it-yourself organisation. 'A district or county council is mainly concerned to provide services for its people; with a parish authority the emphasis is on helping them to help themselves.'[7]

Experience suggested a number of points which the government kept in mind during the consideration of bodies at parish level in the context of reorganisation. In the first place, local communities need a body or bodies through which a collective view can be expressed on matters of local importance; in many instances the parish council provided this focus for public opinion – a very important function which was in addition to any statutory powers. Secondly, elected parish councils would be viable only if they have power to raise money and take action and scope to use that power, even if only on a modest scale; the statutory apparatus of electoral areas, regular elections, and so on, would hardly be justified in order to elect a body which could do no more than talk and protest. Thirdly, the opportunity for a parish council to take action generally exists only in small towns and villages, which do not necessarily need the uniform provision of local government services, where there is scope for existing services to be augmented in ways that suit the needs of the particular locality and where purely local action is within the financial reach of a small body. This last point did not deny the existence of identifiable communities or neighbourhoods within bigger towns or wholly built-up areas but suggested that, in such cases, it might be preferable for local views to be expressed through voluntary or non-statutory bodies which would rely on the district council or county council to take the necessary executive action.

Existing parish councils were retained in being by the LGA 1972, though with some additional powers (for example, an increase in the amount of money – to an amount equal to a rate of 2p in the £ – which each parish council may spend for the general benefit of the area or its inhabitants and the right to be informed about planning applications affecting their area. Indeed the 1972 Act was described in some circles as an Act for the strengthening of parish councils and the abolition of all other authorities. But a number of decisions had to be taken in the process of including parishes in the new structure. Was it appropriate for parishes to continue, or to be created in the future, in the metropolitan districts which (in contrast to non-metropolitan districts) were all primarily urban units? Should parish councils be established for those boroughs and urban districts which were to be abolished on reorganisation? What action should be taken as regards urban parish councils – or neighbourhood councils – in parts of big towns?

The existing law, going back to the LGA 1894, provided for local government parishes only in rural districts; if the whole or part of a rural district was converted into an urban district, or absorbed by an urban district or a borough, then parish government in that area was extinguished. This was a frequent reason (among others) why rural fringes of big towns resisted annexation, and it led the AMC to reach agreement with the National Association of Parish Councils in 1961 on proposals which, had they been implemented, would have permitted communities which were included within urban areas to retain their existing parish councils.[8]

The Redcliffe-Maud Commission also drew a distinction between the built-up cores of the metropolitan counties and other areas, when it came to establishing local councils. While they saw a general need for local councils to succeed all the former boroughs and urban districts outside the metropolitan areas, they thought that, in the metropolitan areas, 'there will not be the same need for local councils in view of the existence of the metropolitan districts'. Here, they thought, local councils should be optional.

Similar reservations about parishes in urban areas were entertained by the Conservative government in 1971. In the White Paper on 'Government Proposals for Reorganisation' they asserted their desire to give every encouragement to the existing parishes outside the metropolitan counties, where their general character should remain unchanged 'as much a part of the social as the governmental scene'. But, continued the White Paper, 'the retention or establishment of parish councils in essentially urban areas raises different problems – in the metropolitan districts, for instance, or in town areas outside the metropolitan counties' (Cmnd 4584, paras 38–40).

One point was speedily resolved soon after the publication of the White Paper when the department's consultation document on the future of parishes made it clear that the government proposed initially to retain existing rural parishes in metropolitan, as well as in non-metropolitan, districts, together with the constitutional arrangements for parish meetings and parish councils; provision would be made, however, for a review of the parish pattern, which the new district councils would be required to undertake (under the general aegis of the Boundary Commission) after the main reorganisation had come into operation. These decisions were given effect in the Act which thus created the situation (which could not arise under the previous system) in which some parts of a district had authorities at three levels and others at only two. This followed logically, however, from the new aim to combine town and country at district level, and to abandon the former distinction between urban and rural authorities.

A more pressing, and very much more difficult, problem was the immediate future of the towns which, prior to reorganisation, were county boroughs, boroughs and urban districts. They were all due to be abolished, and although the larger ones would become new districts on their own without loss of identity this did not apply to the medium or smaller boroughs and urban districts. There were, for instance, 570 non-county boroughs and urban districts with populations below 40,000 and another forty-one between 40,000 and 50,000. These authorities would, after reorganisation, find themselves amalgamated with others in new units; some would be comparatively big fish in their new ponds, others would be only small fish and were apprehensive of the prospect.

The pressure to retain some kind of elected council for the areas of the abolished authorities gathered momentum, assisted by a campaign organised by the Abingdon Borough Council and Chesham Urban District Council, who circulated all boroughs and urban districts with populations below 40,000. Although the idea of local councils akin to parish councils had attracted little support when proposed by the Redcliffe-Maud Commission, the imminence of reorganisation led many towns to view matters in a different light. The possibility of qualifying for a parish council later, when parishes were reviewed, was better than nothing but did not go nearly far enough. There would be a break in continuity, during which the town would be left without any embodiment of its separate identity and without any body capable of taking even the most minor action to meet purely local needs; and in the case of boroughs there would be a loss of civic dignities which had hitherto - and in some towns over many centuries - been attached to the status of a chartered corporation. Hence the pressure for the retention of 'interim parish councils' which would maintain continuity, at least until the general review of parishes.

The proposals for Wales were relevant here, and supported those who pressed for the establishment of interim parish councils. For Wales the Bill adopted the expression 'community' instead of parish, and substituted community councils for all the existing parish councils. Subject to certain listed exceptions, it also gave each of the existing borough and urban district councils the right to apply to the Secretary of State for Wales, before 1973, to have a community council established as from 1 April 1974 for the whole or part of their area.[9]

The government's initial decision not to provide for interim councils was based on a number of considerations. There were practical difficulties in arranging fresh elections to yet another group of authorities, and providing for the reallocation of property. But the most powerful argument was the need to allow the new district councils to get off to a good start, free from the ghosts of the former authorities, and to ensure that existing councillors who wished to remain in local government transferred their allegiance to the new authorities. This objective might be made harder to achieve if the erstwhile boroughs and urban districts remained in shadowy existence, even though deprived of most of their earlier powers. It applied with special force in the case of a borough or urban district which would provide a substantial part of the population and resources of the new district.

The Welsh analogy was not wholly conclusive. The reorganisation proposals for Wales had a longer history than in England; the proposals had been before the public in effect since 1967 and, as fewer authorities were involved, it was possible to define the new districts in the Bill itself. This also made it possible to identify, at an earlier stage, the existing 'excepted boroughs' which, by reason of their size in relation to the districts of which they would form part, were precluded from retaining separate councils at parish level.

But a number of amendments on the future of the smaller towns in England were tabled to the Bill during committee stage in the Commons, and the pressures inside and outside Parliament induced a change of attitudes on the government's part. The problem of borough privileges is dealt with later but, on interim parish councils, the government accepted the need to provide continuity for councils – at any rate in those small towns which compared in size and character with existing rural parishes. If parish councils were likely to be established for such towns as a result of the later review, why not identify them now and retain the town's representative body – especially where the existing borough or urban district constituted only a small element in the new district, so that its continued existence would not be a threat to district unity? There was (in such cases) little chance that ambitious councillors would choose to stay with the parish council of the small town instead of seeking election to the district council, and the practical problems of new elections before 1974 could be avoided by retaining existing members in office to constitute what was now referred to as the 'successor parish council'.

The problem was, however, to identify those small towns which were broadly comparable in size and character with other small towns or villages which already had rural parish councils. Various possibilities presented themselves: to state in the Bill that successor parish councils would be retained in all boroughs and urban districts with populations below (say) 20,000 (but this would catch urban districts which were integral parts of larger built-up areas and also, in some cases, towns which were major elements in new districts); by allowing all towns within a given population limit to choose whether they wanted a successor parish council (this would be in line with the Welsh provisions but had the same drawbacks as the first alternative); by listing select towns in the Bill (but this would add further complications to the parliamentary consideration of the Bill, and there would be political pressures to extend the list); or to bring in the Boundary Commission to advise.

This last solution was the one adopted and it was written into the Bill on report stage in the Commons. The Boundary Commission were required to consult with the existing counties, boroughs and urban districts and the joint committees of existing authorities and recommend which councils should be retained as successor parishes, having regard to guidelines laid down by the secretary of state. The final outcome would be given effect by order subject to negative resolution (part V of schedule 1 to the LGA 1972). There were several advantages in this course. It placed the task in the hands of an independent body, and one which already had a close knowledge of the districts as the result of their work on non-metropolitan district boundaries. And by arranging for it to be carried out as a separate exercise, after the Bill was through, it meant that individual applications for successor parish status could be considered in the light of final decisions on the district pattern.

The guidelines for the Boundary Commission on successor parishes[10] were discussed with the local authority associations, and reflected the government's desire to avoid retaining authorities at parish level which were either so big as not to be comparable with existing parishes or which formed so large an element in their respective districts as to constitute a threat to the unity of the new authorities. Even so, the population figures quoted were generous, bearing in mind that very few existing parishes exceeded 10,000. Boroughs and urban districts which were essentially parts of larger towns or continuously built-up areas should not be selected, but otherwise the guidance gave a fairly broad hint that the claims of towns under 10,000 should normally be allowed. And 'many towns of the order of 10–20,000 might well qualify; but the Secretary of State would expect proposals above this range to be the exception rather than the rule in both metropolitan and non-metropolitan counties'. In addition, however, the Boundary Commission were to take into account the proportion of the district population comprised in the town under consideration. Again, no rigid limit was prescribed but it was suggested that if the town constituted more than one-fifth of the total it should not qualify. These two considerations, on absolute numbers and on the proportion of population, had both to apply – they were not alternatives.

On the strength of the first round of applications the Boundary Commission recommended a total of 269 successor parishes. In response to representations they looked at additional information provided by previously disappointed clients, and made some further recommendations. Finally, they considered some late applications from towns which had not applied in the first instance. In all, 300 successor parishes were identified by the Boundary Commission, and constituted by order.[11]

The last major decision on parish councils was whether the Local Government Act should make any specific provision for parish councils or neighbourhood councils elected for parts of larger towns. The cause of such bodies had been actively pressed by the National Association of Parish Councils and the Association for Neighbourhood Councils. The Redcliffe-Maud Commission had arranged for a study of community attitudes which showed that most people feel some identity with a 'home area' which is usually much smaller than the area of the borough or district in which they live.[12] The Association for Neighbourhood Councils had carried this further by asking the Gallup Poll to carry out a sample survey to find out whether people thought 'it would be a good idea or a bad idea to have a number of local neighbourhood councils . . . to help on such things as local schools, housing, etc'. And Chesterton's *Napoleon of Notting Hill* was romantically prayed in aid.

The Conservative government of the day were cautiously disinclined to take the matter further in the context of reorganisation. Partly this was because the exercise was already sufficiently complex and controversial but partly, too, because of widespread doubts whether there was scope for another level of statutory authorities in wholly built-up areas, where the main local government services were already fully provided. The White Paper had suggested that the views and wishes of neighbourhoods might preferably be represented by non-statutory bodies, to which district councils should be empowered to give financial aid (Cmnd 4584, para. 40), and on this thought the matter rested during the reorganisation period. It is true that the Act provided for the subsequent review of parishes by district councils and covered the possibility of establishing parish councils in areas which did not have them until then – including, in theory, parts of big towns (except London, to which this provision does not apply). But this review would be subject to guidance from the secretary of state, which was to be formulated in the future. The only expression of opinion of the then government was contained in the guidelines on successor parishes which said that it was the government's view 'that statutory authorities should not be established at parish level (at any rate for the present) for areas which are essentially parts of larger towns or continuously built-up areas'. But the further history of this aspect lies outside the scope of the present study.

## THE DIGNIFIED ELEMENTS

Governments who set out to reform local administration become inevitably involved not only in the practical operation of services by executive authorities but also in the retention, adaptation or abandonment of the miscellaneous trappings of earlier regimes. Some of these are connected with counties, some with boroughs; some still faintly reflect the functions and duties of ancient offices, some are now of purely ceremonial significance. Ministers did not make the mistake of regarding these matters as unimportant; in many cases they are the outward symbols of the historical continuity of a county or of a town and, for this reason, they required very cautious handling. The underlying policy was at all times to preserve the links with the past wherever this could be done without weakening the practical operation of the new system, while at the same time taking such modest steps as might be practicable towards the removal of anomalies.

The creation of Greater London and (elsewhere) of a pattern of new counties had obvious repercussions for all aspects of official and unofficial life which, although not connected with the provision of local government services, were organised on a county basis. The administration of justice was, in mediaeval times, part of the whole process of local administration organised under the sheriff in each county and (as already noted) the definition of administrative counties under the 1888 Act owed a good deal, in marginal cases, to whether an area had its own separate quarter sessions. The other inherited characteristic of a county was the possession of a separate militia, and hence a lieutenant and deputy lieutenant.

The gradual tendency has been for local government and the administration of justice to be disentangled from each other, but commissions of the peace are still issued on a county basis and local authorities still have some functions connected with the physical provision and maintenance of magistrates courts. County courts and crown courts, however, are quite separate from local government.

The offices of lieutenant and sheriff survive, though here again they now have little connection with local government. The lieutenant's principal role is to act as the sovereign's personal representative in the county; in addition, and among other things, he is the chairman of the committee which advises on the appointment of justices of the peace, and he usually holds another and even older post as *custos rotulorum* or keeper of the county records.

In recent years the formal duties of the sheriff of the county have chiefly been connected with the supreme court (for example, in executing judgements within the county) but even these have been further reduced by the Courts Act 1970. The post of sheriff is now chiefly of a ceremonial and social character.

Both these posts have survived the centuries, however, and have come to be associated with the county. For this reason–and because the holders of the posts are eminent and influential people holding royal appointments–the repercussions of local government reorganisation had to be carefully pondered.

The pre-existing pattern contained (inevitably) a number of complicating features. The counties for which lieutenants were appointed were not always the same as the counties which had their own sheriffs, and these again were different in some respects from the administrative counties for local government. East and West Sussex (separate for local government) were treated as a single county for the purposes of the appointment of one lieutenant and one sheriff, as were East and West Suffolk and the three Divisions of Lincolnshire. Cambridgeshire and Huntingdonshire, separate for other purposes, shared the same sheriff before 1965. The three Ridings of Yorkshire each had their own lieutenant but only one sheriff between all three (until the creation of the separate shrieval county of Hallamshire[13] under the Criminal Justice Administration Act 1962). Moreover the counties of cities and counties of towns (and Oxford, even though not a county corporate) elected their own sheriffs, though these were generally offices of dignity only. The City of London - a county of a city by prescription - was again different, with its own sheriffs and (exceptionally) its own lieutenancy. The remainder of the administrative county of London (that is, excluding the City) constituted the 'county of London' with its own lieutenant and sheriff (section 40 (2), LGA 1888 and see section 206, London Government Act 1939).

It has been the recent custom, when county boundaries have been adjusted for local government purposes, to provide that the new boundary shall also apply to the areas of jurisdiction of the lieutenants and the sheriffs involved and this, on a much larger scale, was the course adopted on the reorganisation of London government. Greater London was not designated as a county - partly because the governing body would then have had to be the Greater London County Council, which would have given the impression that the LCC had merely been expanded to take over the whole metropolis. Greater London was, however, given its own lieutenancy and shrievalty (under the Administration of Justice Act 1964) as had been the case with the former county of London; the City of London remained outside these arrangements.

Outside Greater London and in Wales Part X of the Act of 1972 retained these ancient offices and effected a rationalisation by providing that the new local government counties should henceforth be the sole pattern of counties for all the purposes mentioned in the preceding paragraphs - for lieutenants, sheriffs, the *custos rotulorum*, commissions of the peace and magistrates courts.

Although logical, this solution had not appealed to everyone and some had argued (and this had also been discussed in the context of county amalgamations under the 1958 Act) that opposition to change would be reduced if it could be said, for instance, that although Rutland and Hereford had become parts of larger counties their identities had been preserved by the retention of separate lieutenancies for the former areas. But this suggestion - to perpetuate the shades of the former authorities - would have run counter to all efforts to encourage the unity of the new ones, and in one way the solution adopted by the Act was helped by the fact that in terms of total numbers the picture remained the same as before. There were previously forty lieutenants in England and thirteen in Wales but after reorganisation there were forty-five in England and eight in Wales - a total in each case of fifty-three. So there were the same number of posts to be filled and prima facie few, if any, of the existing lieutenants would be deprived of their appointments by reorganisation. Some adjustment of appointments was required and not all existing lieutenants could retain their previous posts: where two counties were amalgamated, for instance, only one of the lieutenants could be the queen's representative.

The transition was eased, however, by changing the statutory title from lieutenant to that already in common use, that is, lord-lieutenant, and permitting the queen to appoint additional lieutenants, too. So where (for instance) two counties were amalgamated, the Act made it possible for both existing lieutenants to be retained and to hold direct royal appointments – one as lord-lieutenant and one as lieutenant.

In the case of the sheriffs, here too the Act gave statutory recognition to the term already in common use – high sheriff – but the right to appoint a sheriff, although retained by certain cities and towns as an office of dignity, was no longer a criterion of county status. The concept of a city being a county of itself – a county corporate – disappeared as no longer compatible with the establishment of counties as the class of units responsible for those services which required wide areas embracing both town and country.

At district level the problems connected with borough status, and the preservation of dignities and privileges granted to boroughs, were taken very seriously by ministers, and the Conservative government's White Paper had contained early reassurances on this point (Cmnd 4584, para 43).

The origins and characteristics of boroughs have provided an inexhaustible field of research for constitutional and legal historians and are briefly referred to above (p. 13). At this point it is sufficient to recall that, prior to reorganisation and save in the special case of the metropolitan boroughs created by the Act of 1899, boroughs derived their status from a royal charter (or in some rare cases presumed grant of a charter) and that the charter constituted the area a borough and incorporated all the inhabitants; in the case of other types of authorities the body corporate was the council and not the whole collective body of inhabitants. Originally the practical purpose of a borough charter was to grant the town some element of self-government, and exemption from the jurisdiction of the sheriff of the county. But in modern times borough status has been prized as a mark of distinction rather than for any practical difference it made to the administration of services; in some instances boroughs enjoyed special charter rights, for example, to hold their own markets, but over the years the functions of all types of authorities have come within arrangements laid down by statute.

The distinction afforded by borough status was given tangible expression in various ways, some of which have already been mentioned (see pp. 42–4 above): the chairman of the council was styled the mayor, the clerk of the council became the town clerk, the council was expanded to include a proportion of aldermen (a feature shared with county councils), the borough council had the right to acquire and hold corporate property not earmarked for an express statutory purpose, and the right to elect honorary freemen and, finally, proposals for the alteration of wards in boroughs were dealt with by the Home Office and not by the county council.

In addition, other dignities were enjoyed in certain boroughs by royal grant. There were three royal boroughs in England - Windsor, Kingston and Kensington; forty-five boroughs were entitled to the style 'city'; in eighteen English cities the mayor was entitled to the style 'lord mayor', and the lord mayors of London and York could also use the prefix 'right honourable' (an honour extended to the chairman of the LCC and subsequently to the chairman of the GLC).

All these marks of earlier favour were jealously guarded by boroughs, collectively and individually, and earlier pages of this study bear witness to the extent to which boroughs were differently treated when it cáme to proposals affecting their boundaries and/or status. As a result boroughs were eventually found at all three levels of the old structure - as county boroughs, as non-county boroughs and (under the Local Government Act 1958) among the parishes, as boroughs included in rural districts.

Clearly, and notwithstanding the general desire to retain the traditional attributes of boroughs, there was scope for rationalisation; and the fact that all existing authorities were to be abolished seemed to offer the opportunity. No one contemplated the disappearance of the style 'borough' for a class of local authority, but the question arose whether boroughs under the new regime should still depend on the grant of a royal charter. The London Government Bill, as originally introduced, made no provision for further royal charters but proposed that arrangements with regard to status should be made entirely by ministerial order. It was agreed, however, that the London boroughs would all be large and important authorities which should not be denied the possible grant of a charter. The Bill was amended on this point as it went through Parliament (section 1 (2)) and, in the event, all the London boroughs were incorporated in this way. As the existing authorities were abolished there was nobody who could speak for the new second-tier units until they had been elected. The Act therefore allowed the minister to apply for charters on behalf of the embryonic boroughs, and this he did.

The question was considered again when reorganisation was going forward in the rest of England. Instead of only thirty-two new London boroughs the prospect arose of scores, even hundreds, of new districts petitioning for charters and the right to call themselves boroughs. Was not the time ripe to discontinue the grant of royal charters and constitute all boroughs by statute? Indeed, would it not be an astute move to make all the second-tier authorities boroughs - metropolitan boroughs in the metropolitan areas and county boroughs elsewhere? Such a move might prove attractive to the AMC and might counterbalance any feeling that, as the top-tier authorities were all to be counties, the reorganisation had taken on a form unduly favourable to the CCA.

This piece of official ingenuity did not appeal to ministers, however; some existing boroughs admittedly included large tracts of open country but historically a borough was a town, and not everyone wished to come within town government. It was therefore decided that borough status should continue to depend on the grant of a royal charter but, while retaining this ancient element, the government proposed some ways in which boroughs could be painlessly accommodated within the new system. These were set out in consultations with the local authority associations[14] and were reflected in the Bill when first introduced.

The main ingredients of the proposals at this stage were as follows: all the executive units within the counties would be defined for statutory purposes as 'districts' but, once elected, all district councils should have the right to petition for a charter. That charter would turn the district into a borough, the chairman of the council would become the mayor and the clerk the town clerk. The charter might also retain any previously granted rights connected with ceremonial matters or offices of dignity (for example, the appointment of a sheriff or high steward) but would no longer deal with anything else; wards, corporate property, and any functions previously exercised under charter powers, would in future be dealt with under general statutory provisions and orders. There would, in fact, be no difference (other than in style and ceremonial) between boroughs and other districts; aldermen were no longer to sit on any borough council[15] and the incorporation of all the inhabitants of a borough disappeared too; except in the London boroughs (whose constitutions remain governed by the charters granted under the London Government Act) the corporate body was the council in the case of boroughs as well as all other authorities. Finally, it was left for the council of the new district to petition separately for the renewal of grants formerly made outside the normal scope of charters – especially for city status and the right of the mayor to the title 'lord mayor'.

The government's proposals aimed at preserving borough status, but as no more than a ceremonial embellishment; only district councils could apply but, whether or not they were known as boroughs, all districts were to stand on the same footing as regards constitution, powers and functions. In such circumstances the consultation document circulated by DOE to the associations said that, in future, there would be no public inquiries into charter petitions and 'it would be the expectation that a council's petition for a charter would be acceded to'. In other words: there would be no minimum population for new boroughs and no search for a *de facto* corporate personality. To assist district councils the Privy Council Office later drew up advice on how to apply for a charter, including model draft charters to suit varying circumstances.

Up to this point the proposals were fairly straightforward and were satisfactory from the point of view of those large towns which were, without loss of identity, to be transformed into new districts. But they did not meet the wishes of the small and medium-size boroughs who hoped to retain some evidence of their former incorporated state. Pressure came from these towns, both inside and outside Parliament, during the course of the Bill's proceedings and by the time the Act reached the statute book it had been considerably elaborated in order to preserve the former dignities – especially the office of mayor – of towns which were now included in larger districts.

The case for doing this was most clearly accepted in the case of very small boroughs which would be given 'successor parish' status. In these instances the members of the former borough council were to remain in office as parish councillors and an elected body would visibly represent the community. In order to meet the wishes expressed on behalf of these towns the government now came forward with a proposal that, although the term 'borough' was restricted to authorities at district level, there would be no harm in a successor parish council – or indeed any parish council, whether or not it had succeeded a former borough – resolving to call itself the 'town council' for the area and adopting the style 'town mayor' for the chairman of the council (or 'city mayor' in the case of those very small cities such as Wells and Ripon where the style 'city' was regranted to the parish and not to the whole of the new district).

There remained, however, the intermediate towns which were too big to have successor parish councils but which would not constitute new districts on their own. The outcome here depended on whether the new district council petitioned for borough status for the district as a whole. If it did, then the existing borough would be merged in the new and larger borough, as had happened on many occasions in municipal history and, most recently, when existing boroughs in Greater London were merged in the new London boroughs.

But if the district council did not ask for a borough charter, and chose instead to remain as a plain 'district', then the device of 'charter trustees' came into operation. This innovation was, in effect, a representative body brought into being to support the office of mayor in towns which had formerly been boroughs. The members of the district council elected for the area of the former borough constituted a body corporate known as the 'charter trustees'; they were entitled to elect one of their number to act as town mayor (or city mayor) and to hold historic or ceremonial property – in particular the charters, insignia and plate of the former borough or city.[16]

These arrangements seemed generally to please the towns for which they had been devised – and their councillors. They were obviously open to criticism from other sources as being unnecessarily elaborate and for placing too much emphasis on archaic elements which, if they had been abolished entirely (at any rate at parish level), would soon have been forgotten. This was not the view taken by ministers, however, who wished to soothe ruffled feelings as far as possible, provided it could be done (as here) without affecting the new operational arrangements. About fifty former cities and boroughs emerged from reorganisation with charter trustees, including the cities of Lichfield and New Sarum (Salisbury) and the three boroughs of Bootle, Crosby and Southport in Sefton – the only metropolitan district which did not apply for a borough charter before 1 April 1974 (Sefton subsequently applied for such a charter, which was granted in April 1975 when the charter trustees of the three former boroughs were dissolved).

## KEEPING THE NEW SYSTEM UP-TO-DATE

Several references have already been made to the separate Boundary Commissions established under the Local Government Act 1972 for England and for Wales. The English Commission had immediate tasks connected with the setting up of the new system; they were required to make recommendations for the initial pattern of non-metropolitan districts, for the names of the new districts and for successor parishes. The role of the new Commission in relation to the non-metropolitan district pattern had been outlined in the Conservative government's White Paper which went on to say that 'the government have in mind that the Boundary Commission should form part of the permanent machinery for keeping local government areas and electoral divisions up-to-date' (Cmnd 4584, para. 57).

The establishment of the new system necessarily required a review of the machinery both for future boundary changes and for the adjustment of electoral areas; in each case the existing arrangements were inherently linked to a structure of authorities which was being superseded.

In England (outside Greater London) the dissolution of the Hancock Commission under the Local Government (Termination of Reviews) Act 1967 had left still in force the provisions on boundary alterations contained in the LGA 1933, though the looming shadow of general reorganisation inhibited nearly all further *ad hoc* changes. When announcing his final decisions on the Hancock Commission's proposals, the then Minister of Housing and Local Government (Mr Greenwood) reiterated the substance of an earlier departmental circular[17] that proposals for further changes under the 1933 Act would be entertained only if agreed by the local authorities concerned and if the circumstances were special and urgent. In practice boundary changes made after the Hancock Commission were wound up had mostly been minor adjustments to the boundaries of county districts or parishes.

Under the 1933 Act (as amended over the years) county councils could join together or could join with county borough councils in seeking a ministerial order to make an agreed boundary modification and such an order was not subject to any form of parliamentary procedure (section 143 (2)). But a proposal to change a county or county borough boundary which came from only one of the authorities involved went through the more stringent procedure, normally involving a public inquiry and always requiring an affirmative resolution of both Houses (section 140). Similar provisions had been applied in the case of the boundaries of Greater London, the London boroughs and the City.[18]

Boundary alterations affecting county districts and parishes outside Greater London required an order made by the county council, which had to be confirmed by the minister; a public inquiry was needed in certain cases where objections had been lodged, but no parliamentary procedure was involved.

The power of a local authority to seek a change of boundaries or status by means of a private Bill had been suspended for a period of fifteen years when the Hancock Commission had been set up (see p. 74 above) and this suspension remained in force, notwithstanding the Commission's demise.

The procedure for modifying electoral areas also reflected the historical evolution of the local government system. County electoral divisions were amended by order of the Home Secretary, on the application of the county council or a district council; electoral wards in urban districts, rural districts and parishes were modified by the county council without the need for any ministerial confirmation. But in boroughs outside Greater London the procedure required a petition to the queen because the original warding pattern would have been laid down in the charter of incorporation; such petitions were referred to the Home Secretary for investigation (and a public inquiry was normally held) before changes were given effect by Order in Council. The procedure for amending the wards of the London boroughs had been brought more into line with other local authorities, however, by the London Government Act 1963 (part III of schedule 1), so that these applications were made to and dealt with by the Home Secretary.

The provisions applying to boundary alterations in the London Government Act 1963 represented the application of existing procedures to the new situation in London; they did not attempt to break fresh ground. But the introduction of a new structure in the rest of the country clearly required new machinery through which all local government areas could be kept up-to-date. The opportunity presented itself to rationalise the procedure so far as possible, and to take advantage of the lessons learned from the history of the Trustram Eve and Hancock Commissions; and, in the process, to extend any new machinery to include the London authorities as well.

The Redcliffe-Maud Commission had proposed that the main initiative for bringing forward boundary changes should come from within the local government system itself – and not from any outside body. Their report would have put on the provincial councils the duty of proposing any future changes in the pattern of metropolitan or unitary areas; within the metropolitan area the metropolitan authority would have had responsibility for changes affecting metropolitan districts (Cmnd 4040, para. 307).

Mr Senior dissented from the view that the task of keeping the new system up-to-date should be left to the local authorities themselves. He feared that mutual backscratching between authorities would leave any machinery unused and he advocated the establishment of a permanent independent Local Government Commission for this purpose (Cmnd 4040--I, paras 140-4). The Wheatley Commission on Local Government in Scotland made a similar proposal and went further, by suggesting that such a body should have duties with respect to electoral divisions, too (Cmnd 4150, ch. 37).

Boundary Commissions have been appointed from time to time throughout the modern history of local government. It was true that the outcome had not been wholly successful in the case of the Hancock Commission or even partially successful in the case of the Trustram Eve Commission. But that was not the fault of the Commissions themselves; rather it was due to the failure of machinery and policy to complement each other. The idea of a Boundary Commission still had great attractions as the machinery for the future.

In the first place, an independent body would provide a more obviously impartial forum for the consideration of possible boundary changes and, although it would be difficult (as the Crossman Diaries indicate[19]) to remove such matters altogether from the realm of politics, the recommendations of an independent Commission would carry great weight; ministers would need to be very sure of their ground before acting contrary to the proposals of such a body. But this could have advantages for ministers; they would not only be relieved of the task of undertaking the initial investigation of proposals but reliance on the recommendations of the independent Commission would provide a shield (if they chose to use it) against political pressure groups.

Secondly, an independent Commission whose remit covered the whole field of local government would bring that element of uniformity to the consideration of boundary changes which had been absent from the earlier arrangements, when applications were made by individual authorities and decisions were taken *ad·hoc*.

But if the benefit of these advantages was to be fully achieved the new arrangements also needed to profit from past experience in three further ways.

The new arrangements would need to apply over the whole field of local government boundaries, to the exclusion of any other method of boundary alteration. This meant that the embargo on alterations by private Bill (imposed for fifteen years under the LGA 1958 and due to expire in 1973) would have to be made permanent.

In addition the procedures governing the consideration of boundary proposals would need to be as simple and as speedy as possible, with reliance upon informal conferences rather than on the more legalistic proceedings by public inquiry.

Lastly, provision was needed for regular and comprehensive reviews of boundaries. This did not require the removal of a local authority's right to propose boundary alterations at any time if there was an urgent need, but it did imply the recognition that such applications could no longer be relied on to ensure that the pattern of authorities as a whole was kept in line with changing conditions.

Consultations with the local authority associations resulted in a very broad measure of agreement on the machinery later contained in Part IV of the LGA 1972 and the setting up of the Local Government Boundary Commission for England and a parallel Commission for Wales. Both Commissions are small bodies with a statutory limit of seven members in England (including the chairman and deputy chairman) and five in Wales. Commissioners hold part-time appointments and a proportion of them have direct experience of local government as former officers. None of the English Commissioners are drawn from the ranks of members or former members of local authorities – thus avoiding problems of balancing party affiliations. The secretariat of the Commission are civil servants on loan from DOE and the Home Office.

The Commissions are appointed by the secretary of state – a constitutional expression which includes all holders of ministerial office of that name. In practice, and because the Commission's work covers both local government boundaries and electoral matters, appointments to the English Commission are the result of joint agreement between the Secretary of State for the Environment and the Home Secretary, with the former taking the lead as the minister with overall responsibility for the structure and functioning of local government. This responsibility has attached itself, in modern times, successively to the President of the Local Government Board, the Minister of Health, the Minister of Housing and Local Government and the Secretary of State for the Environment. It was formally enunciated in the White Paper *The Reorganisation of Central Government* which, *inter alia*, announced the intention to set up the DOE in 1970 (see Cmnd 4506, para. 31).

The Commissions are advisory not executive bodies. The English Commission's remit is to make recommendations to the Secretary of State for the Environment (on administrative boundaries) and to the Home Secretary (on electoral arrangements); the example of the Trustram Eve Commission, who were themselves responsible for making the necessary orders, was not followed. The responsible minister has the power to accept the Commission's proposals, to accept them with modifications or to reject them. But the government's intention here was clarified by the Minister for Local Government and Development (Mr Page) during the committee stage of the Bill when he said 'if the Commission is to have any credibility it is essential that we have a convention in the House that the Secretary of State accepts the Commission's proposals, unless there is an exceptional reason which he is prepared to justify to the House for refusing to proceed on those proposals' (Commons Hansard, Standing Committee D, 1 February 1972, col. 1204).

The main provisions in this part of the Act deal with comprehensive reviews of local government boundaries, but the requirements are not the same for all classes of authorities.

The Commission are placed under the duty to review the areas of the main authorities at stated intervals of not less than ten and not more than fifteen years from the last review. This requirement applies to the areas of all counties, metropolitan districts, Greater London, the London boroughs and the City of London. In the case of Greater London and the City, the Commission's powers allow them to make recommendations only with regard to boundaries; they cannot propose the abolition of either the GLC or the City (or the Temples). In other areas their powers include not only boundary alterations but also the abolition or creation of new counties, metropolitan districts or London boroughs, and the conversion of a metropolitan county into a non-metropolitan county or vice versa. The Commission are also empowered to review particular boundaries or areas *ad hoc* between the periodic reviews, but are prohibited from proposing the conversion of a non-metropolitan county into a metropolitan one – or vice versa – before the first comprehensive review. This provision was inserted to prevent an immediate revival of claims for metropolitan county status from those areas which had been unsuccessful aspirants while the Bill was before Parliament.

The period of ten to fifteen years for the obligatory reviews of these main areas is the same as that governing the reviews of parliamentary constituencies under the House of Commons (Redistribution of Seats) Acts. The recent history of parliamentary constituencies has some points of similarity with that of local government areas in that, before the Second World War, there was no machinery for regular review. Disparities between constituencies due to population movements led to a major redistribution of seats in 1918, following a Speaker's Conference, but then nothing was done until the build-up of further gross disparities led to the appointment of the Departmental Committee on Electoral Machinery whose report was published in 1942 (Cmd 6408). That Committee recommended the establishment of four standing Boundary Commissions for the regular review of parliamentary constituencies in England, Wales, Scotland and Northern Ireland. The Committee originally recommended that a review of the state of constituencies, coupled with any necessary proposals for redistribution, should be made during the normal life of every Parliament. The House of Commons (Redistribution of Seats) Act 1944 which set up the Parliamentary Boundary Commissions adopted a different formula and required each of the periodic reports to be submitted not less than three and not more than seven years after the last one. Experience suggested that an interval of this size was too short and, under the Redistribution of Seats Act 1958, it was extended to not less than ten and not more than fifteen years. This, it was felt, avoided the upsets and uncertainties of constant change while being not so long as to allow the development of glaring inequalities. For the same reasons the period of ten to fifteen years was adopted for the review of the main local government areas, coupled with the possibility of *ad hoc* reviews of particular areas in between, if necessary.

The Local Government Boundary Commission are also under a duty to keep the pattern of non-metropolitan districts under review but no special intervals are laid down to govern the timetable for this work.

In all these cases the Commission are also required to consider, whenever it is made, any request for changes in respect of particular areas submitted to them from a county or district council or from a London authority and, if they think fit, to formulate proposals and submit them to the secretary of state. But the authorities cannot go to the secretary of state direct.

Parish boundaries are to be reviewed by the district councils, not by the Commission. But the Commission remain firmly in the picture because the outcome of a review of the parish pattern in any district is a report to the Boundary Commission. On the strength of this report the Commission make proposals formally to the secretary of state, but in doing so the Commission may adopt or reject or modify the district council's suggestions, or may do the job over again (section 48 (8) and (9)).

The Act contains provisions on procedure (section 60) which lean significantly towards informality while specifying some essential requirements to ensure that everyone is fully informed as to what is going on. If an area is being reviewed the Commission must consult with all the local authorities affected, with any body representing local authority employees which has asked to be consulted, with such other public bodies who appear to the Commission to be concerned, and with such other persons as the Commission think fit; except in the case of local authorities and staff bodies the extent of the consultation is left to the good sense of the Commission. There is a power to hold public inquiries but no requirement to do so and the implication is that the Commission will proceed by way of informal conference conducted, if necessary, by an Assistant Commissioner on the Commission's behalf. The Commission's draft proposals and their final recommendations have to be publicised by being placed on deposit in local authority offices but publicity beyond this stage is, again, at the Commission's discretion.

The procedural provisions affecting the actions of the secretary of state are similarly simplified. He is empowered, on receipt of a report from the Commission, to implement it as it stands, to implement it with modifications or to reject it. The only requirement here is that he must allow six weeks to elapse so as to allow for representations (section 51 (2)). The requirement to be found in earlier Acts, for public inquiries held by the minister, is significantly absent.

Finally, the provisions affecting ministerial orders are simplified, too, and take another step away from detailed parliamentary supervision. Changes affecting local government administrative areas and boundaries are all to be given effect by order of the secretary of state on the receipt of a report reaching him from the Boundary Commission. In the case of orders affecting only parishes there is no parliamentary procedure (as before); in all other cases orders are subject to negative resolution. In some instances this means that Parliament has an opportunity to object in circumstances which previously did not go to Parliament at all. Orders giving effect to joint applications for boundary changes between two counties or between counties and county boroughs, for instance, were exempt from any form of parliamentary proceedings; under the new arrangements all orders affecting major authorities can be challenged in Parliament. On the other hand, other orders affecting counties and county boroughs were previously subject to affirmative resolution, and each of these had to be voted on by both Houses before coming into effect. Under present arrangements even the most far-reaching order, for example, for the creation of a new metropolitan county, is subject only to negative resolution and would not come up for discussion unless a Member forced a debate by putting down a prayer to annul the order.

It was upon this question of the creation of further metropolitan counties that some differences were recorded during the initial consultations with the local authority associations. The CCA took the view that such a development, which would have repercussions for the allocation of functions as well as for areas, would be so important that it should be made only by special legislation. As the CCA saw it, the order-making procedure would not be appropriate – possibly (one suspects) because they thought a new metropolitan county might more easily be created by order than by Bill. The AMC, fearing the opposite, would have preferred to retain the right of local authorities to promote private Bills (a right permanently abolished by section 70 of the Act) so that groups of authorities could, in the last resort, seek metropolitan status in this way.

It was a feature of the Trustram Eve and Hancock Commissions that they operated within guidelines laid down in ministerial regulations, both as regards substance and procedure. Inherent in the whole concept of an independent commission is the need for the body in question to be given terms of reference – notwithstanding the difficulty of drafting these in the field of local government. Section 52 of the 1972 Act therefore contains general powers for the secretary of state to give directions about reviews. These may affect the order in which particular areas are reviewed by the

Commission, so that the consideration of any particular area is given priority or is deferred. Or directions may lay down criteria to be taken into account either by the Commission or (in the case of the parish reviews) by district councils. Guidelines of this kind were not a matter of urgency on the passing of the Bill because the first need was for a period of stability while the new authorities established themselves. Partly for this reason proposals for adjustments of county and district boundaries were discouraged, but partly also because the Commission had a separate priority task laid on them by the Act – to review the electoral areas within the new local authorities as, in most cases, these authorities had come into being on the basis of wards devised at short notice for the first elections (see pp. 206-8 below). This work pre-empted the capacity of the Commission in its early years. The review of the parish pattern and some local adjustments to principal areas received attention in the late 1970s but the question of guidelines for the first major reviews of authorities (between 1984 and 1989) is for the future.

## FUNCTIONS: THE SCOPE OF LOCAL GOVERNMENT

It is not intended, in a study of the machinery of change, to look at individual functions in detail, but structure and functions are so closely linked that the main decisions must cover both. Some functional considerations have already been referred to – the difficulty of defining a single pattern of areas suitable for all local government services, the linking of related services in the environmental and the personal groups, the need to combine town and country in the administration of the former group and the population requirements of the latter. These were among the basic considerations which shaped the new structure; central decisions affecting functions involved many other matters, too, including the allocation of functions in a two-tier system, working arrangements for the discharge of functions, and indeed the whole scope of local government.

'By reducing the number of units and creating a new framework of areas, we shall emerge with a pattern of stronger authorities which will be more effective in terms of resources and organisation. Our purpose in this context will be to increase the responsibilities of local authorities not to reduce them.' This declaration by the then Prime Minister (Mr Heath) in 1971[20] can be matched by many other ministerial statements of hope or intent. But disappointment awaited anyone who expected that the reorganisation of local government, either in Greater London or in the rest of the country, would be accompanied by the transfer to the new authorities of some major service comparable to the transfer to local authorities of (say) the functions of the School Boards in 1902 or the Guardians in 1929. Indeed, the terms of reference of both the Royal

Commissions clearly indicated that their proposals should be related to the administration of functions for which local authorities were currently responsible. The Herbert Commission were debarred from looking at either police or water, while the attention of the Redcliffe-Maud Commission was directed to the *existing* functions of local government.

This approach naturally attracted criticism. If local government was to be reformed and strengthened, so that its functions could be extended, the logical move would be to define its wider responsibilities and shape the new structure accordingly; to look forward not back.

But central governments do not usually work so boldly, and would have argued, in this situation, that the practical problems of reorganisation to meet the present and expected needs of existing functions were sufficiently difficult without asking new authorities to take on extra responsibilities at the same time.

Moreover the organisation of government departments militated against such a comprehensive approach to public services. Within central government (as the Herbert Commission had noted - see pp. 93-4 above) responsibility for each of the major services is in the hands of a department whose chief concern is normally to promote the efficient provision of that particular service; in many cases those departments are dealing with other agencies and other forms of administration besides local authorities; only DOE - or more strictly only the Local Government Directorate within DOE - is primarily concerned with the overall operation of the local government system, as distinct from individual services.

Against this background, when the future of a particular service comes up for consideration within central government the initiative lies with the department or (within DOE) with the directorate responsible for the function in question, to whom the general health of local government is only one among many considerations - and then probably not high on the list.

The reorganisation of London government could not itself affect the responsibility for services throughout the country but it might have been the opportunity for the GLC to take over functions which, for historical reasons, had been treated differently in the metropolis from elsewhere. Police was the obvious example, but there was never any intention to alter the old-established position of the Home Secretary as police authority for Greater London.

On the other hand the establishment of the GLC made it possible, a few years later, to give the new authority wider responsibilities for overall transport planning[21] and for the services provided by the London Transport Executive. Under the Transport (London) Act 1969, which made a very rare transfer of a nationalised undertaking to local government, the GLC were made responsible for appointing members of the London Transport Executive and given powers of direction over the Executive, but not day-to-day control. The relationship between the Executive and the GLC is broadly similar to that previously existing between the London Transport Board and the Minister of Transport and to that now existing between the passenger transport authorities and the passenger transport executives in the metropolitan counties (under Part II of the Transport Act 1968 and section 202, LGA 1972).

When local government was being reorganised in the rest of the country the discussion on the scope of local government, far from contemplating its extension, was concentrated on transferring functions away from local government in connection with the personal health services and water. In each case the separate reorganisation of these functions was principally governed by considerations regarded as special to the services in question, and arguments in favour of the retention or extension of local government responsibilities in these fields were outweighed by others.

In the case of the NHS there was a strong prima facie case for involving the local community (through its elected representatives) more closely in the running of the health services, not less. Many of these services had been pioneered by local authorities; some were still local authority functions; health, welfare, the children's service and education were all personal services which concerned individuals and clearly fell within the purpose of local government as defined by the Redcliffe-Maud Commission 'to provide a democratic means both of focusing national attention on local problems affecting the safety, health and well-being of the people, and of discharging, in relation to these things, all responsibilities of government which can be discharged at a level below that of the national government' (Cmnd 4040, para. 30).

As against these general considerations, however, was the hard fact that the costs of the NHS had trebled since 1948 and that nine-tenths of the cost was directly provided by the Exchequer. It would have been quite impracticable for local government to have contributed more towards the financing of the health services from existing sources of revenue, and the central government took the view that it was equally impossible to hand over management of the enormous sums of Exchequer-provided finance to elected authorities. The medical profession, over the years, have also shown themselves hostile to the idea of management decisions in the health service resting with elected members.

The Redcliffe-Maud Commission attempted to meet arguments on both scores by suggesting a special structure within the local government system, akin to that introduced by the Passenger Transport Act 1968. Elected members on the passenger transport authorities are responsible for general policy decisions, while the day-to-day operational decisions are left in the hands of the professionals. But this solution did not commend itself either to the Labour Party, when in office, or to their successors; both White Papers on local government reorganisation came down against a local government solution (Cmnd 4276, paras 26-7 and Cmnd 4584, para. 27).

The National Health Service Reorganisation Act 1973, promoted by the Conservative government, had much in common with the measure fore-shadowed by the Labour government's Green Paper of 1970, *The Future Structure of the National Health Service.*

In the field of water services the considerations were different. Water supplies and sewerage and sewage disposal were old-established local government functions which (except where water companies operated) were still the responsibility of local authorities or joint boards of local authorities. Moreover, they were closely associated with other local government engineering services and with the public health and environ-mental services of local authorities. On the other hand, several develop-ments were raising problems which indicated that water services could no longer be administered satisfactorily within local government boundaries. Water consumption, for domestic and industrial use, had been rising steadily for many years and was placing increasing strains on water resources. These demands were sure to increase further. Industrial wastes, now more often discharged into the sewerage system instead of directly to rivers or the sea, were frequently more difficult to treat. Most water, when used, finds its way back to rivers as effluent, and much is abstracted and used again. A substantial degree of separation had taken place between water supplies (largely in the hands of joint boards and water companies) and sewerage (which remained in the hands of individual county borough and county district councils). While the provision of water supplies and the treatment of effluents were in different hands there were frequent clashes of interest; these conflicts could ultimately be resolved only if all aspects of water services (including water conservation, land drainage, fisheries and navigation) were under the same authority and based on the main river basins, which are the natural units for this purpose.

Although these trends had been discernible for many years there was no question, when the Herbert Commission were appointed, of removing water services from the local government field. It was true that water (in the sense of water supplies - not the whole range of water services) had been excluded from their terms of reference, but this in no way indicated an intention at that time of removing the function from local government. Indeed at one stage, when the London Government Bill was in preparation, the government proposed to dissolve the indirectly elected Metropolitan Water Board and transfer its functions to the directly elected GLC - a proposal which had to be dropped for reasons that are referred to later (see pp. 191-2 below).

Nor, when the Redcliffe-Maud Commission were established, was the drastic reorganisation of water services immediately contemplated; MHLG evidence to the Commission, which was compiled only a comparatively short time after the organisational changes introduced by the Water Resources Act 1963, treated both water supplies and sewerage as continuing local government functions. Indeed the ministry's evidence stressed the desirability of water distribution being in the hands of the same authorities as those responsible for planning the location of new houses and factories, and of sewerage remaining in the hands of the authorities responsible for housing.

But, as already mentioned (p. 125 above), the Labour government had come round to the view, even while the Redcliffe-Maud Commission were sitting, that this earlier assumption could be incorrect and that the whole administration of water services ought to be looked at again. After the Commission's report was published, therefore, the Central Advisory Water Committee were asked to review the future organisation of all water services 'in the light of the report of the Royal Commission on Local Government in England and of technological and other developments'.

The CAWC reported unanimously in favour of establishing a small number of Regional Water Authorities for areas based on river basins; such authorities would be responsible for the planning and co-ordination of all water services in their region. But the Committee were divided on the question whether such authorities should actually take over the executive functions of the existing river authorities, water undertakers and sewerage authorities or whether these bodies should remain responsible for their various services while working within the framework of plans drawn up by the Regional Water Authorities. The CAWC made no recommendation on the ultimate role of the regional water authorities but set out the arguments which they thought the government should take into account in reaching a decision.

Notwithstanding the evidence given to the Redcliffe-Maud Commission on the links between water services and local government functions, and also the avowed object of local government reorganisation to create stronger local authorities, the Conservative government (who promoted the Water Act 1973) came down in favour of concentrating executive functions as far as possible in the RWAs and taking all water, and nearly all sewerage,[22] functions away from local government.

The ultimate outcome, therefore, was that local government reorganisation was the occasion for the loss of local authority functions in connection with both health and water, and responsibility for these services was transferred to bodies – the Area Health Authorities and the Regional Water Authorities – which, although they contained a proportion of elected members from local authorities, were chiefly composed of ministerial appointees and persons representing special aspects, for example, the medical professions on the AHAs.

It is very likely that these developments would have taken place at some stage whether or not local government had been reorganised, in which case it was sensible to make the changes at the same time as reorganisation, rather than subject these services to a double upheaval. No doubt, too, there are powerful arguments in favour of the type of organisation then thought right in each case. But the turn of events did nothing to counter the conclusion that, when individual services are under consideration, those within central government who are responsible for such services prefer to seek efficiency through 'managerial' bodies composed of appointed members rather than try to reverse the centralising trends already referred to by extending the part to be played by elected local authorities. For this reason responsibility at the centre for the general health of the local government system needs to be entrusted to a senior minister with firm convictions of his own and of sufficient weight to influence his colleagues.

## FUNCTIONS: THE ALLOCATION BETWEEN TIERS

The adoption of a two-tier structure for local government is based on the proposition that some functions require wider areas of administration while others are better organised on a more local basis; and that the advantages of having separate elected authorities at two levels, with areas more closely related to the functional requirements of services, on balance outweigh the administrative advantages of unified management in a single pattern of areas which might be too big for some services but too small for others.

The earlier pages of this study have brought out the functional requirements of main services which shaped both the decision in favour of two tiers instead of unitary authorities, and also the general size of the authorities at each level. From the first, both in Greater London and the rest of the country, there were some essential points on the allocation of existing local government functions which (given the type of structure to be established) commanded very general acceptance.

The main decisions on planning, highways and traffic must clearly be for the GLC and the counties; the inadequacy of the earlier local government arrangements in these fields were among the main reasons why reorganisation was being tackled at all. The fire service and (outside London) police were also unquestionably appropriate to the wider rather than the more local units. Next: education and the personal social services needed authorities with a substantial population base, though this did not necessarily point to its allocation to the counties or to the GLC. On the other hand the main housing function and a group of environmental health services normally figured among the functions deemed appropriate to the second-tier authorities.

But while these were the generally agreed essentials of the functional arrangements, a great variety of detailed decisions were needed both as regards the main services themselves (especially if there was any question of their being split between the two levels) and also the less spectacular functions. It is not proposed to catalogue what conclusions were reached in each case, but rather to mention some of the considerations and some of the problems which influenced the final package of functions at each level.

The Herbert Commission had recommended that the primary units of local government in Greater London should be the London boroughs, who should perform all local authority functions 'except those which can only be effectively performed over the wider area of Greater London or which could be better performed over that wider area' (Cmnd 1164, para. 743 (1)). But it is difficult to prove by statistics that size has a very important effect on performance – as the Redcliffe-Maud Commission noted in reviewing the outcome of their research programme (Cmnd 4040, para. 217). Arguments about the allocation of functions (or aspects of functions) for the first or second tier were therefore not always clear cut.

The professionals (not least those in government departments) who are engaged in the administration of particular services will usually see merits in bigger, rather than smaller, units of administration, and in the allocation of functions to counties rather than to districts. The wider area and the greater resources of the bigger authority (it is argued) offer advantages to the community, who will get a higher standard of service through an organisation better equipped to meet the needs of the public, to provide specialised facilities and to attract high-calibre officers. The suggested allocation of functions as between first- and second-tier authorities set out in the MHLG written evidence to the Redcliffe-Maud Commission reflected the strong appeal of this approach, and prompted the chairman's comment during the department's oral evidence that the functions left over for second-tier authorities were 'not very thrilling' and included no essential parts of the major functions.[23]

Against this leaning towards the top tier there had to be balanced a variety of pronouncements declaring that the inclination should be in the opposite direction on the grounds that, in principle, decisions in a democratic society should be taken as far as possible by the people most closely affected. 'In the government's view' (said the Conservative White Paper) 'there will always be conflicts between those who argue for large scale organisation on grounds of efficiency and those, on the other hand, who argue for control by a body close to the people for whom the service is designed. The government must obviously seek efficiency, but where the arguments are evenly balanced their judgment will be given in favour of responsibility being exercised at the more local level' (Cmnd 4584, para. 13). These final words closely echoed the Redcliffe-Maud Commission when discussing the distribution of functions in metropolitan areas, and the Herbert Commission on the need to restore the health of local government (Cmnd 4040, para. 345 and Cmnd 1164, para. 747). In practice these general attitudes were often overlaid and obscured by other more urgently practical considerations.

The desirability of linking certain groups of services together has already been mentioned - education and the personal social services (that is, those studied by the Seebohm Committee) and also planning, highways, traffic and public transport. Similar arguments were adduced to link (for example) the youth employment and the library services with education, while housing has been linked both to the personal group of services and also to planning.

The advantages to be gained by linkages in such cases are based on the interests of the public as consumer. The planning and location of development is so clearly associated with communications (and with water supply and sewerage services - argued the MHLG in their evidence to Redcliffe-Maud) that the right decisions are most likely to be taken when responsibility for all these functions is concentrated in one authority. Similarly, family needs for social services and support take a number of forms which are related to each other; housing, health, welfare, education and employment are often interdependent, and as far as possible services should be provided by the same, and not by different, authorities. But again such arguments, although they were among those taken into consideration, were not always followed. The Labour government's White Paper proposed to separate education from the personal social services in the metropolitan areas and, when in opposition, Labour Party spokesmen proposed amendments to the Local Government Bill which would have had the same effect; the previous Conservative government in fact separated these services in inner London. The LGA 1972 associated library functions with education in the hands of county councils in England, but allowed the possibility of some Welsh districts being designated as separate library authorities (section 207 (2)).

The Local Government Bill also provided that, while functions under the legislation dealing with food & drugs and weights & measures should be county functions in England and (generally) in Wales, individual Welsh districts could be designated by order, in which case they became district functions (sections 198 (3) and 201 (3)). Amendments to achieve a similar result in England were moved during the committee stage of the Bill in the Commons and were resisted, not only on the grounds that both these services had become more specialised since they had been allocated to the London boroughs on the reorganisation of London government, but also because such an arrangement would detract from county responsibilities for these services. The special provisions affecting Wales were a historical survival of the local government proposals which had remained under discussion with the Welsh authorities since the publication of the report of the Local Government Commission for Wales in 1962. But in England the principle had been followed that legal responsibility for each service, or for a defined part of a service, should be placed clearly and wholly with one class of authority or another. It would be open to any responsible authority to make arrangements with another authority (see p. 183 below) for the exercise of any particular function – and this possibility was frequently stressed by ministers during the Bill's progress – but the government resisted all attempts in England to make the bigger non-metropolitan districts statutorily responsible for a wider range of functions than the smaller ones.

There were several obvious reasons for this. First, it would undermine the attempt to simplify and define where the ultimate statutory responsibility lay for each service – an attempt which also aimed to abolish the complications of the former system in which functions could be exercised as of right, or claimed by delegation, by county districts with populations at various statutorily defined levels. Secondly, to accept the claims of big districts to exercise specified functions in connection with (say) planning, education or the personal social services, would have gone a long way towards creating two types of districts and re-creating the situation in which county councils were excluded from exercising functions in those enclaves formerly represented by the county boroughs. Thirdly, there would have been the problem of defining the point at which separate functions should be exercised by the 'excepted districts', with the danger of pressures to reduce the entry point (and hence to increase the number of excepted districts) as had been evidenced in 1888 in the pressure to reduce the qualifying population for county borough status. Lastly, whatever settlement was reached on reorganisation, the way would have been opened for continual agitation in the future to extend both the number of excepted districts and the functions they would exercise, and thus to plant the seeds of continuing uncertainty and dissatisfaction.

A further set of problems arose when it was proposed that a particular service should be split, so that defined aspects were allocated to one tier and the rest to the other. The proposals of the Herbert Commission regarding education in Greater London have already been referred to, and also their rejection (see p. 97 above). The division of a function obviously raises difficulties both in initial definition (where to draw the line between the county and the district responsibilities) and in subsequent operations. There is the danger – perhaps even the certainty – of some degree of friction and duplication; and this can also arise in connection with functions exercised concurrently at both levels – though the concurrent functions, for example, those connected with amenities and recreation, are, by their nature, less likely to cause controversy.

But some services – and planning and highways are prominent in this category – have aspects which range from major issues of county (or even regional) significance, down to the smallest detail of an individual planning permission or the lighting of a country road – issues which may be of intense local interest but are of no significance elsewhere. The development of these two major functions has always reflected both wider and more local interests and, although unwelcome to the professionals, they remained divided between the tiers after reorganisation. Indeed it was partly to admit of such matters being administered at more than one level that the two-tier system was adopted. In the case of planning the main structure plan remains with the GLC and the county councils, together with the determination of certain major planning applications, while local plans and most planning applications are handled by the London boroughs and the districts. In the highways field the statutory role of the districts outside Greater London is much less than it used to be, when non-county boroughs and urban districts were highway authorities for non-county roads and could also 'claim' to maintain and improve county roads if their populations exceeded 20,000. Under the LGA 1972 both metropolitan and non-metropolitan districts may claim a share of the highways function, but only to the extent of carrying out maintenance work in relation to unclassified roads in urban areas.

Attempts to introduce a simple and logical pattern of functions were further complicated by the need to take account of the way in which functions were exercised immediately prior to reorganisation, and to avoid dislocating services. 'The new local government pattern should so far as practicable stem from the existing one. Wherever the case for change is in doubt, the common interests, traditions and loyalties inherent in the present pattern, and the strength of existing services as going concerns, should be respected' (Cmnd 4040, para. 9 (x)). The Redcliffe-Maud Commission may have had boundaries particularly in mind in this, the last of their general principles, but the concept of functions as 'going concerns' had a not inconsiderable influence. In Greater London, for instance, the LCC education service survived under the Inner London Education Authority (though the LCC health & welfare and children's services did not) and the GLC inherited the functions of the LCC in connection with housing, parks and open spaces, and the main drainage functions of the London and Middlesex County Councils – all special to Greater London. In the rest of the country, while the main decisions led to the transfer of major functions and their staffs from county boroughs to the new county councils (in connection with education, the personal social services, the fire service, libraries and other functions), nevertheless the teams of officers built up by county boroughs and county districts in the exercise of planning and highways functions (for example) had a substantial influence on the agency arrangements which are referred to below (see pp. 185–6).

Finally in the catalogue of considerations which affected the allocation of functions was one which stood at the very heart of the concept of a viable system of local democracy. It was set out by the Onslow Commission in their Second Report, on the reorganisation of county districts: 'Efficient administration depends not only on area but also on there being assigned to each unit functions of such variety and importance as will ensure local interest, and secure as members of local authorities persons best fitted to render service' (Cmd 3213, para. 41).

This implies, first, that each level of authorities should be involved in a range of functions in a way which permits members to take decisions and to be responsible for their effective implementation. Naturally there will be limitations, both financial and administrative - these affect all local authorities from counties down to parishes - but within these limitations a council should be able to exercise real responsibility. It should have powers of disposal over its own revenues, and a sufficient range of functions to support an organisation through which action can be taken - a point which is particularly relevant in the maintenance of a technical services department. Secondly, it implies that for democratic reasons - to ensure the maintenance of public interest and to attract members and officers - it may be desirable, within reason, to allocate functions to a class of authority notwithstanding that such functions might be equally well or better administered at a different level. Some doubts were expressed about the credibility of functions allocated to the metropolitan county councils but generally, of course, it was on the range of functions at non-metropolitan district level that the sceptical eye was fixed. Powerful pressures constantly urged the desirability of larger units and/or the concentration of responsibilities in county hands; but would the residue of functions, which formed the district package, sustain either viable democracy or efficient administration at that level?

There was no way in which this question could be answered in advance by reference to scientific data. Essentially it required political decisions by ministers in balancing the great variety of considerations urged upon them from all directions. Naturally the outcome was criticised by those who were rooted in the previous system or by those who, for professional reasons or on grounds of abstract logic, would have preferred their own solution. The two-tier structure necessarily meant that a practical solution had to be sought to the problem of functions - and one which could not be perfect.


## WORKING ARRANGEMENTS FOR THE DISCHARGE OF FUNCTIONS

The statutory provisions governing the way in which local authorities discharge their functions have varied over the years, and because many of them have emerged piecemeal according to the alleged needs of particular services they have presented a confused and contradictory picture. A frequent device of governments wishing to emphasise the importance of an existing service, or to encourage an emerging one, was to lay upon the responsible authority the requirement to appoint a committee solely to deal with that service and/or to create a statutory post for the chief officer. Such arrangements were condemned by the Maud Committee on Management who recommended that authorities should be trusted to arrange their own internal organisation free from imposed requirements of this kind. [24]

Whereas the London Government Act had deliberately made no attempt to alter the general provisions affecting authorities throughout the country, the 1972 Act clearly offered the opportunity for implementing the Management Committee's recommendations. It was also the occasion for reviewing the working arrangements between authorities and the ways in which they might co-operate with each other in the discharge of functions. These two aspects of functional arrangements were given very prolonged study within government circles.

As regards the provisions affecting a local authority's internal organisation, some progress was made towards abandoning the requirements for particular statutory committees, for example, in connection with finance (which curiously enough applied only to county councils), health, allotments, diseases of animals and youth employment. But they were retained in a number of other cases (listed in section 101 (9) of the Act), either because the committees were governed by special provisions affecting their composition (for example, police, sea fisheries and national parks), or because pressures behind particular services were too strong for the government to abandon requirements which were regarded as safeguards (especially education and the personal social services).

Subject to these requirements, however, authorities were given revised and wider powers to set up such committees and sub-committees as they thought necessary, and to arrange for the discharge of any of their functions by such committee or sub-committee or (a new general power) by an officer.

The operative section of the Act, section 101, also allowed an authority to arrange for the discharge of its functions by another local authority - a provision vitally important to the arrangements in the Bill affecting the distribution of functions and relations between authorities.

Basic to the government's approach to functions was the aim to place clear statutory responsibility for each major service with either the counties or the districts, so that there should be no doubt as to where the ultimate responsibility lay for the quality and nature of the service provided, for overall policy and for finance. But this ultimate responsibility did not mean that the statutory authority must itself discharge every aspect of the service. Different services have different operational requirements and so the Act also provided an array of powers by joint action which would allow authorities to co-operate in any way which suited the needs of the area and the requirements of the services. They could establish joint committees, establish consortia, set up joint teams of officers, lend staff or supply goods and services as between authorities. In addition, under section 101, one authority could exercise a function or an aspect of a function on behalf of another.

Delegation is an essential part of day-to-day business in local government, and most decisions are taken by committees, sub-committees or officers acting under delegated powers. But delegation from one authority to another had become an unpopular concept, partly because it was associated with arrangements that were too formal and legalistic, and even more because it had become identified with the contest for power between the county councils and the bigger districts – as a result of which the latter had gained the statutory power to claim to exercise delegated functions in connection with planning, education and health. These arrangements led to a degree of division of responsibility for the service, and a good deal of friction in their operation.

While it is impossible to legislate for harmonious relations the government at least attempted to avoid a division of statutory responsibility, and to get away from the old phraseology. Hence the word 'delegation' is absent from the Local Government Act, which speaks instead of an authority's power to 'arrange for the discharge of their functions' when granting a wide and flexible power for authorities to agree between themselves on such working arrangements as seem suitable. The width of this power, to make what became known as 'agency arrangements', does not derogate from the statutory responsibility of the principal authority who alone are entitled to borrow money or to levy a rate in respect of the function (section 101 (6)); but agency arrangements are excluded in the case of those functions for which statutory committees still had to be appointed – notably education and the personal social services (section 101 (10)).

There were general reasons why agency arrangements would be appropriate in many of the other services. In the first place such an arrangement could help the efficient operation of a service. A specialist team of officers employed by the county council might make it convenient for the county to act as agents for the districts in some aspects of district services. Or, in the reverse direction, the county council might find it best to use the district council's organisation and the local knowledge of district members and officers in the administration of county services. Secondly, there could be managerial and staffing advantages if agency arrangements led to the exercise of related functions being concentrated in the hands of one authority. If, for example, the package of activities in the hands of the districts was extended by agency arrangements it might permit the employment of a stronger team of officers than would otherwise be the case; benefits would then be felt by all the functions exercised by that authority, and not only those subject to the agency arrangements. Thirdly, during the transitional stage of reorganisation, there was the special need to avoid unnecessary dislocation of staff and property and to make the best use of existing experience in the local administration of services.

The long-term aim of the Local Government Bill was to leave all agency arrangements to be worked out entirely by agreement between the authorities concerned - who would need to settle between themselves what functions should be involved, the degree of discretion to be exercised by the agent authority, by whom the necessary staff should be employed, the duration of the agreement and arrangements for its variation. The transitional problems led to this objective being modified, but only in a limited fashion, and in relation to the changeover on 1 April 1974.

The Act provided for the transfer to county councils of a number of functions which had previously been exercised by county district councils, for example, highways, refuse disposal, libraries, and functions connected with consumer protection such as weights & measures and food & drugs. It was a matter of urgent importance to the officers employed on these functions by the old authorities, and also to the members of the new district councils who had to settle their management structure in time for the appointed day, to know whether agency arrangements were to operate in these fields. They feared that the new county councils would be reluctant to enter into such arrangements and, if agency arrangements were to rest wholly on the agreement of both sides, then there was no way of coercing them.

This situation, and the anxieties at district level, prompted some very widely supported proposals which were discussed at report stage in the Commons (Commons Hansard, 17 July 1972, cols 244-65). These would have given a right of appeal to the secretary of state in the case of new authorities whose predecessors had discharged functions now allocated to the counties; if the secretary of state was satisfied that the district council had adequate staff and resources, he could direct the county council to enter into agency arrangements under which the district council would continue to operate the transferred functions. Accepting that there was a real problem, the government later introduced the clause which became section 110 giving a right of appeal - but one essentially connected with the transition to the new system and the need to reassure councils and officers at district level that they would get a fair deal in settling the operational arrangements which were to take effect as from the appointed day. The whole question of agency arrangements was the subject of a lengthy circular which, in the light of consultations with the local authority associations, gave advice on the potentialities for agency arrangements in connection with the former district functions mentioned above and set out details of the right of appeal.[25]

This was not a departure from the long-term aim - that agency arrangements between authorities should be entirely a matter for mutual agreement without central intervention. The responsible minister, if appealed to by a local authority seeking agency arrangements, could direct that such arrangements be entered into and (if necessary) he could dictate the terms of the arrangements too. The direction must be given before 1 April 1974, however, and it operated for not more than five years; it was not a permanent provision but one aimed solely at easing the transition to a new system. After then a new situation would arise.

This right of appeal in respect of agency arrangements was given to all new counties and districts, though in practice (as expected) it was exercised only by districts. The biggest single group of appeals was in respect of highways functions. Only a handful of directions were in fact given (which were not all in favour of district councils); in other instances appeals were withdrawn because agreement had been reached; and in yet other cases the possibility that a district council might appeal would no doubt have assisted the county council to reach an agreed solution.

## NOTES: CHAPTER 6

1    Commons Hansard, 24 January 1963, col. 423.
2    Commons Hansard, 13 February 1963, col. 1360 and Lords Hansard, 13 May 1963, col. 1141.
3    Lords Hansard, 14 May 1963, col. 1211.
4    Since reorganisation that part of the Victoria Embankment which was formerly within the Temples has been included in the City (by the London Government Order 1970, SI 1970 No. 211, article 12).
5    The Temples Order 1971, SI 1971 No. 1732.
6    Research Appendix No. 8 in Vol. III of the Commission's Report, Cmnd 4040 – II.
7    Redcliffe-Maud Commission Written Evidence: Memorandum by the NAPC, para. 3.
8    AMC and NAPC Joint Memorandum *Parish Councils in Urban Areas*, July 1961. But the AMC did not go so far as to embrace the possibility of establishing parish councils in parts of towns which were already boroughs – a process which 'might encourage separatist tendencies'.
9    LGA 1972, section 27. The 'excepted boroughs' were the four county boroughs in Wales and the two biggest non-county boroughs, i.e. Cardiff, Merthyr Tydfil, Newport, Port Talbot, Rhondda and Swansea. Each of these accounted for more than 80 per cent of the population of their respective districts.
10   The guidelines are printed in full in the Commission's Report No. 3.
11   Local Government Boundary Commission for England, Reports Nos. 3, 5 and 8; The Local Government (Successor Parishes) Orders 1973 and 1974, SI 1973 No. 1110, SI 1973 No. 1939 and SI 1974 No. 569.
12   Royal Commission on Local Government in England, Research Study No. 9, *Community Attitudes Survey: England* (HMSO, 1969).
13   Sir Arthur Conan Doyle had created a county of Hallamshire, too, some sixty years earlier; the lord-lieutenant of that county had a brush with Sherlock Holmes in *The Adventure of the Priory School*.
14   Consultation paper, 7 April 1971, on borough status, civic dignities and the office of alderman.
15   The office of alderman was also abolished from the London borough councils and the GLC – but not from the City of London (where alderman are directly elected).

16 LGA 1972, section 246 (4); The Charter Trustees Order 1974, SI 1974 No. 176; DOE circular No. 20/74, 20 February 1974. The charter trustee provisions were developed from suggestions originally put forward by Mr R. H. McCall (Secretary of the AMC and formerly Town Clerk of Winchester).

17 MHLG circular No. 35/66, 27 June 1966.

18 London Government Act 1963, section 6. But the Temples were left in a special position; their boundaries could be altered only as a result of a joint application to which they were a party – they could not be altered on an application made solely by the City or by a London borough.

19 In a number of entries Mr Crossman recorded the extent to which he was influenced by political considerations when, as Minister of Housing and Local Government, he was faced with boundary proposals affecting, e.g., Coventry, Leicester, Northampton, Nottingham, Bath and Plymouth (Richard Crossman, *Diaries of a Cabinet Minister*, Vol. 1, London: Hamilton and Cape, 1975).

20 Addressing the Annual Conference of NALGO at Douglas, IOM, 25 June 1971.

21 See the White Paper *Transport in London*, Cmnd 3686, July 1965. Under section 10 of the London Government Act 1963 the GLC were also given the power to make traffic control orders – a power previously vested in the Minister of Transport.

22 District councils, the London borough councils and the City may provide and maintain sewers on behalf of the water authorities under arrangements governed by section 15 of the Water Act 1973.

23 Redcliffe-Maud Commission Oral Evidence, 14 March 1967, Q. 679 (MHLG).

24 Report of the Committee, paras 203–4.

25 DOE circular No. 131/72, 19 December 1972.

## Chapter 7

# The Legislative Stage

## GETTING THE BILLS DRAFTED

Reports in newspapers regularly allege that such-and-such minister is personally engaged on drafting a particular Bill and, by implication, that the Bill must be of special importance to receive such distinguished treatment. No such event occurs in real life. Save for provisions applying to Scotland[1] government Bills are drafted by counsel of the Office of Parliamentary Counsel on the basis of instructions prepared within the responsible department and transmitted by the department's legal staff. In most cases a Bill is the entire responsibility of a senior draftsman working with a junior colleague. Because the London Government Bill and (even more so) the Local Government Bill were long and complicated measures, additional draftsmen were involved but, even so, the drafting team never exceeded two senior counsel, with the same number of assistants, on either Bill.

The help obtained by departments from parliamentary counsel extends beyond the drafting of the Bill itself; counsel also draft all new clauses and amendments tabled by the government and advise on the wording of other amendments; they maintain contact with the officials of the two Houses, advise on parliamentary procedure and draft all motions affecting the Bill; in addition they attend (as necessary) the actual sittings of the Houses or of their committees when the Bill is being considered in committee or on report. Parliamentary counsel are without doubt among the most skilled and hard-worked operatives in Whitehall. Had it been otherwise, neither of these two Bills could have been ready within the government's timetable.

Government Bills are usually prepared under great pressure because ministerial decisions on the timing and final contents of legislation are rarely taken until the last minute. Both in the case of London government and of the subsequent general reorganisation, the essential decision to proceed with legislation was contained in a White Paper published in one session and announcing the intention to introduce legislation in the next - which meant, in effect, at the beginning of the next session. During a period of eight or, at most, ten months ministers had to take the further decisions of the kind described in the preceding chapter; these decisions had to be translated into instructions to counsel, who then had to turn them into draft clauses. Moreover, because parliamentary counsel are always engaged on Bills of the current session, they rarely have time until about the spring in any year to turn their attention to the Bills which will be introduced in the autumn.

Not uncommonly - and it certainly happened in the case of the two major local government Bills - instructions have to be delivered in instalments because there is no time for the document (and it will ultimately run into hundreds of pages) to be completed before counsel is ready to start work. In such circumstances the important task is to deliver, on time, a first instalment which will give the draftsman an outline of the whole operation so that he can plan the shape of the ultimate Bill.

In the case of the London Government Bill and the Local Government Bill this meant that the instructions on the structure of authorities had to be ready first, so that the functions which would be exercised by the new bodies could be logically dealt with as drafting proceeded. Within government circles a severe organisational problem had to be solved by MHLG/ DOE (in conjunction with the Welsh Office on the Local Government Bill 1971/2), as the department primarily responsible, because so many other ministries were also involved. These had to be cajoled or browbeaten into providing instructions on their particular services (together with details of all the existing legislation in force and the amendments needed) in time, and in the right order.

Within the pressures which shape the timetable of government business, it is usually impossible for a big Bill to be as complete on introduction as its sponsors would wish. It is expanded and elaborated during its progress through Parliament to take account of new policy decisions (the clauses on audit, for instance, were redrafted four times during the progress of the Local Government Bill 1971/2), matters which were omitted (because of lack of time) from the Bill as introduced, or to pick up drafting refinements - especially the consequential amendment or repeal of other legislation. As a result, the London Government Bill was lengthened by some thirty pages during its parliamentary consideration and the Local Government Bill by a hundred pages. The Local Government Bill, in the end, became the longest current Bill (that is, as distinct from consolidation) ever to reach the statute book. The length and complexity of both Bills caused constant anxiety as to whether too severe a strain was being placed on drafting resources and procedures.

The London Government Bill was in fact slightly shorter than it might have been because the provisions on non-administrative aspects - lieutenants, sheriffs, commissions of the peace, and so on - were held over for inclusion in legislation to be promoted the following session (the Administration of Justice Act 1964). In 1971 it had been intended that the reorganisation Bill should also establish the local government Ombudsman but, although this proposal was announced in the White Paper

(Cmnd 4584, para. 52), it was crowded out and had to be enacted later as Part III of the Local Government Act 1974.

The original proposal in 1971/2 was, for political reasons, to promote two Bills, one for local government reorganisation in England and another for Wales – though with the same draftsmen responsible for both. A great many provisions would of course have been common to both Bills and another possible approach (also mooted) was to have three Bills – one for the aspects special to England, one for matters special to Wales and one to contain provisions common to both. These possibilities faded before the practical problems of including the necessary provisions within one Bill, quite apart from spreading them over two or three. Given unlimited time it would frequently be desirable, no doubt, to split up big Bills into more manageable portions, but this course would almost certainly take up additional parliamentary time, and the prospect of legislating by instalments – possibly over two or even three sessions – is normally ruled out by the reluctance of governments to pre-empt legislative time in later sessions (even if they can be certain of still being in office). Once a Bill has found its way into the legislative programme, therefore, those responsible will usually think it prudent to include as much as possible; it may be some time before another legislative vehicle comes along.

This last maxim was followed when consideration was being given to the way in which the Local Government Bill of 1971/2 should approach the general provisions dealing with the machinery aspects of local government – qualification and election of councillors, meetings and procedure of local authorities, committees, officers, expenses, accounts and audit. These had been consolidated in the Local Government Act 1933 but a number of amendments and additions had been made by subsequent Acts. When the London Government Act was drafted there was no question but that the existing law, as it then stood, should generally be applied to the new London authorities. The wider reorganisation offered the opportunity, however, of rewriting these provisions, bringing them up-to-date, repealing the Act of 1933 and starting the new authorities off with a modernised code. But the LGA 1933 was itself nearly 300 pages long, not counting the various later amending Acts. It would clearly be desirable to rewrite this aspect of local government law but the question was whether the draftsmen could tackle the task in the time available.

A fortune circumstance made this practicable. In 1968 the Law Commission had made a start on the consolidation of the Local Government Acts. The work had had to be dropped, but parts of a Local Government Consolidation Bill were available in draft as a foundation for further work.

At this point one other factor might be mentioned which favoured the preparation and handling of the Local Government Bill 1971/2; it was the fact that several of the key individuals among parliamentary counsel, DOE lawyers and administrators had also been engaged on the London Government Bill, which thus constituted a dress rehearsal for the even wider exercise affecting the rest of the country. Their previous experience of reorganisation provided a valuable element of continuity which is not always to be guaranteed in the civil service.

Lastly, when preparing a Bill the possibility has to be watched that it may be regarded as a hybrid. A hybrid Bill is one which is introduced by the government and deals with matters of public policy but which 'affects a particular private interest in a manner different from the private interest of other persons or bodies of the same category or class'.[2] If a Bill, introduced as a public Bill, contains or is thought to contain provisions of this kind, it is referred to the Examiners (who are officials of the two Houses) who report whether or not the Standing Orders affecting private business apply. If they do apply then the Bill follows a course which involves a mixture of public and private Bill procedure. Those provisions affecting particular interests are considered through the private Bill procedure, that is, before a Select Committee which hears evidence and petitions presented by counsel and witnesses. The relevant point in this context is that the procedure followed by hybrid Bills is longer and more complicated and (from the government's point of view) less predictable as to its outcome and timing. Determined opposition on a hybrid Bill would certainly delay that Bill and upset the government's timetable – and possibly achieve its partial or total defeat.

Strict logic has never governed the application of the hybridity rules, however, because government Bills dealing with local government in London, although they single out the metropolis for special treatment in a way differentiating it from the rest of the country, have nearly always been treated as public Bills. This includes government Bills dealing with sewerage in Greater London (of which there were many in the nineteenth century, for example, the Metropolis Management Act 1855) but not Bills dealing with other utilities, such as gas, water or electricity – apparently because the latter were not so closely linked to local government functions. Bills introduced by the LCC, and GLC and by other local authorities are, of course, dealt with as private Bills.

Early versions of the London Government Bill included clauses designed to transfer the functions of the Metropolitan Water Board to the GLC and the danger of hybridity on this point was fully considered. Whereas earlier Bills dealing solely with utilities (including water) in London had been treated by Parliament as hybrid the earlier precedents did not seem conclusive when water was treated as one function among many others in the same Bill.

There is no way, in case of doubt, of obtaining an authoritative ruling in advance on the question of hybridity – the decision is taken by the Examiners only after the Bill has been introduced. But informal guidance may be obtained, and the Speaker's ruling on the London Government

Bill disclosed that it had been sought on this aspect (Commons Hansard, 10 December 1962, cols 46–7). The conclusion reached by the Speaker and his advisers was that the inclusion of such clauses would make it necessary to send the Bill to the Examiners as prima facie hybrid. Rather than risk the procedural hazards of hybridity, these water clauses were dropped from the Bill before introduction. Even so, the opposition argued at length in each House (Commons Hansard, 10 December 1962, cols 37–49; Lords Hansard, 23 April 1963, cols 1099–1122) that the London Government Bill should be sent to the Examiners. This view did not prevail, however, and the Bill proceeded as a public Bill – as did of course the Local Government Bill 1971/2.

## THE PARLIAMENTARY TIMETABLE

When the government's legislative programme is being planned before each session, business managers make anxious calculations of the likely demand of each proposed Bill on parliamentary time – with special reference to those parts which must be taken in the Commons on the floor of the House (including the proceedings taken in Committee of the whole House). This in turn depends, of course, on the length and complexity of the Bill in question and the extent to which it is a source of controversy between the two main parties. Civil servants on the other hand hope, equally anxiously, that the parliamentary proceedings will be so arranged that the Bill is finally passed by a planned date, and in time for any subsequent action which must be taken when the Bill is through. The committee consideration of the areas of the London boroughs was taken in Committee of the whole House to allow the many Members interested to speak. On the same reasoning the English counties and metropolitan districts and the Welsh counties and districts should have been dealt with in this way too. But pressure on the time available in the Chamber prevented this and the whole of the committee stage of the Local Government Bill was taken in Standing Committee upstairs.

The London Government Bill was strongly opposed by the Labour Party as a Conservative plot to gain control of local government in Greater London. The government were unable to reach any informal agreement with the opposition on a timetable for the Bill (see Commons Hansard, 29 January 1963, col. 769) and it soon became clear, when the committee stage commenced, that the government would find it very difficult to get the Bill on to the statute book at all without resort to the guillotine. This was duly moved after a Committee of the whole House had considered only the first clause of the Bill in two full days of debate. As usual, government spokesmen quoted from speeches about earlier guillotine motions made by the opposition party when they had been in office, and vice versa, and a timetable was arranged which split up the consideration of the Bill into minute subdivisions, to ensure that the areas of all the new London boroughs (in schedule 1) and each part of the Bill received separate attention. As a result the Bill completed its parliamentary course through both Houses before the summer recess, and received the Royal Assent on 31 July 1963.

This was one of the main differences between the parliamentary consideration of London government and the subsequent and wider Bill. The Local Government Bill of 1971/2, although disliked by the Labour Party, did not attract the same out-and-out opposition which made informal agreement impossible on a timetable for the committee and report stages. Partly for this reason, and partly because the government were forced to guillotine three other Bills in that session[3] and did not wish to use the guillotine more often than was absolutely essential, the Local Government Bill was not subject to a planned timetable. And because the European Communities Bill occupied a great deal of time on the floor of the House, the report stage of the Local Government Bill was very considerably delayed. After two sittings in April, the report stage was not resumed until July 1972 and the Bill did not reach the Lords until the end of that month. The House of Lords had to sit specially during the summer recess in order to consider the Bill which, having been introduced on the first day of the session, received Royal Assent on the last – much later than had been hoped, and later than was desirable in view of the need to define the pattern of non-metropolitan districts before the end of 1972. Indeed, the concluding stages of the Local Government Bill were so scrambled that a couple of amendments made to the Bill in the second House were accidentally lost in the corridors between the two Houses when the Commons were asked to approve the modifications made by the Lords, and hence they did not figure in the Act as finally published. The omitted amendments (which dealt with compensation which might be payable to employees of homes in the children's service) had to be enacted later and appeared somewhat improbably as section 34, Local Government Act 1974.

In total, the London Government Bill was considered for some eighty hours in committee as against one hundred and twenty-seven hours for the Local Government Bill. The latter Bill was, of course, much longer but the extra time spent on its consideration was not an automatic indication that, in the end, it had been more fully discussed. The Standing Committee occupied seven full sessions (over seventeen hours) on clause 1, for instance, and much of the time was spent on a rehearsal of the arguments for and against unitary authorities as against the two-tier system, an issue which had in effect been settled on second reading. Comparison of the parliamentary handling of these two bills reinforces the suggestion of the then Leader of the House (Mr Macleod), when moving the guillotine motion on the London Government Bill, that the Commons should give further study to the machinery for allocating adequate time to the various parts of all major Bills, instead of governments having to resort to guillotine motions in circumstances which always aroused controversy (Commons Hansard, 29 January 1963, col. 775).

## THE BILLS IN PARLIAMENT:
## THE ROLE OF THE SPONSORING DEPARTMENT

The London Government Bill and the Local Government Bill were both long and complicated, but the work falling to the sponsoring department while each Bill was before Parliament - MHLG in the former case and DOE (with the Welsh Office) in the latter - was not essentially different from that normally involved in legislation, though there was more of it.

In the first place, of course, the department had to provide briefs for ministers at the various stages: second reading, committee, report and third reading. For the debate on second reading the brief had to cover not only the minister's speech in opening the debate, but all the general topics which might be raised and which might need to be dealt with in the winding-up speech of the government spokesman. In the case of the two Bills under consideration, many of the notes on particular services and topics were contributed by other ministries, but it was the task of the sponsoring department to commission these notes and ensure that the final folder was comprehensive and consistent without being impossibly unwieldy.

During the committee and report stages, departmental briefs had to cover both government amendments and those tabled by the opposition and by backbenchers on both sides. These briefs are necessary but ephemeral documents designed for use on one occasion only, and they do not go outside government circles. Again these were produced by whichever department was principally concerned but within the general strategy of the Bill, for which the sponsoring department was responsible.

One particular document is produced in the case of each Bill, however, which has more lasting use - the notes on clauses. These are written by officials for the use of ministers during the committee and report stages in each House, and consist of a detailed exposition of the meaning and effect of each clause together with an explanation of all references in the clause to other parts of the Bill or to other legislation. In addition it is usual for these notes to set out the arguments for and against the particular provision, and thus to constitute a fall-back source of instant reference for ministers if questioned on particular points at any stage in the Bill's progress. This additional material normally makes the notes unsuitable for circulation outside government circles but exceptions were made in connection with both the Bills now under consideration.

The London Government Bill was drafted in a way which, so far as possible, applied to London the various statutes which regulated the constitution, procedure and functions of local authorities throughout the country as a whole. The Bill was therefore riddled with references to other Acts in a way which made it very difficult, even for the specialist, to follow without a great deal of research. In order to ease the task of MPs on the Standing Committee considering the London Government Bill, the minister (Sir Keith Joseph) directed that a special set of notes should be prepared which explained the references in the Bill to other legislation. This was done by extracting the necessary information from the fuller notes on clauses; the resultant document was made available both to the Standing Committee of the Commons and to members of the House of Lords.

When the Local Government Bill was introduced a similar, though more comprehensive, attempt was made to provide a factual guide for the benefit of members of both Houses. This time the notes on clauses were deliberately drafted in a way which made them suitable for circulation, and they were supplemented by notes on major government amendments and by maps of the various areas proposed by the Bill.

This course, which has been followed in only one or two other cases, was specifically commended by the Renton Committee on the Preparation of Legislation[4] as a useful supplement to the more general explanatory and financial memoranda which are attached to all government Bills. The Renton Committee recommended that the practice of circulating notes on clauses should become more general, though they acknowledged the difficulty, in the case of controversial Bills, of ensuring that explanatory material remained entirely free of argumentative material. In the case of the Local Government Bill the notes proved generally helpful to the consideration of the Bill in Parliament by disseminating more widely the background and explanatory material that are generally available only to ministers.

The other main function of the department during the parliamentary proceedings on the Bill is to assist ministers to pilot the Bill through with the essential elements intact. This does not mean that the Bill must emerge unaltered but that, in dealing with amendments, a distinction is drawn between changes which would weaken the main principles on which reorganisation was based, and those which affected only matters of detail and on which some compromise would be practicable. When dealing with a long, complex and controversial Bill ministers are often faced with considerable pressures. On general grounds they do not wish to appear to be inflexible; if an amendment appears to be reasonable, their inclination is to accept it in substance rather than reject it. Amendments proposed by government backbenchers are more difficult to deal with than those put down by the opposition, because ministers have extra reasons for wishing to oblige those on whom they rely for support. The state of the timetable may also affect the situation; if the Bill is moving slowly, and government supporters are restive, there will be a wish to shorten the proceedings by accepting an amendment if possible.

It is the task of the department to appreciate the pressures to which ministers are subject and, while not participating in political decisions, to consider and to advise on alternative courses of action which would be consistent with the essential purpose for which reorganisation was being undertaken. Three matters on which ministers made modifications during the passage of the Local Government Bill have already been referred to – the machinery for designating successor parishes, the retention of civic dignities granted to the pre-reorganisation boroughs and the appeal provisions affecting agency arrangements operating from 1 April 1974. In all these the department suggested ways in which ministers could go some way towards meeting the wishes of MPs without eroding the fundamental provisions of the Bill.

But it was in connection with areas that the department felt most apprehension, with the historical precedent of the 1888 Act in mind. On that occasion the government of the day had originally proposed the creation of ten county boroughs, all with populations of about 150,000 or above. As a result of pressures during the passage of the Bill through Parliament, changes were made which allowed the creation of sixty-one county boroughs – several with populations under 50,000 – thus undermining the new structure before it was established.

In the context of London, the government had adopted certain principles regarding the definition of Greater London (the continuous built-up town) and the size of the London boroughs (with a minimum population of 200,000 wherever possible). Defined principles were also applied in the rest of England to the number and boundaries of the metropolitan counties, and to the size of counties and of metropolitan districts generally (for which a higher minimum of 250,000 was regarded as desirable in 1972). Many amendments proposed to the London Government Bill and to the Local Government Bill ran counter to these principles, and the acceptance of any one of them would have made it almost impossible to avoid accepting others. In the event the government, on each occasion, managed to avoid this particular pitfall. The amendment which kept the Isle of Wight as a separate county (see p. 140 above) was accepted by the government only during the report stage of the Bill in the Lords, when it was too late for further pressures to be brought on behalf of other areas. It is true that the resultant patterns of areas still attracted criticism (and who could expect otherwise?) but they emerged consistent with the bases of the reorganisation proposals.

## NOTES: CHAPTER 7

1  Bills relating wholly to Scotland, and any Scottish elements in Bills which also apply to England and Wales, are prepared by the Parliamentary Draftsman for Scotland who, with his colleagues, are members of the Lord Advocate's Department.

2  Mr Speaker Hylton-Foster, Commons Hansard, 10 December 1962, col. 45. Private interest in this context would include the interest of a local authority or water undertaking.

3  The European Communities Bill, the Housing Finance Bill and the Housing (Financial Provisions) (Scotland) Bill.

4  Cmnd 6053, 1975, para. 15.10. Appendix D to the Committee's Report lists all the types of explanatory documents on the Local Government Bill issued before the Bill was published, while it was before Parliament and after it became law.

## Chapter 8

# Implementation

### THE GENERAL FRAMEWORK OF IMPLEMENTATION

The passing of the London Government Act 1963 and of the Local Government Act 1972 marked the beginning, in each case, of a period of even
more intense activity for the members and officers of the existing and new
authorities because it was on them that the main burden fell of the
enormous amount of work needed to effect the transition from the old
system to the new.

An essential first requirement, of course, was to hold the elections that
would bring the new authorities into being. Then each newly elected
council had to make a vast number of preparations during the ten to
twelve months available to them before the final changeover. The authorities' management structures had to be settled, key officers appointed,
arrangements made to take over services from the existing authorities, to
unify the differing practices of those authorities, to operate those services
without a break as from the appointed day and to prepare estimates on the
basis of which the rate would be levied during the first year of the new
regime. The existing authorities had to maintain services right up to the
last moment and prepare for an orderly transfer of staff and property to
their successors.

In some matters the central government had to take a direct hand (in
naming the new areas, for instance, and in settling the arrangements for
the first elections) whereas in other matters their role was less direct and
consisted primarily in defining the framework within which the existing
and the new authorities would operate – as in the case of arrangements
affecting staff and property. In all cases, however, the main burden fell
upon local government itself and without the unstinting work of local
government members and officers, based upon acceptance of reorganisation as a fact (whether or not they agreed with the form it took),
implementation would have been impossible. The transitional problems
of reorganisation in 1972–4, however, have been more fully described
elsewhere.[1]

The new county councils were elected on 15 March 1973 and thus had
about twelve-and-a-half months of shadow existence before the changeover;
the non-metropolitan districts were elected on 7 June 1973 and had just

under ten months. The GLC, the London boroughs and the metropolitan districts had preparatory periods between these limits. These overlap periods were longer than had been envisaged when the provisional time-tables had first been worked out but, even so, were none too long - indeed were far too short in some views. Opinions differed on this last point. Undoubtedly the shortness of the period meant that many preparations were made hurriedly and imperfectly. If more time had been available plans for complements, staffing structures and the operation of some services would have received fuller advance consideration. But on the other side was the danger of a loss of efficiency in the administration of services while reorganisation was pending and the disadvantage of delaying the final implementation by a full year; this would have extended the transitional period which inevitably put enormous strains on members and officers many of whom were simultaneously engaged in both the existing and the new authorities - and some, in 1973-4, were also involved in the implementation of reorganisation in connection with water and the NHS too. For many local government employees, moreover, this was a period of great worry and uncertainty about their own futures - a period which should be brought to an end as soon as possible. On balance the general opinion was in favour of the timetable as fixed, and a changeover to the new system at the earliest practicable date.

## JOINT COMMITTEES OF EXISTING AUTHORITIES

For members and officers of the existing authorities preparatory work had, of course, started well before the Acts reached the statute book, so that the final overlap months constituted only the last part of a much longer period of planning and implementation, much of this being carried out through joint committees of existing authorities.

These had first come into existence, in the case of the London government reorganisation, when the government's proposals for borough groupings had been published in December 1961.[2] In a number of the proposed groups the borough and urban district councils concerned met to consider their reactions to the government's proposals and, from this beginning, consultations followed on a wide range of matters of common interest.

The advantages of such consultations were obvious, were actively encouraged by the government and were given statutory recognition in section 86 of the London Government Act. The Act contemplated a joint committee composed of representatives of the councils of the counties and county boroughs wholly or partly within Greater London, in order to prepare for the setting up of the GLC, and a joint committee for each of the new London boroughs except Harrow (which was the former borough of Harrow with its boundaries unchanged). The borough joint committees were to include county council representatives, because the new London boroughs would be taking over some of the functions (together with the relevant staff and property) then exercised by the existing county councils. The provision in the London Government Bill was couched in terms that the existing authorities 'may' set up such committees, but it was intended that all of them should do so and there was a reserve power for the minister to require the formation of a joint committee, and if necessary determine its composition.

Inevitably, some joint committees operated more successfully than others depending, *inter alia*, on whether the constituent authorities were of the same political complexion and (especially in the early days, before the new areas were finally settled) on the extent to which they agreed with the proposed groupings. But the value of committees of this kind was clearly proved and the device was adopted from the beginning when the wider reorganisation was undertaken. Ministers took every opportunity to urge the early voluntary formation of joint committees at both county and district level, and the LGA 1972 contained a positive requirement in section 264 that a committee should be formed by the existing authorities for each new county and each new district, again with a long-stop power for the secretary of state to determine the composition of a joint committee in default of agreement – a provision which had to be used in a handful of cases. The Act (supplemented on this topic by DOE circulars[3]) also required, because some functions were to be transferred on reorganisation, that county joint committees should include representatives not only of counties and county boroughs but also of county districts, and vice versa.

In the reorganisation of 1972–4 the role of the joint committees was wider and more clearly defined than in connection with London government. Broadly their functions fell under three heads: they were the channel of communication and consultation between the government and the predecessors of each of the new units on matters such as the warding arrangements for the first elections, the names of the new units and claims for successor parish status; they constituted the machinery through which proposals were formulated for consideration by the new authorities, when elected, on (for instance) management structures, the key posts to be filled, the location of the new authorities' headquarters and the use of available premises, and arrangements for the operation of services; finally they were the forum, even after the new authorities had been elected, in which the existing authorities could keep in touch with each other on the operation of services, on the letting of major contracts and on the disposal of assets during the final months before the changeover.

In practice many of the joint committees operated through sub-committees or working groups of senior officers. Without the preparatory work carried out in this way the new authorities could not have been ready in time.

## NAMES OF THE NEW AREAS

Experience has repeatedly shown what passionate feelings can be unleashed by arguments about the name to be given to a new local authority area. It has not been unknown for two authorities to agree in principle to amalgamate, in order to form a stronger and more sensible unit, and then to withdraw because of a dispute over its name. Where the name of an existing authority is adopted for the whole of a new unit it is often seen as an indication that the other constituent elements have been swallowed up and have lost their identity. Those who believe themselves to be thus ill-treated are not comforted by the reflection that place names for towns and localities will remain in daily use, as before; indeed, taking London as an example, some names which are household words in the social geography of the capital – Bloomsbury, Clerkenwell, Mayfair, Limehouse, Soho, for instance – have never been attached to local government areas in modern times. This was a potentially controversial field, in which the responsibility for settling the names of the new authorities had to be accepted by the central government. To have left the issue to be debated by each new council after they had been elected would in many cases have meant plunging the authority into a fierce internal dispute between factions desirous of perpetuating the former authorities, at a time when the greatest unity was needed in order to launch the new one.

Greater London and the new counties were treated differently in this respect from the London boroughs and the new districts. The importance of these units suggested that their names should be settled by Parliament, and the circumstances made this practicable. There was no alternative to Greater London, and, in the case of the counties, the great majority of new counties were the successors of existing ones. Where this was not so local opinion was canvassed before the government's proposed names appeared in the Bill. Most of these proposals were accepted, though one or two modifications were made in Parliament: Tyneside became Tyne and Wear, Teesside became Cleveland, and Malvernshire was abandoned so that the elements in that disputed county could re-emerge in the name Hereford & Worcester. But in the case of the other main authorities, the question of names was firmly deferred until the period after the groups had been irrevocably settled but before the first elections were held to the new councils.

In London the boroughs were all to be incorporated by royal charter, and this was the normal vehicle for conferring the official name on a new borough. As there was no existing authority to make application for the charter (and whose name could be carried on) the minister had not only to make application on behalf of the new authorities, but also to recommend to the queen what names should be adopted. Consultations with the existing authorities and with the joint committees for the new borough groups were initiated in June 1963, when suggestions were invited. Anticipating the likelihood that the new groups would try to resolve internal differences by suggesting double-barrelled names (of which the Greater London area already had too many) the minister tried to put in a word for the convenience of later generations by saying that he believed it 'to be important that the new boroughs should have short and simple names. Complex names and artificial hybrids will not, he suggests, commend themselves to public opinion nor attract loyalties; and he feels they are best avoided. In many cases it is likely to be obvious that the best name will be the name of the place generally recognised as the centre of the new borough; this will often, but not necessarily, be the name of one of the existing local government areas.'[4]

Many London borough names settled themselves along the lines suggested by the consultation letter. Others produced local names designed to avoid adopting that of any existing authority – Hillingdon (and not Uxbridge), Havering (and not Romford), Redbridge (not Ilford), Brent (and not Wembley or Willesden). In others, historical names were adopted in place of the major element in the new group – Southwark (instead of Camberwell), Merton (instead of Wimbledon). Some of these resulted from local agreement; in other cases ministerial intervention was needed but even the minister (Sir Keith Joseph), despite the feelings attributed to him above, did not entirely avoid double-barrelled names in his acceptance of Kensington & Chelsea, instead of the single name Kensington.

The new districts under the 1972 Act were to achieve borough status, if they so wished, only after (and not before) the first councils had been elected. There was no question of names having to be settled by inclusion in royal charters; after consultations with the district joint committees these were conferred by two ministerial orders, one order for the metropolitan districts[5] and one for the non-metropolitan districts.[6] Consultations on the metropolitan districts' names were conducted by the department, but the names for the non-metropolitan districts were recommended by the Boundary Commission[7] who had already, and separately, made proposals for the boundaries of those districts.

Consultations on district names and the guidelines to the Boundary Commission echoed the earlier exhortations (on the London boroughs) regarding the need for short and simple names; cold water was again poured on hybrid, concocted or double-barrelled suggestions. Names, it was further urged, should be relevant to the geographical, historical and traditional background of the district concerned; and there was a need to avoid two districts finishing up with names so similar as to lead to confusion.

Whenever possible the secretary of state and the Boundary Commission accepted names that were agreed locally, though it had to be admitted that some of the new names (such as Vale Royal, Three Rivers, Forest Heath) give little hint as to where the district is,[8] while others needed getting used to.[9]

The allocation of names to the new areas was not necessarily final. The Local Government Act 1958 contained simplified machinery in section 59 through which counties and boroughs could change their names – machinery which had immediately been used to enable the administrative county of Southampton officially to adopt the name of Hampshire. This was re-enacted and extended to all counties, districts and London boroughs by section 74 of the LGA 1972, but for the first five years after their election (until 1 April 1978) the new county and district councils had to obtain the secretary of state's agreement to any change. This provision aimed at discouraging the new authorities from immediately reopening earlier controversies, but it did not prevent some districts from applying for and the secretary of state (reluctantly) giving his consent to early changes. In nearly all these cases the name originally allocated was abandoned in favour of one which was either less convenient or less imaginative – Tiverton was changed, for instance, to Mid Devon, Pastonacres to North Norfolk, Petersfield to East Hampshire, Basingstoke to Basingstoke and Deane.

## FIRST ELECTIONS TO THE NEW AUTHORITIES

The legislation for London and for the rest of England and Wales defined the long-term arrangements for local government elections, and dealt with such matters as the length of the term for which councillors should be elected, and whether councillors should all retire together or by thirds.

In the case of London the three-year term followed that in force for the country generally, and whole-council elections for both the GLC and the London borough councils followed the arrangements which applied to the LCC (along with all county councils) and to the metropolitan borough councils. The Herbert Commission had in fact recommended (Cmnd 1164, para. 858) that the constitution of the London boroughs should be the same as for municipal boroughs generally, which implied that one-third of the councillors should retire each year. The government did not follow the Commission on this for three reasons (as Lord Jellicoe explained – Lords Hansard, 15 May 1963, col. 1312): because whole council elections commanded the most support among the existing authorities (and all metropolitan borough councils were elected on this basis), because a three-year term free from elections gave councils a desirable period of stability in which to pursue their policies, and because whole-council elections allowed greater flexibility in warding arrangements.

When local government was reorganised in the rest of England the office of alderman was abolished and, to give greater continuity to councils and a longer period in which to develop and apply policies, the length of a councillor's term of office was extended from three years to four. Machinery was also included in section 8 and schedule 2 to the LGA 1972 under which the GLC and the London borough councils (though not the City of London) were later brought into line on this point with authorities elsewhere. The long-running discussion between the merits of whole-council elections, as against retirement by thirds, resulted in a settlement which closely followed the earlier system. County councils were to be elected on a whole-council basis every four years; necessity required this because elections by thirds imply three-member electoral divisions, which would be impossibly big at county level. In compact urban areas reasonably small three-member wards can be defined, so in the metropolitan districts councillors all retire by thirds. Other districts were given the option (previously possessed by urban and rural district councils) to choose which of the two systems suited them best (section 7 (4), LGA 1972). In London, the system of whole-council elections in the London boroughs (specifically retained in 1963) was left unaltered. The final regime ensures that local government elections of some kind will be held each year (to help the political parties keep their machines ticking over): county council and the GLC elections will be held every fourth year; where district councillors retire by thirds these elections will be held in each year in which there is no county council election; in the case of those district councils which have chosen whole-council elections, these elections will be held in the year mid-way between the county council elections.[10]

But special arrangements were needed both in 1964 in London and in 1973 in the rest of the country for the first elections to the new authorities, all of which had to be held, of course, on a whole-council basis to get the new councils launched.

Proposals to amend and to keep electoral areas up-to-date are frequently controversial and the old procedure for dealing with these (and for which the Home Secretary was the responsible minister) normally involved formal public inquiries.

In practice there had been a tendency for the size of councils to grow. New warding proposals originated in the local authority concerned and, when a shift of population indicated the need for one locality to have increased representation, it was usually less controversial to add a few extra members in such areas – but without redrawing ward boundaries so as to reduce the number of councillors elsewhere. The result over the years has been to produce councils of unwieldy size. When the Local Government Bill was introduced in 1971, for instance, there were sixteen county councils and county borough councils in England each with a membership exceeding 100 and another seventeen with 90–100 members. This situation had frequently been criticised and the Maud Committee on Management had suggested that when local government was reorganised no council should have more than seventy-five members.[11]

The formation of new authorities in London and in the rest of the country raised two questions. First: what warding procedure would be practicable within the restricted timetable of reorganisation, and secondly: to what extent should the government attempt to limit the size of the new councils, either by statute or in the process of defining the electoral arrangements (and hence the number of councillors) for the first elections?

Special considerations, needless to say, applied in London. The LCC, alone of all local authorities, were elected on the basis of parliamentary constituencies with three councillors returned for each constituency (a total of 126 councillors in 1962 to which had to be added 21 aldermen). The Herbert Commission saw advantages in retaining constituencies as the basis of GLC elections though with one councillor per constituency instead of three; this would result in about a hundred councillors, which the Commission considered would be adequate (Cmnd 1164, para. 853). This recommendation came in for a good deal of criticism from those engaged in local government who thought that electoral arrangements for Greater London councillors should be based more directly on the London boroughs (see Cmnd 1562, para. 24). On reflection the government adopted both views, and the effect of the London Government Act was to provide that if, after the next review, the constituencies in London were based on borough boundaries then they should be adopted for the purpose of GLC elections; but if constituencies straddled borough boundaries, so that a London borough contained (say) two constituencies plus part of a third, then the Home Secretary had to arrange for that borough to be specially divided into electoral areas for GLC election purposes.[12]

In the event the revision of parliamentary constituencies in 1970 resulted in each London borough containing two, three or four parliamentary constituencies without any spilling over into a neighbouring borough or across the outer boundary of Greater London. So elections to the GLC are now on that basis. But this was not the situation in 1964, when the first elections were held, so these were arranged on a 'whole borough' basis with each borough forming a single electoral unit in which electors voted for two, three or four candidates. The number of Greater London councillors returned by each borough at the first election was laid down in the Bill and, with an eye to the link with parliamentary constituencies, the figures were obtained by dividing the number of local government electors in each new London borough by the parliamentary 'electoral quota'[13] for England and rounding up or down to the nearest whole number.

The metropolitan borough councils in London were also special in that they were the only main authorities whose size was limited by statute. The

London Government Act 1899 had fixed the maximum number of councillors at sixty which, with ten aldermen, meant that no metropolitan borough council could exceed seventy members (or seventy-one if the mayor was elected from outside the council). This limit had been retained by the London Government Act 1939 and was also written into the 1963 Act (section 1 (4)). The government argued that in practice a total membership of seventy should be ample; among municipalities only five of the largest county borough councils had bigger councils and Croydon (the biggest of the county boroughs included in Greater London) had found a council of sixty-four members sufficient. The statutory provision thus reinforced the influence that could be brought to bear through the machinery for settling the initial warding pattern (though it was later repealed by the LGA 1972 when all local government electoral divisions – and hence the size of councils – were brought within the purview of the Local Government Boundary Commission).

The time available for finally settling this pattern was only just over five months – between Royal Assent in July 1963 and the end of the year – so that the new electoral registers to be published in February 1964 could be based on the new wards. But the process had to start much earlier and existing authorities were asked, soon after the Bill had received second reading, to start preparing draft ward schemes for formal consideration as soon as the Act was passed. The five-months period after Royal Assent was just sufficient for the Home Office to follow the essentials of the normal procedure, but it was a tight fit. The draft proposals were published and local inquiries held in each new borough, conducted by independent barristers appointed by the Home Secretary. Final decisions on the ward boundaries were included in the new borough charters sealed in December 1963 and January 1964.

The same questions, regarding the size of councils and procedure for the initial warding arrangements, arose when the new authorities were elected under the 1972 Act. But this time there were far more authorities to cope with, and the period between Royal Assent (which was not given until 26 October 1972) and the deadline for the new electoral registers, to be published in February 1973, was much shorter.

Consultations, as on other topics, had started early and proposals were circulated by the government back in March 1971 (well before the Bill was introduced) both on the size of the new councils and on warding procedures for the first elections.[14] On the first of these topics, the government proposed a range of council sizes for each main type of new authority, devised after considering the number of electors and the responsibilities of those authorities, and the general experience of existing authorities. Drastic reductions in the generally accepted size of councils would certainly have been resisted, so the new county councils (the government suggested) should normally have between sixty and a hundred members, metropolitan district councils between fifty and eighty and non-metropolitan district councils between thirty and sixty. Rigid limits could not be insisted on but these ranges should provide adequate flexibility – and the smaller authorities of each type should normally fall into the lower half of the range concerned.

Most of the new councils were in fact contained within these ranges and the exceptions might well have been even fewer had more time been available. But the timetable made it necessary for the initial electoral arrangements to be based on the rough-and-ready adaptation of existing electoral areas to fit in with a scheme for each of the new counties and districts. In drawing up these schemes care was taken to see that the area of each of the existing local authorities was fairly represented on the council for the new authority, in proportion to their share of the total electorate. Existing wards or county electoral divisions which were too small to fit the new scheme for electoral areas were grouped together, while those which were too large had the number of representatives increased. There was no time to divide existing electoral areas by drawing new lines on maps; this was a matter to be left for the Boundary Commission in the course of their initial review.

Nearly all the preparations in 1971-2 were carried out on a provisional basis while the Bill was before Parliament, and draft electoral schemes had to be changed as modifications were made to the local government areas during the progress of the Bill.

In the case of the counties and metropolitan districts (whose areas were set out in the Bill) the Home Office prepared draft schemes for each area. These were published locally and representations were invited. Such representations were considered by an independent Advisory Committee appointed by the Home Secretary and consisting of a barrister, as chairman, with two former clerks of local authorities.

The non-metropolitan district pattern did not begin to emerge until the Local Government Boundary Commission – Designate published their draft proposals for the new districts in April 1972. The Home Office were then faced with the task of establishing electoral arrangements for the 296 new districts in time for the elections to be held in June 1973. They sought the assistance of the joint committees of existing authorities, as contemplated by section 264 (4), LGA 1972, and invited them to suggest warding arrangements for the new districts. In many cases these were adopted as the draft electoral schemes for the area, with or without modification, though in some cases the Home Office had to devise schemes of their own. These draft schemes were also published locally and representations invited. The Advisory Committee was enlarged by the appointment of eight more former local government officers and they sat as sub-committees in order to consider the large number of representations within the short time available. The Committee then reported to the Home

Secretary, advising him whether or not he should change the draft schemes in light of the representations. No formal inquiries were held, as had been practicable when London government was reorganised, but in a very few cases informal local meetings were arranged to assist the Advisory Committee by providing further information. These meetings were chaired by a former local government officer appointed by the Home Secretary for this purpose.

Both in London and in the rest of England (and Wales) the electoral arrangements devised for the first elections achieved a general equality of representation within each new local government unit. The schemes for the metropolitan districts (where councillors were to retire by thirds) had achieved a pattern of wards all of which returned three members or a multiple of three. But in other areas, and in the London boroughs, there was less uniformity on this point; the circumstances in which proposals had been prepared meant that many new authorities had wards or electoral divisions returning different numbers of councillors (up to seven in some cases). And in all areas there was a need for the first electoral divisions to be reviewed and brought more carefully up-to-date. For this reason the 1972 Act (section 63 and schedule 9) placed a duty on the Boundary Commission to review the electoral arrangements in all districts and counties as soon as possible after the first elections – an exercise which the Commission extended to the electoral arrangements in the London boroughs too.

## INTERNAL MANAGEMENT OF THE NEW AUTHORITIES

It has already been mentioned that the joint committee of existing authorities were responsible for considering the future management structures of the new authorities and for formulating proposals to be considered by the new councils when elected. Final decisions had to wait until the new councils were in existence but, because of the limited time then available, the preparatory work done by the joint committees had a very great influence in shaping the organisational arrangements of the new authorities.

When London government was reorganised the government made no attempt to enter this field. Apart from the existing statutory provisions requiring the appointment of separate committees for certain specified services, and a new obligation on all the London boroughs to appoint a borough architect (an obligation later removed again when section 74 of the London Government Act was repealed by the LGA 1972), matters connected with internal organisation were left very much to be settled by each local authority for itself. And when new local authorities were formed, such as the GLC, the new London boroughs and (under the Act of 1958) certain new county boroughs such as Teesside, Torbay and those in the West Midlands, it usually happened that the organisational arrangements of the dominant existing authority were adopted as the basis for the new one.

But the expansion of local government and of the total numbers employed by local authorities, the interdependence of services, the growing complexity of all governmental functions and, not least, their rising costs, highlighted a number of common weaknesses in existing management methods in local government.

Many of these had been inherited from the nineteenth century when the system developed under which separate committees were appointed to administer individual services, each of which had its own chief officer. There was a tendency for such committees to proliferate in numbers, to operate as separate empires on their own (especially where the committee had a statutory existence, for example, the education committee), and for members to become far too deeply immersed in the details of administration. The increasing need for overall machinery, not only to co-ordinate the work of the separate committees but also to direct the work of the authority as a whole, had been noted long before.[15] In practice many authorities, especially the bigger ones, developed their own machinery for effective co-ordination both at member and officer level, but general uneasiness about the slow adaptation of local government to changing conditions led to the appointment of the Committee on the Management of Local Government (the Maud Committee) in 1964.

The Committee was appointed by the then Minister of Housing and Local Government (Sir Keith Joseph) at the request of the four main local authority associations and their report, published in 1967, gave priority to the question of internal organisation.[16] Not unexpectedly, in view of the fact that many members sat on both bodies, the Management Committee's report was later endorsed by the Redcliffe-Maud Royal Commission (Cmnd 4040, ch. XII).

Very briefly, the main proposals in this field were that the need for a managing body in each authority should be met by the appointment of a central committee to advise the council on its strategy and priorities, to co-ordinate the policies and work of the separate service committees and to ensure that the best management methods were adopted. This recommendation was complemented by others: that functional committees should be reduced in numbers and kept manageable in size, that members should concentrate on policy decisions leaving the operation of services to officers,[17] and (at officer level) that each authority should have a chief executive officer, chosen regardless of his professional background, to head the team of chief officers, that the number of separate departments should be reduced and that chief officers should be responsible for groups of services.

Certain aspects of the Committee's report aroused controversy – notably the proposal that a 'Management Board' should take over all executive decisions (subject to the council's overall control) leaving functional committees to be no more than 'deliberative and representative bodies'. But the general need for better co-ordination of council policies and programmes was widely accepted in local government circles. And so were many of the specific proposals – derived, as they were, from the already established practice in some of the most effective authorities.

Except in so far as central government was urged to remove the statutory requirements for the appointment of certain functional committees and chief officer posts, so as to give local authorities complete discretion to settle their own internal affairs, these recommendations were aimed entirely at local authorities. But they were given a considerable impetus when the Conservative government's reorganisation plans were launched in 1971. The then secretary of state (Mr Peter Walker) addressing the LAMSAC conference (the Local Authorities Management Services and Computer Committee) in March 1971 said: 'It is not enough to legislate, to draw new boundaries and to agree new functions and then just sit back and hope that things will happen and improve. The legislation is important, the agreement on functions and boundaries is vital. But at the end of the day, if local government reform is to succeed it will be because the opportunity of reform will have been grasped by those in local government, to see that the new machinery of administration is far better than anything that has gone before.'[18]

The reorganisation of local government, when management structure and methods were generally under review, created an opportunity for following up and developing the proposals in the Management Committee's report. The action taken led to the publication of the Bains report on the management and structure of the new local authorities.[19] This was prepared by a working group of local government officers, with a member from industry, under the chairmanship of the then clerk of Kent County Council and the overall aegis of a steering committee composed chiefly of local authority members. Both the steering committee and the working group were set up jointly by the Secretary of State for the Environment and the four local authority associations.

The report, like the others quoted above, drew on experience in local government to develop recommendations for the continuing adoption of the corporate approach to management in local government, based not only on modernised committee and departmental structures but also on improved personnel management and on better management services generally.

Management in local government is a topic authoritatively discussed in many recent works.[20] The aspect for special mention here is that the central government, in conjunction with the associations, took a new and positive initiative in this field. Hitherto central intervention had been limited to specific requirements on aspects of particular services, but the Bains report dealt with management as a whole. Mr Walker's foreword to the Bains report echoed his address to LAMSAC: 'I look upon this report as being one of the most important and vital aspects of local government reform'. The report was published in 1972 in time to be considered (as was its aim) by the joint committees of local authorities preparing draft management proposals for consideration by the new authorities. Local authorities were already moving towards corporate management and the Bains report gave the new authorities a powerful shove in that direction.

## STAFF AND PROPERTY

Even small adjustments in local government boundaries involve a formidable array of consequential and transitional arrangements, always required when territory is transferred from one authority to another. These supplementary provisions are voluminous and, when the boundary adjustment is being effected by order, most of the statutory instrument is taken up with articles on all manner of details – which may range from the registration of births and deaths to amendments of the rating valuation lists, and from the transfer of staff and property to the enforcement of local Acts and byelaws. In the past each separate order has contained this long catalogue of consequential provisions but, to obviate the need for this recital in future, section 67 of the LGA 1972 contained a power permitting the Secretary of State for the Environment to make regulations of general application covering the supplementary matters which have to be dealt with in boundary orders. These regulations have now been made and they will operate with future boundary orders instead of reproducing all the provisions in each order.[21]

Most of these consequential and supplementary matters were also dealt with by order on reorganisation, and two of these were of special importance – the transfer of staff and property from the existing authorities to the new ones.

They were, of course, the subject of prolonged consultations with local government bodies (which in the case of staff included a wide range of unions, staff associations and professional bodies) and the outcome were separate orders on each topic. But two general points can be made which applied to both.

In the first place: amalgamation gives rise to far fewer problems than division. To take a straightforward case – under the LGA 1958 the two administrative counties of Cambridgeshire and the Isle of Ely were amalgamated to form a single new county. No changes of functions were involved. The new county simply took over the functions of its two predecessors and also their properties and staff. The problems arise when the area of an existing authority is divided, or when its functions are split. In such circumstances it becomes necessary to allocate both property and staff to separate successor authorities. When areas are divided and functions are simultaneously reallocated, the problems multiply rapidly.

Secondly: in neither of these fields was it desirable or practicable for the central government to make individual decisions. Only the local authorities had the necessary knowledge of conditions on the ground and only they could make the detailed arrangements. The role of the central government, after full consultation, was to define the framework within which the existing and the new authorities should sort things out for themselves. As far as possible local authorities were left to reach their own decisions.

The main lines of action applying to staff and property were the same in 1965, for London, and 1974, for the rest of the country. Looking at property first, it has to be kept in mind that 'property' in this context includes not only land and buildings but also equipment, vehicles, records and stores, cash balances and capital funds and all kinds of rights and liabilities arising from contracts. The main orders[22] were necessarily complex documents but the two main principles from which they started were simple. First: property which was *held* by an existing authority in connection with the exercise of a function in any area (such as education or housing) was transferred to the authority which would be exercising that function in the area after reorganisation. Secondly: all property not transferred by specific rules, including 'general purpose' properties such as council offices, was transferred to a named authority at the same level; the designated successor to each county council was one of the new county councils and, similarly, for each county borough and county district council the successor was a new district council.

While the two basic principles were simple they needed a great deal of elaboration to meet the problems created by the division of areas and the reallocation of functions – problems which were dealt with (in the wider reorganisation of 1972–4) in two special explanatory memoranda published by DOE and sent to all local authorities with the main property orders.[23] Properties might, for instance, be held for more than one purpose or they might not be held for any specific purpose; in such cases there might be a need to determine the principal *use* to which the properties were being put. And in cases where use was relevant to transfer, temporary uses might need to be disregarded – where, for instance, land acquired for building was being used in the meantime as a car park. Or where (for instance) land was being used for refuse tipping that could be used later for recreation when tipping was complete, the transfer might need to be based on the ultimate, and not the present, use. In addition it might be necessary to safeguard the right of one new authority to continue using accommodation in a building transferred to a different new authority. Particularly difficult problems arose where the personal social services were transferred from county councils to the London boroughs and to the metropolitan districts, in allocating the future ownership of residential homes in the welfare and children's services and the right to use accommodation in these homes.

In some instances the authorities concerned might agree that a particular property should be transferred to an authority different from the one suggested by the general rules, and this was made possible in the order. Special rules were evolved, too, in respect of capital and revenue balances in cases where an area was split; instead of the balance going wholly to the specified 'legatee' authority they were divided between the new authorities inheriting the parts of the existing area on the basis of the rateable values of the respective parts, while balances in the housing revenue accounts were apportioned on the basis of the number of houses transferred to each of the new authorities.

The reallocation of property was pre-eminently a matter for officers to consider and, if possible, to reach agreements for ultimate recommendation to their councils. And, in the great majority of cases, details were settled in this way. No special machinery for the settlement of disputes was written into the order dealing with the transfer of property on London reorganisation. These were left to arbitration (under the general law) or, in the last resort, to the courts. In 1974, however, the order interposed arbitration at the behest of one of the parties to a dispute between authorities. Local authorities could agree between themselves on the appointment of an arbitrator or, failing agreement, could ask the secretary of state to appoint one; but in no instance was the duty placed on the secretary of state himself to decide any such dispute.

As regards staff: when London government was reorganised the number of local authority employees affected was in the region of 200,000; in the wider reorganisation, in the rest of England, the number was some 2 million. Most local government staff remained doing the same job as before in the same place - teachers, firemen, manual workers, for example - and for them the abolition of their employing authority and their transfer to a new one was not generally a matter of alarm or anxiety. But in other cases, particularly among the administrative professional, technical and clerical officers, reorganisation aroused very genuine and understandable worry - not so much because of the threat of redundancy (which was recognised from the first as only a remote danger) but because a period of uncertainty might be followed by a change of workplace, altered career prospects and possibly (especially among chief and senior officers) a loss of status when appointments were made to the reduced number of new authorities.

The task facing the government in 1963-5 and in 1972-4 was therefore twofold. Machinery had to be devised through which officers of the existing authorities would, in a fair and orderly fashion, become officers of the new ones and, at the same time, staff interests must be safeguarded and anxieties allayed. That ministers took these tasks very seriously is evidenced not only by their frequent public reassurances but also by the fact that on each occasion staffing matters were among the earliest topics on which consultations were opened.

From the start the government made it clear that there were certain aspects in which they were determined not to become involved. These included all matters such as pay, gradings and conditions of service, which were normally dealt with by the permanent negotiating machinery between local authorities, as employers, and the various unions and staff associations. On this aspect a special problem arose in London because most officers of the APTC grades employed by the LCC belonged to the LCC Staff Association, not to NALGO. The terms and conditions of service they enjoyed had been negotiated direct with the LCC and were in many respects different from (and they would say better than) those applying to other local authorities, which had been settled through the national negotiating machinery (to which the LCC Staff Association did not belong). A strenuous attempt was made to require the GLC to adopt the LCC terms and conditions of service and the government suffered their only defeat in the Commons on this point. An amendment carried against them in committee was deleted at the report stage, however, and the GLC were left to settle their own terms and conditions of service in consultation with the various bodies representing GLC employees.

Equally, the government, on each occasion, determined not to intervene in the detailed decisions which the new authorities should properly take for themselves – on management and departmental structures, for instance, on staffing complements and on appointments to individual posts. As in connection with property, the role of the central government was to set the framework within which local authorities conferred and took their own decisions.

But the numbers of staff affected and the human problems of each individual involved led to a demand for special machinery, and hence to the appointment of the London Government Staff Commission and (later, in 1972–4) to separate Staff Commissions for England and for Wales, as well as Commissions for the staff involved in the reorganisations of water services and the NHS.

The idea of 'an independent body to watch over the interests of staff during the period when transfers and appointments to the new authorities are taking place' was referred to by the Minister of Housing and Local Government (Sir Keith Joseph) in August 1962, as a possibility which was then being explored by the department with the associations representing local authorities and their staffs (Commons Hansard, 2 August 1962, col. 138). The proposal was developed during these consultations and during the parliamentary proceedings on the London Government Bill; the later Staff Commissions appointed in 1972 followed very closely on the arrangements worked out in London.

The London Government Staff Commission was a small body of three members,[24] supported by a secretariat seconded from the civil service. It was an advisory, not an executive, body set up with the intention that it should operate by persuasion and discussion, though there were initial differences on this point. From the staff side it was urged that the Commission's role should go further than merely to lay down rules and give advice; the Commission should have powers of direction over local authorities, to make sure that its rules and advice were observed. From the local authorities' side it was argued that such a power of direction would be an excessive derogation from the responsibility of each authority for its internal affairs. The resultant compromise retained the Staff Commission as a body essentially operating by persuasion but with a power of enforcement in the background to be exercised, if necessary, by the minister; the minister (in 1972 the secretary of state) was given powers of direction over both existing and new authorities, to make sure that the Commission were supplied with all the information they needed and that their advice was followed. This power was formally invoked only once – in London.

The various stages and main problems arising in connection with staff appointments and transfers are described in detail in the final reports of the Staff Commissions.[25] Very briefly there were three main aspects.

The first related to staffing decisions of the existing authorities before they went out of existence. In the ordinary course of events vacancies would continue to occur – vacancies which would need to be filled if services were to be maintained. But when reorganisation was only a short way off it was necessary to avoid, as far as possible, any action that would prejudice the chance of existing officers being considered for posts (especially for senior posts) with the new authorities. This could happen if last minute promotions or appointments were made within the existing authorities. In some cases it would be feasible to defer an officer's retirement, or to double-up posts and avoid making any new appointment at all; or promotions might be on a temporary basis; and, if candidates had to be sought from outside the existing authority, they should be sought only from within Greater London or (in the later exercise) only from restricted and local recruitment areas which excluded Greater London. The Staff Commissions gave advice on this aspect, and stressed the need for full consultation about new appointments through the machinery of the joint committees of existing authorities.

Another way in which employees of one existing authority might be prejudiced by the action of another was in connection with gradings and salary scales. The upgrading of jobs, or the late improvement of salaries, might give some officers an advantage on the final changeover as against colleagues who would be joining them from other authorities. Again, close consultation between existing authorities was the main method relied upon to prevent action which might be regarded as unfair, but some late increases of salaries paid to employees of existing authorities in London prompted more specific action on this point in the 1972 Act following a recommendation of the Redcliffe-Maud Commission (Cmnd 4040, para. 562). Section 261 of the LGA 1972 set out a procedure to supplement and back up a voluntary vetting scheme initiated by LACSAB (the Local Authorities Conditions of Service Advisory Board) and machinery was devised under which unjustified salary increases, made in anticipation of reorganisation, could be disregarded for the purpose of the salary (or compensation) to which an employee might be entitled after reorganisation.

The second aspect of staffing matters related to the filling of posts by the new authorities between the date of their election and the final changeover. Devising rules and procedures on this aspect of reorganisation was one of the main tasks of the Staff Commissions. The appointments made during this period included, of course, the key posts in each of the new authorities but in many cases went much lower in the hierarchy too.

In 1972 the Local Government Staff Commission for England, when setting out the general principles to be observed in filling these posts, said, 'in approaching our task we have regarded the operation as basically one of redeploying the present staff'[26] – an approach which had underlain the rules laid down by their predecessors in London, too. On each occasion the chief rule was that, initially, candidates should be sought only from a limited catchment area, that is, from among the officers of existing authorities affected by reorganisation. If it was necessary to go beyond that catchment area (because of the importance of the posts in question or because suitable candidates were not forthcoming) then the agreement of the Staff Commission was needed. On this basis the chief posts with the London authorities were initially open only to officers affected by the reorganisation, including officers of the county councils partly inside Greater London; and, outside Greater London, candidates were to be sought from officers already serving in the area of the new county or new district. Exceptions to this rule were the chief and deputy chief officers of the GLC and the chief executive officers of the new counties (outside Greater London) and of the metropolitan districts. The GLC were enjoined to give first consideration to officers of the London and Middlesex County Councils but with power to advertise more widely and without the specific agreement of the Staff Commission if unable to make an appointment from this field (though still to give preference to officers employed in Greater London). Outside Greater London the chief executive posts in the counties and metropolitan districts were thrown open to any local government officer serving in England (outside Greater London) or Wales, and the Local Government Staff Commission for England themselves acted as the agency through which preliminary applications were made, even before the elections to the new authorities.

The Redcliffe-Maud Commission would have gone further. They took the view that the selection of the chief executive of each of the new principal authorities was such an important decision that the authorities should not be left to take it unaided. They proposed that an Advisory Commission should be established and that the new authorities should be required to seek its advice before making their chief executive appointments (Cmnd 4040, para. 565). This proposal met with little enthusiasm in local government circles and was not pursued.

The third stage in the staffing aspects of reorganisation was reached on the appointed day, when all officers of the existing authorities who were not due to retire on that date or who had not already been individually appointed to a post with one of the new authorities were transferred under the terms of the general staff order.[27]

This main staff order - both in Greater London and then in the rest of England - had two principal objectives: to make sure that all local government staff were transferred to one or other of the new authorities (and that no one was left without an employer) and to lay down certain safeguards for those who were transferred in this way.

The principles of transfer were similar to those applying to property. Staff engaged on a local government service in a particular area went to the new authority responsible for the service in that area, and schemes were needed to allocate officers engaged on more than one service or on services which were being divided among more than one new authority. Such schemes required much local consultation and, as far as possible, individual preferences were followed. To make sure that no one was missed out a 'residuary legatee' (new) authority was named in respect of the staff of each of the existing authorities.

The Staff Commissions were closely consulted by the department, along with the local authority associations and staffing bodies, both on these provisions and on the main safeguards; the latter were fully discussed in Parliament and were written into the statutes themselves.[28] The purpose was to ensure that any officer transferred to a new authority by the order should, while he was engaged on duties which were similar to his previous job, enjoy a salary and a salary scale not less favourable than he enjoyed before reorganisation; and that, whether his new duties were similar or not, his other terms and conditions of service (for example, hours of work, sickness and leave arrangements) should also remain 'not less favourable'.

The extent of this safeguard (which was in fact an advance on those contained in earlier legislation) was discussed at great length during the passage of the London Government Bill when the government were pressed, especially by the LCC Staff Association, for a full 'no detriment' guarantee – that no matter what job the officer might have after reorganisation he should be guaranteed indefinitely a salary at least as high as the one he was earning on that date. But this was resisted. Local government and their officers could not be absolutely protected from changing circumstances – and certainly not by the central government. Local government officers are employed by the various local authorities, not by the central government, and it must be left to each local authority to take the final decision as to how each of the transferred officers should be employed and remunerated. If an officer was finally allocated to a job carrying a lower salary than he had earned previously – or if he was declared redundant – then he would be entitled to compensation (on a scale determined by regulations) but this was a decision which the employing authority must take, not the government. The forecasts that there would be very little redundancy were borne out by figures quoted in the final reports of the Staff Commissions; a total of 172 officers were declared redundant in Greater London and about 900 in the rest of England. In the great majority of cases these officers were declared redundant by arrangement with the individuals concerned.

Both in London and in the rest of the country the new appointments and the transfer of staff were accomplished far more smoothly than might have been the case. Basically this was due to the work of the local authorities, their officers and the various staff bodies who made all the detailed arrangements. But at the centre much of the credit went to the Staff Commissions. Not only was there general acceptance of the principles they laid down and acceptance, too, of their advice on the innumerable specific points constantly raised with them, but their mere existence constituted a reassurance to all local government employees; staffing matters were visibly seen to be under the supervision of an independent and impartial body, established to ensure that everyone would be treated fairly and (vitally important) treated alike. On their side, the Commissions rightly placed great emphasis on the need for full consultations between local authorities and their staffs, and on the paramount importance of keeping everyone informed about the staffing arrangements. If people were not told about the preparations being made their anxieties would be needlessly magnified. The Local Government Staff Commission for England played a direct part in reducing this danger by themselves preparing and publishing a series of bulletins which were made available to all local government staff affected.[29]

Finally on staff, a good deal of criticism was levelled against arrangements made by the new authorities in connection with their staffing complements, the number of chief officer posts and the salaries they attracted (notwithstanding that such salaries were subject to general pay policies then in force under the supervision of the Pay Board). Some of this censure was also aimed at the government for making arrangements which were too favourable to staff interests, and for failing positively to encourage a more efficient deployment of staff. Criticism on these lines was perhaps only to be expected after the changes had taken place, but it needs to be recalled that the climate of opinion was quite different when preparations were going forward for London reorganisation - an upheaval on a size then without recent precedent - and the even wider exercise in the rest of the country. At the time the emphasis was all on safeguarding staff interests, on the need to reassure local government employees and on the need to keep up morale - not least in the interests of maintaining public services in the difficult transition period. Pressures in Parliament an and outside were overwhelmingly in this direction; Sir Keith Joseph, the then Minister of Housing and Local Government, demonstrated his close concern with London staffing problems by personally addressing meetings of the LCC Staff Association, at County Hall, and of NALGO at the Albert Hall.

A particular problem affected officers who had held chief and senior posts with the former authorities. They could not all remain chief officers after reorganisation, when there would be very many fewer authorities. On the occasion of London reorganisation a departmental circular said, at an early stage, that the new authorities could well need extra staff to help them with the special problems likely to arise immediately after the changeover when the system was getting under way. The minister therefore proposed to bring to the attention of the new authorities, when they had been elected, 'the desirability of retaining some staff in an advisory or supernumerary capacity'.[30] The London Government Staff Commission also supported this course of action and their report records that some forty chief officers and deputy chief officers of existing authorities who had not obtained comparable appointments were eventually retained in this way. The Redcliffe-Maud Commission criticised the appointment of 'associate' chief officers in such circumstances, and suggested that the early retirement of such officers with 'generous compensation' would be better for both the individuals and for local government (Cmnd 4040, para. 564). Heedful of this advice the LGA 1972, and regulations made under it,[31] allowed chief and deputy chief officers who had reached the age of 50 by 31 March 1974 to choose to retire immediately, with superannuation benefits enhanced as if pensionable service had continued to the age of 65. Some 2,800 officers took advantage of these arrangements and prompted the Local Government Staff Commission for England to comment that 'the retirement of so many experienced officers from the top ranks . . . represents a serious loss to local government which will not be fully made good for some years'.[32] All of which suggests that it is easier to be wise after the event.

## LOCAL ACTS

The adaptation and rationalisation of local Acts as part of reorganisation is rarely mentioned in books about local government – understandably in view of the arid and technical nature of the subject. But within specialist circles it received a good deal of attention and is not without importance. The topic has only limited appeal, however, and is dealt with here only in fairly general terms.

Local legislation played a very big part in laying the foundation of many local authority functions during the latter part of the eighteenth century and throughout most of the nineteenth. Local authorities, Improvement Commissioners and other *ad hoc* bodies promoted thousands of private Bills to authorise the construction of works (for example, in connection with highways, drainage and sewage disposal), to run public utility undertakings (gas, water and electricity) or to regulate local activities (in connection with building standards, public safety and a variety of public health matters). With the extension of general legislation giving powers and functions to all local authorities the need for local Acts has greatly diminished, but a steady trickle of such Bills are still presented annually to Parliament.

In some cases individual local authorities have reviewed local legislation in force in their area, and have promoted consolidating Bills which repealed defunct provisions and kept the rest up-to-date. But this task had never been tackled comprehensively, with the result that an enormous mass of local legislation remains on the statute book, even though by far the greater part is spent, obsolete or superseded by general legislation. In an ideal world each general Act on (say) highways or housing would have included a schedule repealing earlier local Act provisions on the same point, but in practice there is never time for the widespread research needed to track down all the local Acts that might be relevant. The task has been tackled on one occasion in recent years – in part III of schedule 9 to the Weights and Measures Act 1963, which is the exception which proves the rule. Local Act provisions were repeated in 155 Acts going back to 1824.

Local government reorganisation raised immediate problems because, both in Greater London and then in the rest of England, the areas within which local Acts applied were being abolished and superseded by a very different pattern. Not everything in the field of local legislation had been rendered obsolete by events; some provisions were very much alive and had to be retained in force. Reorganisation also presented the opportunity to reduce the enormous mass of local legislation, to repeal what was obsolete or unnecessary, to revise the residue so that it harmonised with more modern general legislation, and to produce a corpus of local Acts which was relevant, intelligible, accessible and capable of being kept up-to-date.

As an initial holding operation both the London Government Act (section 87 (1)) and the LGA 1972 (section 262 (1)) contained an omnibus formula which ensured that local Acts would remain in force in precisely the same areas to which they applied before, and with the necessary substitution of the new authorities for their predecessors.

But this did nothing to improve the situation and, by itself, would leave many of the new authorities with local Acts which applied in some parts of their areas but not others. The wider and long-term task of rationalising local Acts was tackled in two different ways.

MHLG had traced some 500 local Acts still in force in the Greater London area promoted by local authorities or their predecessors (and there were many more promoted by such bodies as the Metropolitan Water Board, the statutory water companies, drainage authorities and the Port of London Authority). At a very early stage in London government reorganisation the department set up a section working full-time on analysing the contents of the local authority Acts, as a preliminary to deciding whether they needed to be retained. Then, under the order-making powers in sections 84 and 87 of the London Government Act and in laborious consultation with officers of the authorities concerned, a series of long and highly technical orders were made, cutting out much of the dead wood and applying the provisions which remained to the areas of the new authorities and to the new division of functions as between the GLC and the London boroughs. These orders were made before 1 April 1965 and resulted in each of the new London authorities starting off with a set of local Acts which had been very substantially rationalised.

The process was not complete. Within each new London borough any inconsistencies between the local Acts of the former constituent authorities had been eliminated, but the possibility remained that a local provision dealing with (say) highways might apply in one borough while a different provision applied next door. The London Government Act contemplated a further stage of rationalisation covering all the local legislation in Greater London and provided the machinery for this to be done by order. Such further rationalisation could not avoid substantial changes in local legislation affecting the rights of individuals and not necessarily flowing from reorganisation; for this reason the provisional order procedure, which provides opportunities for petitions from objectors, was judged appropriate. The intention was that the process should be initiated by the Minister of Housing and Local Government (or any other minister responsible for particular services) in consultation with the local authorities concerned but, save in one connection,[33] no part of central government has yet had the time or inclination to tackle this task.

The time and effort expended on even an initial tidying-up of local Acts in Greater London convinced the department that this type of exercise could not be repeated by the central government for the rest of the country. The 1972 Act took the essential steps to preserve existing local Acts in force but then placed on the new authorities the duty of reviewing their own local legislation, that is, those Acts, currently in force in the area, which had originally been promoted by local authorities. To provide the necessary spur to action it was further enacted that all such existing local legislation applying within the metropolitan areas would automatically expire at the end of 1979 and in the rest of England (outside Greater London) and in Wales at the end of 1984. There are more local Acts in force in urban areas; the metropolitan authorities were given a shorter deadline of five years so that these were tackled first. The ten-year deadline for the other authorities aimed to make sure that the exercise is tackled with reasonable expedition.

The first 'rationalisation' Bill to be promoted (in the 1974/5 session) was presented to Parliament not by a metropolitan authority but by the South Glamorgan County Council. The Bill, as first deposited, was of formidable length (287 clauses) and the prospect of a spate of such Bills raised fears that the attempt to rationalise local legislation within the time-table laid down by the 1972 Act might place too great a strain on Parliament. There had, of course, been full discussions between government departments and officers of the two Houses when the Local Government Bill was being prepared but the practical problems involved were further examined by the House of Lords Select Committee on Practice and Procedure whose report[34] also reprints the report of an official working party on local legislation.

The first ground for apprehension was the sheer number of Bills that might, theoretically, be promoted by the 422 new county and district councils in England and Wales (outside Greater London). But in practice the number of Bills will be much smaller than this because of the widespread adoption by the local authorities concerned of the practice of including provisions applying to district councils in Bills promoted by county councils. It is now clear that, with very few exceptions, all the rationalisation Bills will be presented by county councils; a total of some fifty such Bills, spread over ten years, is prima facie a manageable total.

The smaller number of prospective Bills also reduces the extent of another problem connected with local legislation – discrepancies in the details and drafting of clauses dealing with the same subject matter. This is a long-standing problem and parliamentary committees have spent much time and effort over the years in trying to standardise provisions in different Bills. Consultations between officials of the two Houses, government departments and parliamentary agents have led to the preparation, from time to time, of 'model clauses' which may be included in private Bills, where need can be proved, and the most recent anthology of such 'common clauses' was published in December 1977 with the consolidation Bills particularly in mind.[35]

But the existence of a 'model clause' does not (or should not) mean that it will be allowed by Parliament in a private Bill without there being a clear need for the provision in the area of the promoting authority and it is on this point – proof of need – that the rationalisation of local legislation creates the biggest problem for Parliament.

Private Bills require the reconciliation of two points of view which can stand in opposition to each other. Provisions in local Acts have often been pioneering precedents for general legislation, later extended to all authorities. But it is also true that a local authority promoting a Bill is likely to want to use the opportunity to seek powers, or to modify the general law in its locality, in order to meet needs which may be insubstantial or merely hypothetical. The public, on the other hand, are entitled to expect that laws will not be passed unless they are genuinely needed and will be effective; there is enough law already on the statute book without unnecessarily adding to its bulk or creating local differences.

Where local legislation is involved the sympathies of government departments are on the side of the strict examination of private Bills and against variations or extensions of the general law unless there is a proven need – in which case the need will often apply to all local authorities and the best course will be for the government to promote general legislation on the point. The difficulty here is that useful provisions precedented in local Acts are unlikely to be either urgent or politically rewarding and hence will be given only a low priority when the government's legislative programme is drawn up. The Public Health Acts of 1890, 1907, 1925 and 1961 were all substantially based on local Act clauses, however, and each greatly reduced the work falling on private Bill committees of the two Houses. Opportunities for such legislation do not recur frequently but the most recent general Act of this kind, the Local Government (Miscellaneous Provisions) Act 1976, was brought forward with the object, in part, of assisting the wider rationalisation of local legislation. It is an Act of more than eighty sections ranging over such topics as highways, housing, land acquisition, places of entertainment, parking, computers, and the licensing and operation of taxis, and its passage means that these particular provisions will no longer appear in separate private Bills.

But while miscellaneous provisions Bills of this kind can reduce the pressure on private Bill committees they will never remove the need for local enactments to meet genuinely special local circumstances. Nor will they prevent authorities from seeking further statutory powers in their search for solutions to social problems. Excessive applications will be encouraged if additional powers are easily obtained; but, conversely, local authorities will be more modest and realistic in their applications if they know that they will be required strictly to prove the need for extra powers when their Bills are examined in committee.

For this reason the parliamentary proceedings on the County of South

Glamorgan Bill were important. The Bill was presented during the 1974/5 session but, because of the need for very thorough examination (as the first 'rationalisation' Bill), proceedings were not completed and had to be carried over into the 1975/6 session. In the House of Lords the unopposed provisions were examined by a specially appointed Select Committee, presided over by the Lord Chairman, instead of the Lord Chairman sitting alone (as was the usual procedure, though Standing Orders have since been amended to allow the Lord Chairman to select other Lords to sit with him on Unopposed Bill Committees in the future). The committee stage of the Bill, in the Lords, lasted fourteen full days and twenty-six mornings, and there were lengthy hearings in the Commons too. Some of the clauses in the South Glamorgan Bill were overtaken by general provisions in the Local Government (Miscellaneous Provisions) Act 1976 but many more were disallowed on the grounds that Parliament found them either unnecessary or undesirable. In the event the Bill which had started off with 287 clauses was reduced to 68. In its final form the South Glamorgan Bill re-enacted only about 1 per cent of the local statutory provisions previously in force and thus gives a revealing glimpse of the extent to which the field of local legislation has become overgrown, and of the beneficial result which will follow from a determined scrutiny by private Bill committees.

The immediate consequence of the rigorous examination and pruning of the South Glamorgan Bill was that the metropolitan county councils (all six of whom deposited their rationalisation Bills within five years of the LGA 1972 coming into operation) restricted themselves to clauses whose need could be justified and they were careful to consult fully with government departments when the Bills were being prepared. As a result these Bills were much shorter than would otherwise have been the case and their examination in Parliament correspondingly less protracted.

The combination of these three aspects – the reduction in the number of likely Bills by the inclusion of district provisions in county Bills, the general enactment of a number of potential local Act clauses in the Miscellaneous Provisions Act of 1976 and the realistic attitude of promoters, warned by the strict parliamentary examination of the South Glamorgan Bill, encourages the view that the rationalisation of local legislation set on foot by the Act of 1972 will be completed within the broad timetable laid down. Crucial to the whole exercise, however, is the attitude of private Bill committees of the two Houses. If they continue strictly to require promoters to prove the need for the powers sought, whether or not petitions have been lodged against those provisions (as they did in the case of the South Glamorgan Bill), then local legislation will be reduced to a manageable and proper part of the complete corpus of statute law, and the basis laid for keeping it that way in the future.

## NOTES: CHAPTER 8

1 The transitional problems of reorganisation in 1972/4 were reviewed in prospect by Joyce Long and Alan Norton, *Setting up the New Authorities* (London: Knight, 1972) and in retrospect by Peter Richards, *The Local Government Act 1972: Problems of Implementation* (London: Allen & Unwin, 1975).
2 MHLG circular No. 56/61, 16 December 1961.
3 Advice on the setting up and work of the joint committees was contained in three DOE circulars: No. 68/72, 4 July 1972, No. 121/72, 28 November 1972 and No. 50/73, 9 April 1973.
4 Official letter from MHLG to the London authorities dated 21 June 1963.
5 The Metropolitan Districts (Names) Order 1973, SI 1973 No. 137.
6 The English Non-Metropolitan Districts (Names) Order 1973, SI 1973 No. 551.
7 Local Government Boundary Commission for England, Report No. 2.
8 These three are respectively in Cheshire, Hertfordshire and Suffolk.
9 For example, Tameside (Greater Manchester), Kirklees (West Yorkshire), Dacorum (Hertfordshire).
10 But not the elections to the London borough councils which will continue (as before) to be held in the year following the GLC elections: The London Councillors Order 1976, SI 1976 No. 213.
11 Report of the Committee, para. 331.
12 London Government Act 1963, schedule 2, para. 7 and the Greater London (Electoral Areas) Order 1972, SI 1972 No. 924. The City and the Temples are deemed to be part of Westminster for this purpose.
13 As defined by section 3, House of Commons (Redistribution of Seats) Act 1958.
14 Home Office consultation letter dated 31 March 1971 sent to the local authority associations, the societies representing the clerks of local authorities and the political parties.
15 For example, by E. D. Simon (later Lord Simon of Wythenshaw) who urged the need for a strong standing committee of co-ordination and control in each authority: *A City Council from Within* (London: Longman, Green, 1926).
16 *The Management of Local Government*, Vol. 1: The Report of the Committee (HMSO, 1967).
17 The implementation of this recommendation was facilitated by the new power (in section 101, LGA 1972) formally allowing local authorities to delegate to officers.
18 Local Authorities Management Services and Computer Committee conference at Eastbourne, 29 March 1971.
19 *The New Local Authorities: Management and Structure* (HMSO, 1972).
20 For example: J. D. Stewart, *Management in Local Government* (London: Knight, 1971); *The Responsive Local Authority* (London: Knight, 1974); Royston Greenwood and J. D. Stewart, *Corporate Planning in English Local Government* (London: Knight, 1974).
21 The Local Government Area Changes Regulations 1976, SI 1976 No. 246, modified by the Local Government Area Changes (Amendment) Regulations 1978, SI 1978 No. 247.
22 The London Authorities (Property etc.) Order 1964, SI 1964 No. 1464; The Local Authorities (England) (Property etc.) Order 1973, SI 1973 No. 1861 supplemented by the Local Authorities etc. (England) (Properties etc. Further Provision) Order 1974, SI 1974 No. 406.
23 DOE circulars No. 149/73, 11 December 1973 and 63/74, 2 April 1974.
24 Including the chairman, Sir Harold Emmerson, formerly Permanent Secretary, Ministry of Labour. The Local Government Staff Commission for England had seven members, including the chairman Lord Greenwood of Rossendale, formerly Minister of Housing and Local Government.

25    London Government Staff Commission Report (HMSO, 1965); Report of the Local Government Staff Commission for England (HMSO, 1977).

26    Local Government Staff Commission circular No. 6/72, 19 December 1972.

27    The London Authorities (Staff) Order 1965, SI 1965 No. 96; The Local Authorities etc. (Staff Transfer and Protection) Order 1974, SI 1974 No. 483. The essential elements of the transfer and protection provisions worked out in the context of local government reorganisation have since been applied to the transfer of 'homelessness' functions from the counties to the districts in non-metropolitan areas (see The Housing (Homeless Persons) (Property and Staff) Order 1977, SI 1977 No. 1821) made under the Housing (Homeless Persons) Act 1977, and to future boundary changes by the Local Government Area Changes Regulations 1976 referred to at p. 211 above.

28    London Government Act 1963, section 85 (3); LGA 1972, section 255 (3).

29    There were eleven such bulletins. Several are reprinted in Appendix E to the Commission's Report.

30    HMLG circular No. 6/63, 8 January 1963, para. 10.

31    LGA 1972, section 260 and the Local Government (Retirement of Chief Officers) Regulations 1973, SI 1973 No. 1260.

32    Report of the Staff Commission, para. 179.

33    Ministry of Housing and Local Government Provisional Order Confirmation (Greater London Parks and Open Spaces) Act 1967.

34    First Report from the Select Committee of the House of Lords on Practice and Procedure, Session 1977/8 (155).

35    House of Lords, Session 1977/8 (28). *Private Legislation: General Powers Bills: Common Clauses.*

## Chapter 9

# Concluding Thoughts

## THE CHANGES MADE SINCE 1888

This study covers a period of some eighty-five years, from the LGA 1888 to the implementation of reorganisation in England and Wales in 1974. During that time there was a tremendous expansion of governmental functions at the centre, through local authorities, and through a variety of nationalised bodies and governmental agencies. In response to the social, economic and political developments briefly noted in the first chapter, the structure of local government has been adapted to meet new needs and new demands. At first, individual local authorities were left to initiate such changes as they desired for themselves. Then systematic efforts were made through the county reviews, the Trustram Eve Commission and the Hancock Commission to improve the map of local authorities, though without departing from the original county/county borough framework. Finally, comprehensive changes were made by direct action of the central government in Greater London, and then in the rest of England and in Wales. A vast amount of discussion, time and effort went into devising successive pieces of machinery for change, and then into considering and implementing the proposals that emerged. The first questions to ask, therefore, are how far the structure was in fact modified during this period, and how far the system in 1974 differed from that at the turn of the century?

One clear difference is in the number of main authorities. In 1900 there were over 1,800 counties, county boroughs, boroughs and districts in England and Wales. The comparable figure in 1974 was 456, a reduction to a quarter of the earlier total.[1] And the new authorities, besides being on average much bigger than their predecessors, fluctuate less wildly in size because the very small units have been merged to form larger ones. The main feature in this reduction of total numbers was the elimination of the smaller authorities, especially at district level. In 1927, out of a total of 1,698 county districts in England & Wales, 972 had populations of less than 10,000; the present position is that out of a total of 296 non-metropolitan districts in England only ten are below 40,000.[2]

And on two other matters, among those noted earlier as legacies from the nineteenth century (see pp. 19-20 above), a substantial degree of modernisation has been achieved. First: the differences between the functions of urban authorities and rural authorities, which formerly differentiated non-county boroughs, urban districts and rural districts, has disappeared. With bigger authorities, many of them including both town and country, there is no longer a clear physical demarcation between urban and rural authorities at district level. And, in addition, the demand for uniform and higher standards of services has led to all non-metropolitan districts having the same powers and duties. Secondly: the special constitutional position of boroughs has been greatly modified. Immediately before 1974 boroughs figured at all three levels of local government – as county boroughs, as non-county boroughs and as boroughs included in rural districts. Boroughs are now found only at district level and (outside Greater London) are legally identical in constitution and powers with other districts in the same county. Borough status has been retained (as have titles granted under the Prerogative[3]) and is still granted by royal charter, but it may be sought with confidence by any district – whether urban or rural in character – and its consequence is of only ceremonial significance. No longer does a borough charter incorporate all the inhabitants; the body corporate in a borough (other than a London borough) is now the council, as in all other principal authorities too. Nor do aldermen now sit as members of borough councils.

The details of local government boundaries still present problems. The nineteenth century system was one in which areas had been created in different ways, at different times and for different purposes. Not only did areas vary greatly in size within the same classes of authorities, but the boundaries were very often eccentric or outdated. This last characteristic had never been comprehensively tackled. The London Government Act 1963 and the LGA 1972 both defined new patterns of major areas which, in broad substance, met the objectives of reorganisation in so far as conflicting considerations made this possible. But in detail the boundaries, being (save in a very few instances only) those of existing units, still exhibited many local anomalies. Within the former county of London there had been no review of boundaries since the metropolitan boroughs were formed and the London Government Act 1899 had in fact contained no machinery for boundary alterations. Outside London the county reviews had been undertaken but with varying degrees of thoroughness – and in any case some forty years had passed since then. The Hancock Commission had examined county and county borough boundaries, and their work had resulted in many useful improvements; but they had not completed their review of the whole country before they were dissolved. So boundaries, after reorganisation, retained many anomalies – especially where urban development had spread across the boundaries of those larger towns which remained as districts on their own (a problem which the Local Government Boundary Commission for England had deliberately left untouched when proposing the new pattern of non-metropolitan districts in 1972 – see pp. 144-5 above).

On the other hand the consequences of this point should not be exaggerated. Some boundaries still need to be reviewed, but because there are now fewer authorities there are consequently fewer boundaries; and local irregularities are less important in the context of a complete pattern of new authorities which in broad substance is far more uniform and rational than before. It is, moreover, an aspect on which absolute perfection is not to be expected. Patterns of development and of movement are always changing and it would be impossible (and undesirable) to adjust boundaries too frequently. Regular review at reasonable intervals has now been planned and written into those provisions of the 1972 Act which established the Local Government Boundary Commissions but, in between reviews, local problems can be overcome as necessary with the help of those powers in the Act which enable one authority to act (by agreement) on behalf of another (see pp. 183-5 above).

The most important point on which the present structure differs from the previous system is, of course, the adoption of two tiers everywhere and the disappearance of one-tier administration in the county boroughs. The concept of the county borough was (as already noted at p. 13 above) a natural one when local government services were essentially local and when the main emphasis was on the environmental problems of urban areas. And the concentration of responsibility for all local government services in the hands of a single authority was always the potential source of great administrative strength. But increased mobility (made possible by the internal combustion engine), the development of new services, the wider needs of functions connected with planning, transportation, education and the personal social services, and the demand for uniformity of standards both in urban and rural areas, have altered the social background to the nineteenth century structure. No longer is it realistic to think of big towns as entities which can be governed within self-contained boundaries, separate from their surrounding hinterlands. Local government must bring town and country together, not keep them antagonistically apart – a principle which was one of those on which the Redcliffe-Maud recommendations were based, even though their proposed unitary authorities owed much to their desire to retain the organisational strength of the all-purpose authority.

Leaving on one side the polarisation of political argument between the Labour Party (which is generally stronger in the towns and which supported the solution which looked to the big towns as the basis for the main operational units) and the Conservative Party (which is stronger in the counties, where there have always been different levels of authorities) it is possible to identify some factors which tended to favour the adoption of a tiered solution rather than a system based on all-purpose authorities.

The much wider range of local authority services automatically leads to organisational problems. The operational requirements of different services are not the same and, as standards rise and as more emphasis is placed on efficient management, it becomes increasingly difficult to devise a single pattern of areas within which all services can be satisfactorily accommodated. The difficulty of organising water services within local government areas (which was formerly possible) instead of river catchment areas (which is now regarded as essential) was a major reason for removing this function from local government.

Moreover, even where overall plans and organisational arrangements need to be geared to wide territorial areas, local government services often involve decisions which are of purely local significance and which arouse the strongest possible public reactions on the spot. Planning offers obvious examples in the contrast between the structure plan (which needs a wide area) and local plans and individual planning decisions, but other examples in other services can readily be quoted. The purely functional view is that all responsibility should be concentrated in the authority for the wider area, and all decisions settled by them – after taking account of local views and representations. The contrary arguments are related to the belief that 'a genuine local democracy implies that decisions should be taken – and should be seen to the taken – as locally as possible' (Cmnd 4584, para. 8) by authorities with genuine functions and powers.

A further factor has a bearing on the discussion between all-purpose administration and a tiered structure. It emerges from the general developments which have produced the situation in which local authorities, to a much greater extent than in earlier decades, are involved in the administration of social services within national programmes for which the central government is responsible – housing, the welfare and children's services, and education, for example. The Herbert Commission made the point (see pp. 93–4 above) that departments in general, other than the then Ministry of Housing and Local Government, were chiefly concerned with the administration of their particular services and only incidentally, if at all, with the health of local government. Not unnaturally, as greater political emphasis at the centre is placed on these services, so the voice of these departments and of their ministers are given greater weight in central decisions. This can be illustrated from earlier pages of this study. When the county reviews were initiated no account was taken of the possible repercussion on county education arrangements of the creation of larger county districts – an omission which had to be specially dealt with by separate legislation (pp. 54–5 above). Such a situation would now be inconceivable, and indeed the operational needs of the education service were among the most important topics considered by the Herbert and the Redcliffe-Maud Commissions. The relevant point here is not that the central departments responsible for services needing wide areas of administration have positively favoured two-tier arrangements – many professional administrators in both central and local government incline towards all-purpose authorities – but that they are inevitably predisposed towards the biggest units for their own particular services. This inclination would lead them to support large county organisations, and to oppose the break-up of existing county services (for example, the LCC education service on the reorganisation of London government). Indeed it might be said that the growing importance of the counties during the present century, and their stronger position in the local government structure, is directly related to the growing political importance at the centre of functions for which counties are responsible and which (in the eyes of the professionals) need the largest available authorities for their planning and administration.

But although the county/county borough dichotomy had disappeared, it may well be that a new one has emerged – between the metropolitan areas (including Greater London) and the rest of the country. If so, it is a division which springs not so much from the form of local government organisation as from the different social and economic problems facing these two groups of authorities. Both in the metropolitan and in the non-metropolitan counties local government is, of course, organised on the basis of two tiers. The bigger non-metropolitan districts would like to exercise the wider range of functions in the hands of the metropolitan districts, and boundary claims may in due course be put forward for the extension of metropolitan authorities into non-metropolitan areas. But these are less likely sources of future tension than differences arising from the fact that authorities in the conurbations face particularly urgent problems connected with the social changes taking place in the inner areas of cities, such as urban renewal, homelessness, unemployment and ethnic minorities – problems for which these authorities will claim special priority and special financial treatment in the allocation of central funds. It is not without significance that this possible line of demarcation was given institutional embodiment when the local authority associations were re-formed after reorganisation into the Association of Metropolitan Authorities (which embraces authorities at both levels in all the conurbations including Greater London), the Association of County Councils and the Association of District Councils (whose membership is composed of authorities in the non-metropolitan counties).

## GENERAL THOUGHTS ON CHANGE IN LOCAL GOVERNMENT

A comparison between 1888 and 1974 indicates the extent to which the local government scene has altered but it is equally interesting to note that many features of the system have recognisably survived, not only from the nineteenth century but from far more remote eras, too. The country is still divided into counties for whose areas appointments are still made to the offices of lord-lieutenant and high sheriff. Within the counties are a second level of authorities clearly descended from the boroughs and the hundreds of earlier times, with civic dignities and titles of honour carefully preserved. And at the lowest level parishes remain as the grass-roots bodies, virtually untouched during the period of this study, and still holding the parish meeting inherited from the open vestries of past centuries. In short, the period has seen great changes of substance but coupled with an emphasis on the continuity of institutions and outward forms. This situation prompts certain general reflections about the processes of change, some of which have been anticipated in earlier pages.

The first needs no further elaboration: that the most important changes of substance to the structure, functions and finance of local government have come about in response to pressures and influences affecting society as a whole – changes in the size and distribution of the population, techno-logical change (especially as it affects mobility), changes in public expectations as regards the provision of services by public bodies, and changes in political organisation. Change comes about to meet concrete needs rather than to satisfy abstract logic.

Secondly, although functions and finance have been continually adapted, the time-scale for changes in areas and the structure of local government is long, and changes come about only slowly. Partly (as noted at p. 2 above) this is due to the practical problems in making changes of this kind – in defining boundaries and in making consequential and transitional arrange-ments; but it is also because changes in the machinery of government have never been lightly or precipitately undertaken by any of the main political parties. The Acts of 1888, 1894 and 1899 were preceded by many years of public debate and abortive legislative proposals. The discussions which led up to the changes since then have been equally long drawn out before action was attempted. Caution is proper and desirable when changes are proposed to complicated administrative organisations which provide personal services to the public, but more fundamental is the belief that, in a democratic state, changes to the machinery of government should be made by agreement – agreement that change is needed and agreement on what changes should take place. A consensus on the first of these two points is usually easier to reach than on the latter, and it is often in this situation that Royal Commissions are appointed: when everyone accepts that something must be done and when an authoritative review of possible courses both clarifies debate and provides the final stimulus for action.

It is not to be expected that there will ever be complete unanimity when proposals for change affect complex social and political situations, but such changes have little chance of being successfully carried through or retained unless backed with a sufficient degree of acceptance both within local government and elsewhere. As the Minister of Health (Mr Bevan) said during the second reading debate on the Local Government Boundary Commission (Dissolution) Bill, 'It must always be the hope of this House that, whenever we try to reform local government, we should try to carry local government opinion with us. After all, we have to live with these people, who are an important part of our constitution, and we must try to get the highest common measure of agreement' (Commons Hansard, 2 November 1949, cols 515-6). The moment at which it is judged that a sufficient measure of agreement exists is likely to emerge only very slowly, and after exhaustive public discussion, where matters connected with the machinery of government are concerned – and illustrations on this point could equally be drawn from the history of changes affecting the franchise or the composition and powers of the House of Lords.

The third general point is not unrelated to the second. Changes are more readily accepted if they are (or appear to be) natural and logical developments, based upon past experience and using the foundations of existing institutions. Sir William Jowitt's views on local government reform have already been quoted above (p. 58). More recently the then Prime Minister (Mr Heath) speaking, shortly after the passing of the LGA 1972, at the banquet to mark the centenary of the foundation of the Association of Municipal Corporations, said 'a hundred years is a notable milestone in the history of the AMC; but a short time in the long evolution of local government whose roots stretch back to the period before the rule of a central authority was established in this country. And it is by evolution rather than by revolution that we are proceeding now. This is the method we have always adopted in this country.'[4] Mr Heath might have quoted Edmund Burke to the same effect in epitomising the approach to government reform which experience suggests to have been the most acceptable – and the most successful – in England: 'A man full of warm speculative benevolence may wish his society otherwise constituted than he finds it; but a good patriot, and a true politician, always considers how he shall make the most of the existing materials of his country. A disposition to preserve, and an ability to improve, taken together, would be my standard of a statesman.'[5]

Burke's prose provides a dignified umbrella for some more mundane devices frequently to be found within governmental activities at all levels – and not only those associated with the gravest kinds of constitutional reform. One of these is the principle of precedent. Where something has been done once, it is safer to do it again – or something similar – rather than experiment with the unfamiliar or untried. It was suggested earlier (p. 95) that the method of approaching London government reorganisation in 1963 was rendered more acceptable because, in broad outline, a similar approach (with a new overall authority and the strengthening of the second-tier units) had been adopted twice before in the last century.

Similarly, in procedure the present machinery for boundary changes established by the 1972 Act, with a Boundary Commission and comprehensive reviews at intervals of ten to fifteen years, was more easily digested because the concepts were familiar from earlier local government Boundary Commissions and from the machinery of the periodic reviews undertaken by the Parliamentary Boundary Commissions. Another principle is that which retains the appearance of continuity while effecting changes of substance within the familiar framework. This has been illustrated in local government by the elaborate lengths to which successive governments have gone to retain links with the ancient origins in the counties, the boroughs and the parishes while changes of substance, to functions and finance, have often attracted less attention.

Finally, among general thoughts on change, is one which has formed a recurring theme of this study - the interrelation between machinery and policy. Machinery is no substitute for policy but must be devised for the purpose of achieving objectives which have already been fully discussed and clearly defined. In the field of local government one kind of machinery may be best for the purpose of modifying and adapting the pattern of local units within the existing structure of authorities, but quite different machinery may be needed for a more thorough-going reform of the system.

## ADJUSTMENTS WITHIN THE EXISTING STRUCTURE

Machinery for the systematic adjustment of local authority areas is the creation of the twentieth century, and reflects the changing position of local authorities in the governmental scene. As bodies responsible for the local administration of major social services they, and the areas within which they operate, attract the positive attention of the central government whose policies embrace the services for which local authorities are responsible (and who are always anxious to claim the credit when those services are successfully provided). So although it remains desirable that individual authorities should be able to make representations on *ad hoc* adjustments to meet urgent local problems, it is impossible to contemplate returning to the situation, however reasonable it was in 1888, in which this is the only effective way of initiating change. After various experiments the device of the independent Boundary Commission is having its third trial since the Second World War, and it is worth while considering how the present model differs from the Trustram Eve and Hancock Commissions, and in what circumstances an independent Commission of this kind is most likely to succeed.

A preliminary point to make, however, is that, while the general task of the present Boundary Commission is broadly similar to that of their predecessors - to review and to keep local authority boundaries up-to-date within the existing structure - the background to their work is different.

The Trustram Eve and Hancock Commissions went to work after several decades in which changes at county and county borough level had been made on a piecemeal basis, and in which the pattern of districts, despite the county reviews, still exhibited many shortcomings inherited from their mixed ancestry in the nineteenth century. The real job that needed to be done was much wider than the one contemplated by those who framed the legislation under which these two Commissions worked and hence, despite the fact that the approach had in each case been generally agreed between the government and the local authority associations, there were plenty of critics of these two exercises and of the adequacy of the Commissions' powers.

The present situation is different. The upheavals in London and then in the rest of the country produced a new pattern of authorities which most people, both inside and outside local government, accept as a working basis for the immediately foreseeable future. It will not last for ever, and will no doubt need further radical change in due course, but no one is looking to the present Boundary Commission for proposals of that kind. The Commission's role is more firmly understood and accepted, and analogies are helpful here with the Parliamentary Boundary Commissions – bodies which are now well established. For this reason the Local Government Boundary Commission for England have started their career in reasonably propitious circumstances. How events turn out in the future will depend on matters not all of which are under the Commission's control.

For the purpose of subjecting the local authority map to regular and comprehensive reviews the Commission's field of reference extends to all authorities. They will themselves be directly responsible for reviewing the boundaries of the counties and districts and the London authorities; in the case of parishes, the reviews will be carried out by the district councils but the Boundary Commission are involved because they were consulted on the guidance issued by DOE to district councils on such reviews,[6] and because they are the channel through which proposals will be put forward from the district councils to the secretary of state. The Hancock Commission, it will be recalled, had no jurisdiction over districts outside the SRAs, and neither they nor the Trustram Eve Commission had any responsibilities with regard to parishes.

Because regular reviews are contemplated the present Boundary Commission are a permanent body, as are the Parliamentary Boundary Commissions. The Trustram Eve Commission were intended to be permanent, too, but declared that the system was too far divorced from current needs to be put right within the powers they had been given. The task of the Hancock Commission was to modernise the map of existing authorities in a single one-off effort, after which they were to be dissolved without the nature of any future machinery being then clearly defined.

Procedurally, the present situation owes much to experience gained in the earlier exercises. The present Boundary Commission (unlike the

Trustram Eve Commission) are an advisory, not an executive, body and thus follow the normal line of earlier precedents. Proposals for boundary changes are submitted to the minister generally responsible for the local government system and given effect by orders made by him. But there are now very few specific requirements as to detailed procedure, other than the Commission's obligation to consult local authorities and staff bodies and to publicise their draft proposals and formal recommendations. The Commission and the secretary of state both have the power to hold formal public inquiries but neither are required to do so, and the emphasis is now on less formal consultations and conferences rather than on proceedings of a quasi-judicial nature. Gone, too, is the cumbrous procedure written into the LGA 1958 under which the minister was obliged to hold inquiries into objections to the Hancock Commission's proposals, thus creating a two-stage process under which the minister in effect had to traverse the same ground as that trodden by the Commission.

Parliamentary control has also been further modified, as part of the gradual movement away from the detailed parliamentary hearing of arguments for and against individual proposals by Select Committees of the two Houses. The power of local authorities to seek changes of boundaries or status by private Bill had now been completely abolished (by section 70, LGA 1972), as a logical consequence of the establishment of the Boundary Commission as the permanent body for the examination of proposals in this field. No boundary orders are now subject to detailed parliamentary consideration under the Special Parliamentary or the provisional order procedures. Orders (other than those affecting only parishes) are still subject to the ultimate control of Parliament, but no distinction is now drawn between orders of different degrees of importance, or between orders affecting different levels of authorities. All orders which have to be brought before Parliament are now subject only to the negative resolution procedure, that is, they may be considered and voted on in the chamber (not in committee) but solely on a take-it-or-leave-it basis, and then only if a Member takes positive action within a given period to move that the order be annulled.

This gradual change in the way boundaries are handled in Parliament reflects the changing view of local authority areas. Against the broad background changes to the scope of governmental activity, the emphasis is placed on local authorities as a pattern of administrative units which must be looked at as a whole; modifications to that pattern need to be considered in the light of general administrative and political principles applied to all authorities, and not treated as isolated conflicts to be decided by judicial processes between two adjacent contending parties.

So far it may be said that the arrangements governing the Local Government Boundary Commission and their work have taken heed of the practical operation of their predecessors. But there are two aspects on which their long-term success will be influenced by events which are still in the future. The first of these is whether the convention is allowed to establish itself that the recommendations of the Commission, as an independent body without any party ties, are accepted and implemented by the government, whether or not the government agree with them. This point was foreshadowed by the remarks of the Minister for Local Government and Development already quoted (see pp. 168–9 above) when the Bill was before Parliament. There are strong practical reasons why, in the long run, this convention would work in favour of the minister who has to take the decisions on local government boundaries – and of the Home Secretary in relation to electoral divisions; consistent reliance on the recommendations of an independent body is a wholly reputable defence against pressure groups (or even colleagues) who may urge intervention to produce a different result, especially when political considerations are involved, and avoids the slippery slope of re-opening the investigation and the ultimate and inevitable charges of gerrymandering. But ministers are traditionally susceptible to political arguments; short-term advantages often appear irresistible, and of course it will always be urged that the particular case in question has features which are so special that it would be not only politically safe but also publicly desirable to disagree with the Commission. The strength of the Boundary Commission's role will depend, to some extent, on whether ministers are able to resist arguments of this kind.

The second matter still in the future is the guidance, which has yet to be formulated, on the basis of which the Commission will undertake the reviews of the main local authority areas. This study has several times stressed that the device of an independent Commission is a piece of machinery well suited to the formulation of proposals within the limits of agreed principles. As a corollary this means, in the local government field, that the Commission's function cannot include new policy decisions (for example, on a completely new structure of authorities or a new distribution of functions) because such decisions, affecting a vitally important part of the whole machinery of government, ought not to be taken except by Parliament itself. But if the Boundary Commission are to be successful in keeping areas up-to-date in response to changing conditions, then the guidelines within which they are to work must give them clear directions. In earlier exercises the guidance was often vague or ambivalent, leaving so much to the discretion of the reviewing bodies that, in the absence of a clear lead, much effort was spent in producing insufficient results. In so far as this was the fault of successive central governments, it derived from their understandable desire to avoid becoming too deeply involved in the difficult and unprofitable work of local government reform, and their hope to get by with modifications which could be made on an agreed basis.

Obviously there will always be the need to seek agreement on broad principles with associations representing local authorities and their employees, but if the local government system is to be modified in line with continuing and rapid social developments it would be idle to think that this can be done without changes which may be both substantial and controversial in particular areas. For instance, when the Boundary Commission tackle their first major review of counties and metropolitan districts, and London authorities, in the period 1984-9, they will be faced with many conflicting claims and arguments about the boundaries of the metropolitan areas, including Greater London, and - most controversial of all - on the possible creation of additional metropolitan counties. And both before then (on an *ad hoc* basis), and in the subsequent reviews of non-metropolitan districts, contentious problems will need to be resolved regarding the boundaries of those big towns which became districts in 1974 without alteration of their then (often outdated) boundaries.

On these matters it is unlikely to prove effective for the guidelines merely to give the Commission a list of factors which they should take into account, and then urge them to do their best. That would serve only to indicate that policy is lacking, and that local authorities who resist change will have a good chance of succeeding. In the very short term that situation might enable the government of the day to avoid difficult or unpopular decisions, but it will be a recipe for allowing the system to fall behind current needs. The success of the Boundary Commission will substantially depend, therefore, on the clarity of the guidance given them for their main task of adjusting local government boundaries, on the extent to which that guidance meets the real needs of the system and the operation of services, and on the degree of determination indicated by the government that they will back the Boundary Commission by implementing proposals - even proposals arousing local opposition - which are based on that guidance.

## MAJOR REORGANISATION

Changes to local authority areas, and to the local government system, are necessitated by wider changes in society and in the whole machinery of government. Future developments of this kind will in due course lead to the situation when adaptation within the existing structure will no longer be a sufficient response to changing conditions - when the structure of local government will need to be reshaped once more.

Major reform must be a matter falling to the direct responsibility of the central government. As part of the wider apparatus of government, local authorities have to be considered within the framework of the whole public scene - the place of state activity, as against reliance on private effort; the types of bodies through which public services are provided; the constitution of those bodies, and the role of elected as against appointed members; the financing of public bodies and the interaction between them.

Two obvious examples figured earlier in these pages, regarding the administration of the NHS and of water services, both of which had (and still have) close links with local government; in each case changes in these services took account of local government reorganisation. Finance, and the whole pattern of central and local taxation, have to be considered in the context of the national economy. The structure of local government, with different levels of compendious authorities, have to be seen against the increasingly complex picture of governmental agencies, to which the organs of the EEC must now be added.

Problems affecting local government are not made easier at the centre, however, by the way in which the central government are themselves organised. Although local authorities have been urged in the Bains report to progress in the direction of corporate management, so that functions operate within co-ordinated plans covering all services, resources and priorities, the central government are far from achieving a similar unified approach to local government as a whole. Major aspects of local government are the responsibility of different departments – Environment, Treasury, Home Office, Transport, Education, Health and Social Security; Employment, Agriculture and others. Except in the case of DOE, the interest of these departments in local government is chiefly related to the provision of particular services, and not to the functioning of the local government system as a whole – they are concerned with local authorities as pieces of administrative machinery rather than with local institutions as part of the democratic framework of government. This is a situation in which it has happened only too often that authorities have received conflicting advice from different departments.

The Maud Committee on Management, echoing a similar plea from the Royal Sanitary Commission in 1871, urged the need for an inquiry 'in the hope that it may be found possible to appoint a single Minister who would be responsible for coordinating the policy of the central government insofar as it bears on the functions of local authorities'.[7] To some extent this recommendation was met by the formal acknowledgment in the White Paper *The Reorganisation of Central Government* that the newly formed Department of the Environment would be responsible, at the centre, for the structure and functioning of local government (Cmnd 4506, para. 31). And an embryo piece of machinery has been established – the Consultative Council on Local Government Finance – on which ministers from the government departments chiefly involved regularly meet representatives of all types of local authorities under the chairmanship of the Secretary of State for the Environment.

But the development, by the central government, of a completely consistent and co-ordinated attitude to local government, will be a slow process which is liable to be deflected by economic emergencies, political pressures or the personal influence of individual ministers.

Major changes to the local government system are rightly contemplated only at long intervals. Local authorities, like all social institutions, develop slowly and are harmed by too frequent change - and also by the uncertainty created by the prospect of change. But when such major changes become necessary, the decisions have to reflect many considerations besides those directly bearing upon the administration of particular local government services. Research can sometimes contribute (though not always very conclusively) towards relating size to efficiency in local government, and socio-geography may offer fruitful contributions. But, in the last resort, the decisions which have to be taken are political in character - not party political (one would hope) but political in the sense of embracing all aspects of government. The course decided upon will be the result of the exercise of political judgement, and not dictated by scientific tests or infallibly deduced from irrefutable data. It will be a decision on what is deemed 'desirable' in the light of all the circumstances, including the practicability of carrying the proposed changes through Parliament and then implementing them.

Practicability, it has already been suggested, requires a sufficient measure of agreement where changes affecting the machinery of government are concerned, and this, in turn, is linked to the need for full and (usually) lengthy public debate. But when the point has been reached at which the government of the day are clear as to the changes they wish to achieve, and have satisfied themselves that there is adequate support for these changes, both within local government and elsewhere, there are still two further necessary ingredients of success. The first is that the government should be possessed of sufficient time in office, and sufficient political resolution, to carry through a process which from the announcement of firm decisions to the final implementation is unlikely (on the basis of experience in Greater London and then in the rest of England) to take less than three or four years. The second requirement is that, when the changes have taken place, the new authorities should be allowed adequate time to settle down. This process is also bound to take a matter of years, while new organisations are built up and while members and officers adjust themselves to new attitudes and new inter-authority relationships. There will be no immediate benefits, and those who were quick to condemn the 1974 reorganisation within months of its coming into effect were usually displaying political naïvety, a hope of scoring political points or the desire to blame the introduction of the new system for the effects of inflation - or all three.

When the government have taken the decision to proceed with a major measure of local government reform they will be undertaking a task of formidable complexity - and one which is likely to become even more complex, if the past expansion of public services is continued in the future. The simultaneous reorganisation of local government, the NHS and water services, all of which took final effect in April 1974, constituted the biggest single administrative upheaval ever attempted in this country. It placed a very severe strain on the central government but even more on local members and officials who were responsible for implementing the changes in each locality. If these measures had been further complicated there would have been a real danger that the legislation might have proved too unwieldy for Parliament to have handled within the timetable and that the total package, even if enacted, would have created a serious risk of administrative breakdown.

This is one half of the answer to those critics who have said that the reorganisation of local government areas and authorities should never have proceeded without the simultaneous reform of local government finance. It is true that in 1888, and again in 1929, financial measures were an integral part of the changes then introduced. But it needs also to be recalled that the earlier changes were far less complex than those attempted in 1974 and on neither occasion was the local government map redrawn.

The other half of the answer is that no concensus existed on what financial reforms needed to be made. It would be extremely foolish - at any time and not only as part of wider changes including areas and the distribution of functions - to legislate on such a complex subject as finance without a sufficient measure of agreement, based on long discussion and preparation. It has been urged that areas, functions and finance ought not to be considered in isolation from each other; this is true in theory but, in practice, there are limits to what can be done in a single operation, and if all change waited for every aspect to be dealt with in a comprehensive pattern nothing would ever be done at all. The White Paper on London government took a robust line on finance which is worth quoting: 'Obviously the financial implications of any reorganisation of local government must be carefully considered. In the Government's view the financial arrangements should follow consequently on changes which are necessary for other reasons' (Cmnd 1562, para. 51).

Precisely what problems will need to be tackled in the future, and what machinery will need to be called into existence, can hardly be foreseen at this stage, but some general maxims are suggested by the experience of reorganisation in Greater London and in the rest of England and in Wales. These are not necessarily special to local government; some are obviously applicable to central government action in all fields.

In the first place, the complete operation and its timetable must be seen as a whole, and all aspects related to each other from the beginning. This requirement is no more than is needed for the prudent planning of any complicated exercise; but, in relation to local government reorganisation, it may indicate that some aspects which logically should follow in sequence will nevertheless have to be pursued concurrently to meet the requirements of the timetable (for example, the simultaneous consideration of counties, districts and electoral areas in the 1972–4 changes). Where this involves the existing local authorities, their members and officers, it also requires that the timetable is fully appreciated and accepted by everyone concerned.

Secondly, there is the need, once the decision has been taken to embark on reform, to carry the exercise through as speedily as is possible. Political considerations, and the timing of the next election, will probably encourage this anyway but within local government, too, there are very strong grounds for pushing ahead. The imminence of reorganisation makes it difficult to maintain services in the meantime, and impossible to plan for the future; uncertainty is upsetting to the individual local government employees who will be personally involved, and will also affect recruitment; and as the members and senior officers of local authorities will be simultaneously engaged in running the existing authorities as well as preparing for the new ones, this period of special strain should not be allowed to continue any longer than is absolutely necessary.

Thirdly – though this is obvious – the government must proceed in full consultation with local government bodies representing authorities, staff and the professions affected by the changes. Staff interests have to be considered from the very beginning.

Fourthly, the principle of equal treatment must be observed both as regards authorities and individuals. When there is general agreement that radical reorganisation is needed, then the consequences – which may well be drastic (so far as authorities are concerned) and may involve inconvenience or hardship (for individuals) – will generally be accepted, provided everyone is in the same boat. But nothing would so certainly destroy any hope of general acceptance, or of a smooth transition, than the belief that some are being treated differently from others or are gaining some sort of advantage. It was for this reason that, both in London and in the rest of the country, the reorganised authorities were all *new* authorities; their predecessors were all abolished, and the course was deliberately rejected of retaining some existing authorities and expanding them at the expense of others. For the same reason it was a major objective of the Staff Commissions to lay down general rules to govern the appointment and transfer of officers to the new authorities, and to ensure that these rules applied fairly and equally.

## TOPICS FOR THE FUTURE

It would be rash to attempt to forecast the pace or direction of future change but some general points have been made during the course of this study which may continue to apply. 'The best way to suppose what may come is to remember what is passed. The best qualification of a prophet is to have a good memory.'[8]

In particular, it has been argued that changes in local government, and in the whole machinery of government, are made in response to general social, economic and political developments. These have led to a general expansion of governmental activities – including local government services. The trend has been for those services to become increasingly specialised, and more expensive to provide as standards rise. In the field of central/local relationships the influence of the central government has increased; the rising cost of local government services has forced the central government to assume a greater responsibility for financing them and, to an increasing extent, local authority services are provided within national programmes, for the overall implementation of which people look to the central government and to national (rather than local) political leaders. The general, and increasing, involvement of the central government in the management of the national economy constrains them, for economic as well as for social reasons, to exercise a considerable degree of control over local authorities, the functions they perform and the level of the services they provide.

These general background considerations have not been altered by local government reorganisation, and will operate to influence future developments as they have in the past. This thought needs to be kept in mind when considering the arguments of those who advocate (even if not in the immediate future) a further reorganisation of local government on a regional basis.

Proposals for regional government have a long history. Many of those who gave evidence to the Redcliffe-Maud Commission included regional bodies in their suggestions for the future structure of local government – as, of course, did the Commission themselves, and Mr Senior in his Dissenting Memorandum. The concept was given additional backing when the terms of reference of the Commission on the Constitution specifically itemised 'the several countries, nations and regions of the United Kingdom'.

A great variety of regional models have been constructed including those described by the Commission on the Constitution (Cmnd 5460) and by Lord Crowther-Hunt and Professor Peacock in their Dissenting Memorandum (Cmnd 5460 - I), but a system including the features which commonly recur would be based on two levels of authorities: regional (or provincial) councils and district councils – both directly elected.

The regional authorities would not be merely advisory bodies; they would have substantial executive functions and would be allowed a considerable degree of autonomy, thus giving a tangible and representative personification to existing regions which already have (it is argued) regional identities and a considerable *de facto* array of organs of regional government. The functions of the regional authorities would include services which they would take over from the existing county councils on the grounds that areas larger than the counties are needed for their effective administration, for example, broad issues connected with planning and communications, major constructional works, the police and fire services and national parks. They would also take over the advisory and planning functions of the Regional Economic Planning Councils. They would become responsible for functions now exercised on a regional basis by *ad hoc* and substantially appointed bodies, for example, the NHS and water services, and would be given some influence over (if not responsibility for) the activities of nationalised industries, where these are organised on a regional basis. They would acquire, by devolution from the centre, a number of central government functions, and would become responsible for the decisions now in the hands of the existing regional outposts of central government departments (the regional offices of DOE, the Department of Industry, and so on). Finally, the regional authorities would have substantial powers in relation to finance in deciding their own financial priorities, possibly exercising some financial control over district authorities (for example, in relation to their investment programmes) and even (in some models) having their own sources of revenue.

The district authorities would succeed to all local government functions which do not need to be exercised at regional level (in particular, education and the personal social services) and also the local management of the health service.

The advantages claimed on behalf of a regional system of this kind fall into three broad groups. First, there would be functional advantages for the services which, in a regional context, would be brought together to be administered within the wide areas which such functions require. Secondly, there would be democratic advantages, in that many activities now in the hands of nominated or appointed regional boards would be brought back under the direct control of elected councils; and, at district level, the authorities responsible for education and the personal social services would be smaller, and more locally responsive, than the present counties. And thirdly, by devolving a substantial degree of responsibility and decision-making to regional bodies, Parliament and the central government would be able to concentrate on major policy issues; far too much detailed work has become concentrated at the centre and it would be for general benefit if this were more widely dispersed.

Regional proposals need careful study, however, and the first impression is that they tend to claim too great a degree of support from what are alleged to be manifestations of regional identities, or regional feelings, in England. In the process, the point becomes blurred that regions exist – or are advocated – for at least three quite separate purposes, which may be in conflict with each other. In the first place regions may be administrative subdivisions of the country on the basis of which government departments (or nationalised industries) find it convenient to disperse their organisations. Lord Crowther-Hunt and Professor Peacock made the point that there are twice as many civil servants working in departmental regional and local offices as at headquarters, and proposed that most of these offices should be 'hived-off' to the control of the regional authorities.[9] But the regional and local offices of (say) the Department of Employment, or of Health and Social Security, are not administering separate regional policies in respect of unemployment assistance or national insurance; they (and other departments) are operating national and uniform services through offices which are administratively dispersed for the convenience of their clients, but all of which need to follow precisely the same rules and procedures.

Secondly, regions have been defined for purposes of economic planning, which embraces not only the formulation of the type of broad regional plan to which reference has already been made (p. 109 above), but also positive policies for grants and other forms of financial assistance aimed at promoting investment and employment in those parts of the country which suffer from persistent problems of high unemployment. But such policies are *national* policies for the regions; assistance is deliberately given to some regions to favour them at the expense of others. The main decisions on this point could not be taken separately in each region, outside or apart from a national policy. In fact only a national authority can carry into effect a policy of economic regionalism.

Thirdly, regions have been (and still are) advocated as the top tier in a redrawn structure of local authorities. On this the view of the Redcliffe-Maud Commission was that regions (or provinces) are not the right areas for the operation of local government services - a view which the then government accepted (see pp. 123-4 above).

If pursued, a regional approach of the kind outlined above would need to overcome some very difficult problems with regard to areas - problems reminiscent of similar problems already referred to in this study. The first requirement in order to settle the pattern of regions would be the need for clear criteria on the basis of which the new pattern would be devised. Regions in England lack the national foundation underlying the devolution proposals for Scotland and Wales. In so far as a regional consciousness has been manifested in England in recent years it has seemed to take the form of a determination in some parts of the country (especially in the north) to make sure that the establishment of Scottish and Welsh assemblies did not result in those countries achieving extra economic help and public investment, at the expense of areas in England which may have problems of equal or greater severity. Local loyalties in England are more discernible - and more widely spread - as loyalties to counties.

In the absence of a generally accepted pattern of regions, inspiration might be sought from the requirements of the water services (basing regions on river basins) or the broader requirements of physical and economic planning (which will have regard to general population and employment patterns and major communications). The map annexed to

Mr Senior's Dissenting Memorandum and adopted by Lord Crowther-Hunt and Professor Peacock followed the former, and offered a pattern of five provinces in England related to catchment areas; the Redcliffe-Maud Commission followed the latter, and produced a map of eight provinces very closely based on the existing economic planning regions. In each case, however, the south-east region is totally disproportionate to the others, and dominates the country in population, wealth and economic influence. But if this particular problem is reduced by subdividing the south-east region (for example, by separating Greater London from the Home Counties, or by dividing the whole region – and possibly Greater London in the process – into four quarters) then one of the main purposes of the regional approach – to facilitate physical and economic planning – is jettisoned; the main effect of such a reorganisation would then be merely to replace one two-tier system by another on a larger scale.

At district level the area problems would be entirely familiar. Most of the existing non-metropolitan districts are well below the population thought desirable for authorities responsible for education and the personal social services, so the district map would need to be redrawn. But even if the minimum population for the personal group of services was substantially revised downwards, from the figure of 250,000 adopted by the Redcliffe-Maud Commission (which was itself well below what DES would have preferred for education), it would still be impossible, in some places, to avoid districts which would be geographically big and remote. So one is back again with the problems thrown up by the Redcliffe-Maud proposals for unitary areas.

Quite apart from the problems of areas, there are more general considerations which militate against the adoption of a regional form of government in England, if this implies that the country would be subdivided into a small number of large provinces, each exercising a substantial degree of autonomy as regards finance and services, and responsible for functions devolved from the central government.

Such a system would require a reversal of many of the long-term trends which have already been noted as influencing the development of local government and of government in general. These trends have been in the direction of greater national cohesion based upon the expansion of public activity at many levels, the development of interrelated social services, the central direction of the economy and the concentration of political influence at the centre. These pressures are now reinforced by British membership of the EEC, where the United Kingdom, as a single entity, is in constant touch with her European partners.

Proposals for devolution to Scotland and Wales also run counter to these trends. But such proposals have been based on the claims of separate nations in two countries which already have the nucleus of separate governments with their own secretaries of state, and separate government departments with headquarters in Edinburgh and Cardiff. To create similar separate administrations within England would have massive drawbacks, without the justification that these must be accepted to satisfy claims based on nationhood.

The point has already been made that the present regional economic policies are in fact national policies with regional implications. The need to preserve the economic unity of the UK has been a constant theme in the development of proposals affecting Scotland and Wales. But separate regions within England would make that task more difficult, especially if annual calculations had to be made and balance struck to demonstrate how far each region had contributed towards national prosperity, and how far each was entitled to share in the benefits of public expenditure. Indeed, a regional subdivision of the country hardly makes sense against the background of modern industrial and commercial organisation. For such purposes the trend is towards all parts of the UK becoming more closely meshed together economically, and for organisations to expand on an international basis – not to contract into a regional framework.

Nor is it possible to believe that ministers, in either their individual or collective capacities, will easily convince themselves that they should relinquish or weaken their responsibilities for the nationalised industries, the NHS or for national programmes in the fields of the social services. A regional structure which allowed the possibility of markedly different policies in different parts of England in connection with (for instance) the health services, the welfare services for the elderly, or education, would generate very little enthusiasm in governmental circles.

And, in so far as the proposals involved the administration of education and the personal social services by district councils which would be more numerous and often smaller in size than the existing authorities responsible for these services, there would be additional resistance from those departments who urged the need for even bigger authorities in their evidence to the Redcliffe-Maud Commission.

Finally, the establishment of regional administrations would mean setting up authorities that, in certain parts of the country, would have permanent majorities in favour of one or other of the two main parties. This happens now at county and district level, but the disadvantages would stand out even more clearly in the eyes of ministers if regional bodies exercised significantly greater discretion than is accorded to existing authorities as regards finance, or the types and standards of services.

Turning now from regionalism, however, it would be fitting to conclude with a brief mention of political considerations – which are never absent from decisions affecting change in the machinery of government. Local authorities are part of that machinery and, being directly elected bodies, they stand with Parliament as primary elements in the democratic framework. Indeed, the value of local government as it has developed in this country is derived as much – or perhaps more – from its representative basis as from the importance of the services it administers.

Members of local authorities and Members of Parliament are elected under essentially the same electoral arrangements. These arrangements, which have a bearing on several topics dealt with in this study, simultaneously illustrate two matters which have already been referred to: the increasingly strong political links between central and local government, and the interrelationship between machinery and policy. There is no aspect of the electoral system, whether it be the franchise, the timing of elections, the method of voting, the counting of votes, the definition of constituencies or the limitation of expenditure by candidates, in which machinery is not closely related to the sort of result that is desired – or in which change is not resisted by those political parties who think they would be worse off if elections were held in any other way. In particular, this point is bound up with the discussion of proportional representation, on which local elections have willy-nilly followed parliamentary elections.

The merits or demerits of the first-past-the-post system are usually argued entirely in the context of parliamentary elections. The main claim is that the system has in practice worked satisfactorily, by enabling one or other of the two main parties to form a government with a clear majority in the Commons, thus providing stable and accountable government. Taking the country as a whole, even comparatively small swings of opinion usually result in more substantial changes in parliamentary seats, and this continues to provide the successful party with an adequate working majority. Some degree of unfairness results in that smaller parties are under-represented, but (it is argued) this is a small price to pay if a more accurate representative system led to a proliferation of small parties, the permanent need for coalitions, a stultification of governmental initiative and the clouding of political responsibility.

But, even if all these claims were accepted, it does not necessarily follow that the same considerations apply with regard to the election of local authority councillors. In the first place, there is not the same need for the identification of a strong 'government party' at local level, where the main policy issues affecting the major services are discussed increasingly at national level, with local authorities broadly working within national programmes. This is not to deny the need for responsibility and accountability in local authorities, whose decisions are of great local importance and who are responsible for raising and spending enormous sums of public money. But, with an increasing range of services, the functions of local authorities – especially in the fields of personal services – impinge upon individuals and groups of individuals in a detailed fashion which is quite different from the broad issues considered at the centre. For this reason there is a far stronger case for the adequate representation of minority views in the council chamber, and for the accurate reflection of local public opinion. The increasing influence of party politics in local government has had certain advantages, but it has very definite disadvantages, too, especially when all details of administration are settled on a basis of party doctrine at private group meetings.

A second reason for electoral reform in local government and for the adequate representation of minority parties follows from the first. While a swing of opinion throughout the country may result in a change of government in Westminster, there are many local authorities in which one party is in so preponderant a majority that no conceivable swing could change the prevailing political complexion of the council. Authorities in this position could exhibit some of the characteristics which the Royal Commission on Municipal Corporations condemned in 1835 in that all effective decisions are taken in the closed circles of the party, instead of in the council which should represent the community as a whole. And, in the context of authorities which are now responsible for a wide range of detailed decisions which may involve considerable financial consequences (in connection with planning decisions, land acquisition and the letting of contracts, for instance) the permanent predominance of one party, faced with an inadequate or non-existent opposition, provides the conditions in which malpractices and corruption are more likely to be found as has been pointed out, for example, by Mrs Ward-Jackson in her Addendum to the Report of the Royal Commission on Standards of Conduct in Public Life (Cmnd 6524).

Many efforts have been made to change electoral arrangements in local government but they have failed to prosper because it is feared, by politicians, that to admit the need for improvement at local level would encourage those who seek changes in parliamentary representation, too. In fact, however, the spur to reform at the centre is provided by events because, in practice, the claims of the present system are now seen to be offset by persistent disadvantages.

Stable governments with working majorities (the main virtue claimed for the first-past-the-post) have not been assured; on three occasions since the Second World War governments have survived for only eighteen months or less before having to call another general election and the Labour government elected in October 1974 remained in office only with the help of the Lib-Lab pact. On no occasion during this period have the government of the day received as many as half the total votes polled; in this sense all recent governments have been minority governments. Such a situation would not have had major disadvantages in the nineteenth century, when the range of governmental activity was comparatively restricted and when there was a considerable degree of common ground between the two main parties on what governments should prudently attempt to do. But since then the field of government action has enormously extended itself and now covers all aspects of social and economic life; politicians have developed a passion for regulating and improving everything by legislation, and the tactics of political life have led to a permanent state of confrontation. Differences are exaggerated between the main parties, who give the appearance of opposing for the sake of opposing, and each in opposition pledges itself to undo much of whatever their predecessors may have attempted. This state of affairs leads to a considerable amount of tiresome bickering, the scoring of purely party points and a destructive belief that confrontation and antagonism should be regarded as normal and appropriate in other fields too, such as industrial relations. These results would be bad enough if governments were backed by a majority of the electorate; they are doubly to be deplored when they result from the actions of governments supported by only a minority of total votes. But it is not difficult to see why the two main parties both oppose change in the electoral system, and deny that representation could be improved without automatically leading to stagnation and chaos.

Any influence which tends to promote instability and uncertainty – as does the present electoral system – must have damaging effects throughout the country as a whole, its present prosperity and its future aspirations. And local government suffers, along with the other elements of society. Local authority services – housing, education, social work services, transportation – are made the subject of doctrinal argument and changes of policy which are injurious to those services, to the morale of those who provide them and indeed to local government as a whole, which is subjected to stricter central controls by successive governments anxious to produce rapid changes of direction. In addition, policy changes can, of course, be enormously expensive in terms of money and manpower. And in a wider context – reverting to the main subject of this study – local government change becomes a matter for inter-party polemics. It surprises no one that political parties resist proposals which they think cut across their interests in defined circumstances – as did the Labour Party in wanting to preserve the LCC, or the Conservative Party in opposing wide boundaries for the metropolitan counties. But if, as has been argued in this study, local government reorganisation is ultimately the product of long and widespread discussion, and becomes practicable only when there is sufficient general agreement in local government circles and at the centre, then it is not credible to pretend that some alternative and better solution was always just round the corner, nor helpful to hint that the pot will be stirred again as soon as the swing of the political pendulum creates an opportunity.

Change in local government requires the wise exercise of political judgement and a balance of many different considerations in the long-term public interest. Local authorities are part of the whole machinery of democratic government whose maintenance will best be assured by emphasising the beliefs and ideals – and the practical and material interests, too – which people have in common, rather than those which divide.

## NOTES: CHAPTER 9

1 The full figures are: in England, counties 45 (metropolitan 6, non-metropolitan 39), districts 332 (metropolitan 36, non-metropolitan 296), London authorities 34 (the GLC, the City and 32 London boroughs); and in Wales: counties 8 and districts 37.
2 In Wales, seven of the thirty-seven districts have populations below 40,000.
3 The Royal County of Berkshire, the Royal Boroughs of Kensington and Chelsea, Kingston upon Thames, and Windsor and Maidenhead (in England) and the titles 'city' and 'Lord Mayor'.
4 At the Guildhall, 13 December 1972.
5 *Reflections on the Revolution in France* (1790).
6 DOE circular No. 121/77, 12 December 1977.
7 Report of the Committee, para. 298.
8 Halifax, *Thoughts and Reflections* (1750).
9 Except for Defence, Customs and Excise and the Inland Revenue (Cmnd 5460 – I, paras 7, 211 (a) and 226).

## Select Bibliography of Official Publications

(All published by HMSO)

### REPORTS OF ROYAL COMMISSIONS AND OF COMMITTEES APPOINTED TO MAKE RECOMMENDATIONS ON POLICY ISSUES

Royal Commission on London Government (the Ullswater Commission). Report Cmd 1830, 1923.

Royal Commission on Local Government (the Onslow Commission). First Report (on the constitution and extension of county boroughs) Cmd 2506, 1925; Second Report Cmd 3213, 1928; Final Report Cmd 3436, 1929. Minutes of Evidence (oral evidence and written memoranda) published in 14 parts, 1923-9.

Royal Commission on Local Government in the Tyneside Area (the Scott Commission). Report Cmd 5402, 1937.

Royal Commission on Local Government in Greater London 1957-60 (the Herbert Commission). Report Cmnd 1164, 1960. Written memoranda of evidence: 5 volumes, 1962. Oral evidence: 70 days hearings (published separately) and Appendix containing supplementary memoranda, 1959-60.

Royal Commission on Local Government in England 1966-1969 (the Redcliffe-Maud Commission). Vol. I the Report of the Commission Cmnd 4040, 1969; Vol. II Memorandum of Dissent by Mr D. Senior Cmnd 4040 - I, 1969; Vol. III Research Appendices Cmnd 4040 - II, 1969. Written memoranda of evidence, oral evidence (13 days) and Research Studies published as separate series, 1967-9.

Royal Commission on Local Government in Scotland 1966-1969 (the Wheatley Commission). Report Cmnd 4150, 1969.

Royal Commission on the Constitution 1969-1973 (the Kilbrandon Commission). Vol. I Report of the Commission Cmnd 5460, 1973; Vol. II Memorandum of Dissent by Lord Crowther-Hunt and Professor Peacock, Cmnd 5460 - I, 1973.

Royal Commission on Standards of Conduct in Public Life (the Salmon Commission). Report Cmnd 6524, 1976.

Committee on the Preparation of Legislation (the Renton Committee). Report Cmnd 6053, 1975.

Committee on the Management of Local Government (the Maud Committee on Management). Vol. 1 The Report of the Committee; Vol. 2 The Local Government Councillor; Vol. 3 The Local Government Elector; Vol. 4 Local Government Administration Abroad; Vol. 5 Local Government Administration in England and Wales, 1967.

*The New Local Authorities: Management and Structure* (the Bains Report) 1972.

Committee on Local Authority and Allied Personal Social Services (the Seebohm Committee). Report Cmnd 3703, 1968.

Committee of Inquiry into Local Government Finance (the Layfield Committee). Report Cmnd 6453, 1976.

Central Advisory Water Committee: *The Future Management of Water in England and Wales*, 1971.


## GOVERNMENT WHITE PAPERS AND CONSULTATION DOCUMENTS

Ministry of Health, *Local Government in England and Wales during the Period of Reconstruction*. Cmd 6579, 1945.

MHLG, *Local Government: Areas and Status of Local Authorities in England and Wales*. Cmd 9831, 1956.

MHLG, *Local Government: Functions of County Councils and County District Councils in England and Wales*. Cmnd 161, 1957.

MHLG, *London Government: Government Proposals for Reorganisation*. Cmnd 1562, 1961.

MHLG, *Reform of Local Government in England*. Cmnd 4276, 1970.

DOE, *Local Government in England: Government Proposals for Reorganisation*. Cmnd 4584, 1971.

Welsh Office, *Local Government in Wales*. Cmnd 3340, 1967.

Welsh Office, *Local Government Reorganisation in Glamorgan and Monmouthshire*. Cmnd 4310, 1970.

Welsh Office, *The Reform of Local Government in Wales: Consultative Document*. 1971.

Scottish Office, *The Modernisation of Local Government in Scotland*. Cmnd 2067, 1963.

Scottish Office, *Reform of Local Government in Scotland*. Cmnd 4583, 1971.

Civil Service Department, *The Reorganisation of Central Government*. Cmnd 4506, 1970.

MHLG, *Local Government Finance (England and Wales)*. Cmnd 209, 1957.

MHLG, *Local Government Finance: England and Wales*. Cmnd 2923, 1966.

DOE *et al.*, *The Future Shape of Local Government Finance*. Cmnd 4741, 1971.

Ministry of Health, *National Health Service: The Administrative Structure of the Medical and Related Services in England and Wales*. 1968.

DHSS, *National Health Service: The Future Structure of the National Health Service*. 1970.

DHSS, *National Health Service Reorganisation: Consultative Document*. 1971.

DHSS, *National Health Service Reorganisation: England*. Cmnd 5055, 1972.

Welsh Office, *National Health Service: The Reorganisation of the Health Service in Wales*. 1970.

Welsh Office, *National Health Service Reorganisation in Wales*. Cmnd 5057, 1972.

Scottish Office, *Administrative Reorganisation of the Scottish Health Services*. 1968.

DOE and Welsh Office, *A Background to Water Reorganisation in England and Wales*. 1973.
DOE, Welsh Office and MAFF, *Review of the Water Industry in England and Wales: A Consultative Document*. 1976.

## OTHER REPORTS, ETC.

Local Government Boundary Commission (the Trustram Eve Commission):

Report for the year 1946. HC 82, 1947.
Report for the year 1947. HC 86, 1948.
Report for the year 1948. HC 150, 1949.
Practice Notes, First Series, 1946.
Practice Notes, Second Series, 1947.

Local Government Commission for England (the Hancock Commission). Reports and Proposals were published for the following Special Review Areas and General Review Areas:

Report No. 1 (West Midlands SRA) 1961.
2 (West Midlands GRA) 1961.
3 (East Midlands GRA) 1961.
4 (South Western GRA) 1963.
5 (Tyneside SRA) 1963.
6 (North Eastern GRA) 1963.
7 (West Yorkshire SRA) 1964.
8 (York and North Midlands GRA) 1964.
9 (Lincolnshire and East Anglia GRA) 1965.

Local Government Commission for Wales. Report and Proposals for Wales, 1962.
Local Government Boundary Commission for England. A continuing series which includes

Report No. 1 (Pattern of new districts in the non-metropolitan counties) Cmnd 5148, 1972.
2 (Names for the non-metropolitan districts) 1973.
3 (Boroughs and urban districts to be constituted successor parishes) 1973.
5 (Successor parishes, further proposals) 1973.
8 (Successor parishes, late applications) 1974.
286 (Parish boundary reviews: procedures and programmes) 1978.

*London Government: The London Boroughs.* Report by the Town Clerks of Cheltenham, Oxford, Plymouth and South Shields, 1962.
London Government Staff Commission. Report, 1965.
Local Government Staff Commission for England. Report, 1977.

# Index of Persons and Places

# Subject Index

FORESTRY COMMISSION BULLETIN 83

# Seed Manual for Forest Trees

*Edited by A.G. Gordon*

LONDON: HMSO

ISBN 0 11 710271 7
ODC 232.31:(021)

KEYWORDS: Seed, Forestry

Enquiries relating to this publication
should be addressed to:
The Technical Publications Officer,
Forestry Commission, Forest Research Station,
Alice Holt Lodge, Wrecclesham,
Farnham, Surrey GU10 4LH

**Front cover:** Sitka spruce seed; Queen Charlotte Islands origin, UK region of
provenance 10. (*40275*).
*Inset:* Female flowers of Sitka spruce. (*A. M. Fletcher*)
    Germinating Corsican pine seed during a routine test. (*39333*)

Sitka spruce and Corsican pine are major conifer species planted in the forests of upland
and lowland Britain respectively.